Ite
The lo
is a w
Fine
ov
D

08.
28.
08. DEC
31. MAR
3RD APRI
25TH

22.

D1341976

Comhairle Contae County Council

Dun Laoghaire Rathdown Libraries
Deansgrsnge

Customer name: O'Leary, Patrick
Customer ID: **********1229

Items that you have borrowed

Title: All you need to know... World War One :
the most catastrophic event in 20th
century European history
ID: DLR27000027416
Due: Saturday 4 December 2021

Title: Somme 1916.
ID: DLR20001033892
Due: Saturday 4 December 2021

Title: The Victorians : Britain through the
paintings of the age.
ID: DLR22000007930
Due: Saturday 4 December 2021

Title: They shall grow not old : Irish soldiers
and the Great War / Myles Dungan.
ID: 18518234769006
Due: Saturday 4 December 2021

Total items: 4
13/11/2021 10:52
Borrow 4
Overdue: 0
Hold requests: 2
Ready for collection: 0

Thank you for using the SelfCheck System.
GD02

dlr

Comhairle Contae County Council

Dún Laoghaire Rathdown Libraries
Deansgrange

Customer name: O'Leary, Patrick
Customer ID: *********1229**

Items that you have borrowed

Title: All you need to know : World War One :
the most catastrophic event in 20th
century European history
ID: DLR27000027416
Due: Saturday 4 December 2021

Title: Somme 1916
ID: DLR20001093393
Due: Saturday 4 December 2021

Title: The Victorians : Britain through the
paintings of the age
ID: DLR22000007930
Due: Saturday 4 December 2021

Title: They shall grow not old : Irish soldiers
and the Great War / Myles Dungan
ID: 1851823476008
Due: Saturday 4 December 2021

Total items: 4
13/11/2021 10:32
Borrow: 4
Overdue: 0
Hold requests: 2
Ready for collection: 0

Thank you for using the SelfCheck System
G002

They Shall Grow Not Old

They Shall Grow Not Old

IRISH SOLDIERS AND
THE GREAT WAR

Myles Dungan

FOUR COURTS PRESS

Set in 10.5 on 12.5 point Ehrhardt
and published by
FOUR COURTS PRESS
Fumbally Court, Fumbally Lane, Dublin 8
E-mail: info@four-courts-press.ie
and in North America by
FOUR COURTS PRESS
c/o ISBS, 5804 NE Hassalo Street, Portland, OR 97213.

A catalogue record for this title
is available from the British Library.

ISBN 1–85182–347–6

Printed and bound in Great Britain by
MPG Books Ltd, Bodmin, Cornwall

To Lany

They shall grow not old, as we that are left grow old,
Age shall not weary them, nor the years condemn.
At the going down of the sun and in the morning
We will remember them.

Lawrence Binyon, 'For the Fallen'.

Contents

List of Abbreviations

AIF	Australian Imperial Force
AEF	Australian Expeditionary Force
Anzac	Australia and New Zealand Army Corps
ASC	Army Service Corps
Bn	Battalion
BEF	British Expeditionary Force
Connaughts	Connaught Rangers
DCM	Distinguished Conduct Medal
DSO	Distinguished Service Order
Inniskillings	Royal Inniskilling Fusiliers
IWM	Imperial War Museum
Leinsters	Leinster Regiment
MC	Military Cross
MM	Military Medal
RA	Royal Artillery
RFA	Royal Field Artillery
RAMC	Royal Army Medical Corps
RAP	Regimental Aid Post
RDF	Royal Dublin Fusiliers
RIF	Royal Irish Fusiliers
RIR	Royal Irish Rifles
RIReg	Royal Irish Regiment
RMF	Royal Munster Fusiliers
VC	Victoria Cross

Preface

Two years ago I wrote *Irish Voices from the Great War*. It was always intended as the first of two volumes and concentrated on the memories of Irish soldiers of what were, for this country, significant battles in the First World War. This sequel, companion volume, or what you will, was intended to take a thematic rather than a chronological approach to the war and look at different areas of the conflict rather than offer a reconstruction of battles as seen from an Irish perspective. It is based on much the same set of sources as *Irish Voices* though in the intervening period many new ones have come to hand.

Long before coming to the end of the research for *Irish Voices* it was obvious to me that a lot of interesting material would have to be excluded for reasons of space. It seemed a shame to have to ignore so many aspects of the Irish experience of the war, hence the second volume. Unfortunately, and inevitably, I have had to be almost as selective on this occasion as well in order to avoid a sprawling and incoherent volume. But if there is a third part to this story it must take a very different form. There is still room for an analytical work which assesses the Great War and modern Irish memory. I do not know if I am the person to approach that theme, but I have left this volume relatively free of any detailed examination of the subject in order to encourage myself or, hopefully, someone else, to attempt it.

Let me be clear about the intention of this work. It is designed merely to keep before the public eye a neglected area of historical research and evaluation and to bring some more anecdotal material into the public domain in an edited, organised and palatable form. It may be of some assistance to academic historians as a short-cut or a pointer to a particular body of documentation, but it does not seek to analyse or draw many conclusions from that data. In other words it is not a work of academic history. It is based on too narrow a corpus of sources for any analysis it might contain to be taken too seriously. I have not consulted, for example, the Liddle collection except at second hand. I have not incorporated any of the relevant files on World War I veterans which are available in our own Public Record Office. Accordingly, any reader looking for thorough historical research and insight will be sorely disappointed – as will anyone looking for additional information on the 36th Ulster Division. For reasons of brevity this volume focuses to a far greater extent than did *Irish Voices* on soldiers from what is now the Republic of Ireland.

Since writing *Irish Voices from the Great War* I have been struck by the upsurge in interest in the subject. The newly established Dublin Fusiliers Association has done a lot of excellent work in preserving and displaying Irish writings and artefacts from the Great War. It is to be hoped that this organisation will grow and will do for the Republic of Ireland what the Somme Association has done for Northern Ireland.[1]

Despite all my caveats I hope the reader who has decided to buy, borrow or beg a copy of this book will enjoy it and will share my affection for the ordinary men who lived or died in an extraordinarily ugly and obscene conflict, orchestrated with all the cynicism at its disposal by an establishment in which some of the minor participants might actually have believed they had a stake. But it was a far more exclusive club than they realised!

My thanks are due to a number of people for their help in assembling and compiling the material on which this book is based. To Kevin Healy, Director of Radio Programmes, RTE, for permission to use material from the Sound Archive, to Kieran Sheedy (from whose work in 1973 the bulk of the taped recollections comes), to Joe Little and Jim Fahy for allowing me to use material from programmes they have compiled over the years and to Ian Lee for patiently winkling out what was there and copying it for me. I am also grateful to Pat Ryan for some awkward tape transfers.

To Billy Ervine of the Somme Association for his continued support and advice. Richard Doherty, has been very generous in letting me have access to the tapes on which one of his excellent 'Sons of Ulster' programmes on World War I was based. I would also like to thank the administration of Leopardstown Park Hospital for access to the late Joseph Cahill and Jack Campbell, two Great War veterans whom I interviewed there.

Without the help of historian John Connor the chapter on Irish soldiers in the Australian Army would never have been written. He supplied me with a huge amount of material and undertook a number of searches and additional research through the documents of the Australian War Memorial. I am especially grateful to Eilis Lambe for allowing me access to the letters of her late grandfather William O'Reilly, as indeed I am to John and Marian Maxwell for access to the diary of Douglas and Cecil Gunning. Gerald Morgan of Trinity College, Tom Burke and the Dublin Fusiliers Association have been especially helpful with advice, encouragement and documents.

A wealth of material was made available to me in the Imperial War Museum in London and I would like to acknowledge the help of Nigel Steel of the Dept of Documents in tracking down the copyright holders for the many memoirs and diaries from which I have quoted. C.M.F. Coleman granted permission to reproduce extracts from the diaries of Guy Nightingale, Cdr. V.M. Lake from the papers of his father W.V.C. Lake, D.E. McElwaine from the papers of his father, Mrs J.P. Brennan from the memoirs of her husband, Rose Hunt from the memoirs of her father Charles Cecil Miller, and Peter Kirkpatrick from the Ivone Kirkpatrick papers. Dr Peter B. Boyden, Head of the Dept of Archives, Photographs, Film and Sound at the National Army Museum, allowed the inclusion of material from that source, most notably the diaries of Capt. Noel Drury. Some additional documents relating to Guy Nightingale and others were researched at the British Public Record Office in Kew. Permission to quote from Frank Hitchcock's *Stand To* was granted by Gliddon Books, who recently re-published the volume, and Lavinia Greacen allowed me to quote from *Chink*, her work on the life of General Dorman O'Gowan. Despite every effort having been made, it has not been possible to obtain permission from the copyright holders of all the collections used.

I would finally like to offer heartfelt thanks to Bernard and Mary Loughlin and the Board of the Tyrone Guthrie Centre, Annaghmakerrig, Co. Monaghan, for taking me in and allowing me a vital four days' peace and quiet in which to get this book finished.

BACKGROUND NOTE

The following background note proved useful to readers of *Irish Voices from the Great War* I reprint it now for the benefit of those who are about to plough through this companion volume.

The use of military terminology and jargon is unavoidable in an enterprise like this, so herewith some background information which may be of assistance in the reading of this book. Some, but not all, is repeated elsewhere in the text.

Before 1914 the small British Regular Army was composed of Regiments which, in the main, consisted of a 1st and 2nd Battalion of about 1,000 men each. A third battalion was often attached to the Regimental HQ and was used for training purposes. From 1914 to the beginning of 1918, with the creation by the Secretary of State for War, Lord Kitchener, of a huge volunteer Army (compulsory conscription in England, Scotland and Wales came later), the Regular Army battalions were augmented by Service battalions of fresh, inexperienced troops. Thus the Royal Irish Fusiliers had its two original battalions, a third and fourth battalion based at home and responsible for training and recruiting and seven service battalions (5th to 11th) at different times during the course of the war.

Battalions, as a rule, were divided into four companies; these in turn were further subdivided into platoons. Before the officer corps became badly depleted, a battalion would normally have been commanded by a lieutenant-colonel, a company by a major or captain and platoons by a full lieutenant. A second lieutenant (also known as a subaltern) might have commanded a 'section' within a platoon, though, depending on numbers command of sections would often fall to a non-commissioned officer (sergeant major, sergeant etc.)

Battalions were banded, in groups of four, into Brigades under the command of a brigadier general. In early 1918, because of the extent of casualties brigades were reduced to three battalions each. Above brigade level was the division, consisting of three brigades. The 10th (Irish) Division, for example, the first Irish division to be recruited, was made up of the 29th, 30th and 31st Brigades. A division was usually commanded by a major general. Above that again was the corps, there were three or four divisions within this unit, which was under the command of a lieutenant-general. Four combined corps made up an army, under the command of a General. At the outset of the war, in 1914, the British Expeditionary Force which went to France, had two armies. This number had grown to five by 1917.

The first commander of the British Expeditionary Force was Field Marshal Sir John French. He was succeeded in December 1915 by General Sir Douglas Haig, who was elevated to the rank of Field Marshal in 1917. He held his position until the end of hostilities in November 1918. When it became clear that the war was not going to be swift and decisive, a general proclamation was issued by the British government calling for 100,000 men to volunteer for three years service. This force, raised by Lord Kitchener became known as K1 and included the first Irish division, the 10th. Further proclamations followed and the Second New Army (K2) included the other nationalist division, the 16th. In the Fifth New Army was the Loyalist 36th (Ulster) Division.

The period from the arrival of the British Expeditionary Force (the bulk of the Regular Army at the time) until just before the First Battle of Ypres saw the beginning of the destruction of the famous Irish units of the old Regular Army. This process continued with the destruction of the 1st Dublins and 1st Munsters at Gallipoli in April 1915 at the V Beach landing.

The numbers of Irishmen involved in the war then grew exponentially with the introduction of the first volunteer unit, the 10th Division, at the Suvla Bay landing in Gallipoli in August 1915. Later that year the 36th (Ulster) Division and the 16th (Irish) Division were introduced to the Western Front. These two divisions were Unionist and Nationalist mirror images, based on the politically oriented militias of the Ulster Volunteer Force and the National Volunteers. Both would suffer appalling casualties at the dismal Battle of the Somme in 1916, the 36th on 1 July, the opening day of the offensive and the 16th in the September attacks on the tiny French villages of Guillemont and Ginchy.

The 10th Division, unlike the two other Irish divisions, became engaged in hostilities against two of Germany's allies, the far-flung Ottoman Empire of Turkey and the Bulgarians. After being withdrawn from Turkish territory in Gallipoli, the 10th found itself assisting the Serbians against an opportunistic attack by their traditional Bulgarian enemies towards the end of 1915. The division was based in Salonika in neutral Greece. By 1917 it had been moved to Palestine to assist General Allenby remove the Turks from the Holy Land.

Meanwhile the two other Irish Divisions found themselves side by side in the 2nd Army of General Plumer (who ranks alongside Allenby as one of the few capable British commanders of the war) and took part in the successful offensive at Messines-Wytschaete in Belgium, a prelude to the long, wearisome and bloody Third Battle of Ypres (often referred to as Passchendeale). Here the 16th and the 36th came under the wing of the Fifth Army, led by an Irishman, General Gough (one of the least competent British commanders). The result was a disastrous erosion of morale and manpower and the continuation of the loss of the 'Irish' character of the two divisions as events at home (in the aftermath of the Easter 1916 Rising and the ill-advised attempt to introduce conscription in 1918) reduced recruitment to a trickle.

Things got worse in 1918 when the war was almost lost to a massive German advance in March of that year. The Fifth Army, with its numbers greatly depleted, bore the brunt of that assault, and the 16th (Irish) Division division ceased to exist. Many of the Service battalions which had been recruited during Kitchener's 1914 initiative were merged or disbanded. What was left of the 36th Division stayed together, but the battalions which made up the nationalist divisions (10th and 16th) were spread throughout the Army, giving rise to accusations of lack of trust in their committment to the cause for which they had signed up to fight.

I Taking the Shilling

In a society where military service was an integral part of the cultural landscape and where wars of one kind or another had been fought in each generation, the rush to 'join up' after the declaration of hostilities in 1914 was understandable. The armed forces had long been a 'proving ground' where men tested their courage and endurance, in a sense their very 'maleness'. The relatively small British Regular Army did not permit many to undergo such a rite of passage. Therefore the mass recruitment drive of late 1914, undertaken when it became clear that the war would not be over in a matter of weeks and could not be won by the British Expeditionary Force alone, afforded a unique opportunity for thousands of men to 'test their mettle' without the necessity of making the army or navy their career.

But Ireland was not such a society. The country had no great military tradition of its own,[1] and by the early 1900s most of its soldiers were merely an adjunct to the army of its near neighbour and coloniser. Granted, Irish regiments had a long and distinguished history in the various colonial wars of the British empire, but this could never have accounted for the large numbers of Irishmen who, like their British counterparts, embarked on the war against Germany with marked enthusiasm.

In addition to the Irish battalions in the Regular (standing) Army, Irish recruits filled three volunteer Divisions, the 10th (Irish) – southern but not exclusively nationalist, the 16th (Irish) – southern and almost exclusively nationalist, and the 36th (Ulster) – northern and overwhelmingly unionist. They did so for a variety of reasons. In the case of most of the northern unionists who filled the ranks of the 36th Division the motives were straightforward: they were fighting in defence of the Union, of a unionist and Protestant Ulster.

Spread throughout the 36th was, undoubtedly, a representative sprinkling of men whose motives for enlisting were more economic than political in nature. Soldiers serving in the Great War were often able to earn more in combat than they would have in menial employment back home, and their families were entitled to 'separation allowances' which, in many cases, saved them from the most abject poverty. But this was more especially true in what is now the Republic of Ireland. In the early 1900s industrial wages were almost double in Belfast what they were in Dublin, and work was much

easier to obtain. The Lockout of 1913 had left many working-class Dubliners
virtually destitute. The prospect of the 'separation allowance' and of what it
would mean to their families was sufficient to persuade many thousands of
men (urban dwellers in particular) to take their chances in the trenches.[2]

But economics alone cannot explain why thousands of southern Irishmen
took up arms either. For a few (mostly members of the Protestant Ascendancy
class, the so-called 'Anglo-Irish') it was the logical extension of a family
military tradition. For many of the latter and more besides it was also an
opportunity for adventure and the ultimate 'test of character and manhood'.
The extent to which World War I killed off romance and idealism can be
exaggerated, but many young men did follow this particular Holy Grail in an
era where it was still possible to harbour rather than merely cling to illusions.
For some it was a gesture of support for 'little Catholic Belgium', a neutral
state portrayed as having been pillaged and raped by a marauding German
army which had poured across its borders like one of the Gothic tribes of
historical legend. The author's own grand-uncle, smitten by a sermon at
Sunday mass, joined up for just that reason and died on the Somme in 1916.
This appeal to Irish Catholicism was often combined with blatant propaganda. Tales of the rape, murder and evisceration of Belgian nuns abounded.
Recruitment campaigns often displayed Germans as monsters. A Leitrim
nationalist party MP was quoted as saying at one meeting that 'He had it
from Cardinal Mercier himself that priests were shot down as you would
shoot dogs ... and the nuns hunted or killed.'[3]

But most Irish nationalists joined the British armed forces *en masse* for
precisely the opposite reason to the northern unionists, to weaken the Union.
That other 'Holy Grail', Home Rule, had been fought for and achieved by
John Redmond's Irish Parliamentary Party at Westminster. It had been suspended for the duration of the war. Redmond, in his famous Woodenbridge
speech, had advised the Irish people, and especially the members of the
National Volunteers, to join in the European war and to do so as citizens of
a new European nation-state.

In an often gushing Introduction to Michael McDonagh's propagandistic
The Irish at the Front, published in 1916, Redmond elaborated on his call to
arms. He makes a cloying reference to 'these soldiers of ours to whose
keeping the Cause of Ireland has passed to-day. It was never in worthier,
holier keeping than that of these boys, offering up their supreme sacrifice of
life with a smile on their lips because it was given for Ireland.'[4] Redmond's
preface was part of the drive to recruit more Irish nationalist volunteers to
the sixty odd Irish units involved in the fighting. He did so by appealing to
the vanity of those who might be undecided, describing the Irish as 'the
cream of the Army' or the '*corps d'elite*'. He also attempted to establish some
sort of blood relationship between Ireland and France. 'The Irish people, like

their racial kinsmen the French, Redmond asserted, 'are one of the peoples who have been endowed in distinguished degree with a genuine military spirit, a natural genius and gift for war which produces born soldiers and commanders, and which is the very reverse of the brute appetite for slaughter'[5] – the latter being a clear reference to the 'marauding Hun'.

Redmond was careful to stitch into his text the basis upon which, as far as he is concerned, the Irish regiments were fighting. He pointed to the rights won back from England and to the passage of the Government of Ireland Act, signed by the King in 1914:

> Thus when the war arrived Ireland had at once a charter of rights and liberties of her own to defend ... The war by a most fortunate conjunction united in a common cause the defence of England against a mighty danger and the defence of principles for which Ireland, to be true to herself, must be ever ready to raise her voice or draw her sword.[6]

The alternative to this course of action was too awful to contemplate, an alliance with, and domination by, the autocratic Prussian menace! 'The Irish people ... put a national army into the field ... for the express purpose of defending Ireland from such a fate and of doing their share in helping to rescue the unfortunate and heroic peoples who have already fallen under it.' He emphasised the importance of his religion (by which he clearly meant the Roman Catholic religion) to the recruit: 'The Irish soldier, with his limpid faith and his unaffected piety, his rosary recited on the hillside, his Mass in the ruined barn under shell-fire, his "act of contrition" in the trench before facing the hail of the assault, his attitude to women, has been mostly a singular impression.' He makes this association of religiosity with Catholicism even though the numbers of those enlisting in Southern regiments would have included a disproportionate percentage of Protestants

Ironically, in making his booster recruiting pitch he actually foresaw what would happen by 1918 – a drastic decline in numbers enlisting in the aftermath of the 1916 Rising, increased disillusionment with the war *per se*, the absence of conscription and the hamfisted attempt to introduce it. Redmond asked how Irishmen would respond to this fresh call to arms:

> The ranks of their brothers in the field are thinning under the wastage of war. Will they keep them filled? Aye will they! I should be untrue ... if I could harbour for a moment the idea that the young men of Ireland could think unmoved of the wistful bewildered faces of their noble brothers while they held back, could watch the ranks of the Irish armies thinning, and the glorious regiments, brigades, and divisions gradually filling up with others than Irish soldiers until their character as Irish

armies finally vanished and ceased to exist – and something, I fear, would
go with that character which Ireland might never get back.[7]

By 1916, even in the months prior to the Easter Rising, the war was becoming
a 'hard sell'. There was a sophisticated awareness by then of what conditions
at the front were really like and what the war was actually about which did
not make it immensely attractive. Despite his own brother William's enlistment ('I prefer to say to my fellow countrymen "Come" instead of "Go"')
there were some murmurings about the wisdom of Redmond's recruiting role
by 1916. These were expressed as open defiance when the Volunteers split but
were more subtly encapsulated in the words of a contemporary satiricial song:

> Come all ye scholars saints and bards
> Said the Grand Old Dame Brittania
> Will you come and join the Irish Guards
> Said the Grand Old Dame Brittania
> Now Johnny Redmond you're the one
> You went to the front and you fired your gun
> Well you should have seen those Germans run
> Said the Grand Old Dame Brittania.

Generally, however, Redmond's call was greeted with enthusiasm. The colourful Frank 'The Pope' Flanagan joined up, 'not for King or country, or for
poor little Belgium. I had met many of the Belgians and I certainly had no
idea of fighting for them. I was in the Irish Volunteers and a follower of John
Redmond ...'[8] Emmet Dalton, who would return from the front a decorated
war hero and would then join the IRA, felt that 'such was the confidence
that was reposed by the people of this country in their representatives that
they believed implicitly that the obligations entered into by the British would
be honoured.'[9] Jimmy O'Brien joined the 10th Battalion of the Royal Dublin
Fusiliers in December 1915, at the age of eighteen. He recalled a sense of
excitement in Dublin at the time: 'There was plenty of feeling for the war.
People were very patriotic, they wanted to join the Army. There was a good
pro-British feeling at the time.' This enthusiasm was especially evident among
the membership of the National Volunteers (set up to counter the threat to
Home Rule from the Ulster Volunteer Force). As soon as war was declared,
more than 7,500 members of the Volunteers who were reservists were obliged
to return to their units, but by 1916 the Force had contributed more than
24,000 to the British Army. Thanks to the unionist sympathies and insensi-
tivity of Kitchener, the National Volunteers were not allowed to form their
own units – as had the UVF, when it became the 36th (Ulster) Division –
but this appears to have had little if any impact on recruitment, as the 16th

(Irish) Division was, effectively, the equivalent of the 36th.[10] (Kitchener did allow the 16th to adopt the shamrock as its emblem!)

The 10th Division, the first Irish division to be formed, reflected more accurately the political and religious mix in the south of the country. Its ranks included far greater proportions of Protestants and southern unionists than did the 16th. Major Bryan Cooper, the historian of its troubled campaign in Gallipoli, wrote floridly of this 'alliance' that:

> many of the officers and men had played, or, at least, had relatives who had played, an active part in the agrarian and political struggles that have raged in Ireland for the last forty years. Yet all this went for nothing; the bond of common service and common sacrifice proved so strong and enduring that Catholic and Protestant, Unionist and Nationalist, lived and fought and died side by side like brothers. Little was spoken concerning the points on which we differed, and once we had tacitly agreed to let the past be buried we found thousands of points on which we agreed ... It is only to be hoped that the willingness to forget old wrongs and injustices, and to combine for a common purpose, that existed in the 10th Division, may be a good augury for the future.[11]

Noel Drury, himself a unionist, joined the 10th (the 6th Dublins) as a lieutenant and was struck by the variety of classes and occupations which had coalesced into one military entity:

> The peace time jobs of some of my men are extraordinarily varied. Here are a few taken at random from my list, footman, gardener, baker, labourer, butcher, book-keeper, bar tender (Buenos Aires), broker's clerk, ship's steward, merchant tailor, provision broker, electrician, postman, carpenter, fireman (Rathmines brigade), musician, railway porter, miner, boot operative, carter, blacksmith, photographer, flax dresser, hosier, printer, seaman, painter, bricklayer, hotel boots and 'student'.[12]

The 7th Dublins included a group of middle-class rugby players recruited at Lansdowne Road as well as a contingent of Dublin dockers.

Some fought out of economic necessity; others, principally Irishmen who enlisted in England, might conceivably have been attracted by the bonus often paid by patriotic employers to those who gave up their jobs to enlist. Michael Collins was working with the Guaranty Trust Company in London at the outbreak of the war. A member of the Irish Republican Brotherhood, faced with the prospect of fighting for England or being labelled a conscientious objector he simply quit his job, telling his bosses he was going to join up. He duly received an extra week's salary which he proceeded to hand over to the IRB![13]

After going through the holocaust that was the Great War, many of its participants must have lost sight of why they had joined up in the first place. (In the case of all but a few Irishmen resident in Britain after the introduction of conscription, enlistment would have been voluntary.) James Phillips, from Wexford, as a member of the Royal Navy Reserve, had little choice; he was called up 'like thousands and thousands of others, I suppose … fighting for the freedom of small nations I was supposed to be.'[14] Interviewed sixty years later he still sounded sceptical. Others however, went to some lengths to get into the army. Pat Farrelly was a 34-year-old civil servant when the war broke out. He attempted to join up in 1915 but was turned down because he had varicose veins. Instead of taking the line of least resistance he went into hospital to have them removed and presented himself again. This time he was accepted into the 7th Leinsters, where he became a sergeant major.

Frank Laird was also a 35-year-old civil servant with varicose veins. It took him a while to overcome his reluctance to enlist:

> Every day word came that someone had joined up … I had never considered soldiering as at all in my line. Besides I had a house to keep going, with a sister to keep it for me. So for a while I contented myself with the fact that Kitchener had set the limit at thirty-five years and sat tight. It soon went up to thirty-eight and then I saw I was up against it … I was naturally a man of peace. On the other hand was the awkward question of how my friends would regard me afterwards if they found me still at home when the war was over. It seemed a poor affair to be peaceably pen-pushing while men were fighting and dying out yonder. There was the reflection, too, that a Civil Servant's life, though agreeable, did not offer great variety. Here was a chance to get out of the groove with a vengeance.[15]

Pausing only to have his varicose veins dealt with and to become engaged, Laird (a Protestant with unionist sympathies), responding to peer-group pressure and some sense of adventure, took the 'King's shilling' (or two and ninepence, to be meticulously correct).

The writer Monk Gibbon was son of the Church of Ireland rector of Taney parish in Dundrum in Dublin when war broke out. His innate pacifism (later to reassert itself) was overcome by a combination of factors:

> We were filled with angry horror by the accounts of German atrocities in Belgium; there was even supposed to be a Belgian refugee on the far side of Gorey with both hands cut off at the wrist. But our patriotism did not need these artificial stimuli … These were the days when, even in Dublin, young women were capable of presenting a white feather to

a strange young civilian when they met him in the street, as a token of his cowardice. It was an ingenious form of moral blackmail which must have given its original inventor a considerable degree of patriotic and at the same time malicious pleasure.[16]

It was propaganda rather than peer pressure which finally decided Gibbon that he should enlist: 'Reading one day in the paper that the Germans had crucified a Canadian soldier with bayonets on the doorway of a barn, I had presented myself shyly in the doorway of my father's study and had told him that I must go to the war.'[17]

Thousands of Irishmen were already part of the British war effort in August 1914; these were the soldiers of the British Expeditionary Force ('The Old Contemptibles') which was rapidly despatched to France as soon as war was declared and which was forced backwards just as rapidly. Not all those Irishmen were in the recognisably Irish regiments (the Royal Dublin Fusiliers, the Royal Munster Fusiliers); many, like Jack Campbell, were in units such as the 1st Royal Highlanders (the Black Watch). Campbell was one of five working-class Dublin brothers who had made a career in the British army:

> ... the eldest fellow was a long headed type; when the other four of us would be reading fairy tales or that kind of thing, he'd be reading the *Handsworth History of the World*. I think it was his influence really that made us join the army, because he was always on about the 'far horizons' and the different countries and different people. We all got the bug anyway, that it'd be nice to be able to get out and see these people and mix with them. Not having the money to do these things, we figured, through his suggestion, the best way of doing it would be to join the British army; then you'd go to different countries.[19]

Campbell had plenty of time to reflect on the downside of army life as he participated in the retreat from Mons in 1914.[20]

Terence Poulter was one of three brothers who served during the Great War, though from motives entirely different to those of the Campbell clan. Poulter's family had moved from England, and he and his two brothers, Harry and Edgar, had been educated at St Andrew's College. Terence was only 16 when war broke out, and had to wait until 1916 before he could enlist: 'I trained with the Dublin Schools Cadet Corps and then went into Trinity OTC and from there I was posted to the 7th Officers Cadet Battalion stationed in Fermoy ... where I did the three months' training satisfactorily and got my commission.' The teenage Poulter was delighted to be emulating his brothers:

> This sort of King and Country thing didn't so much apply as the enthusiasm to get into the army, to 'do or die' because the rest of the

family had gone ... That you were going to get killed never entered
your head, even though you knew the casualties were very heavy ... It
was like trying to get an international rugger cap. The enthusiasm was
to get to the top. I went to endless trouble to get into the army because
I had great difficulty in passing the doctor in the first instance and my
father went to a lot of trouble.

Poulter had had problems with one of his hands since childhood, and his
father, himself a recruiting officer, had to use his influence to have his son
accepted, even in 1916 when the army had become far less selective. Once in,
however, the desperation for personnel with even the barest minimum of
training, asserted itself. Poulter had been passed fit for home duties only and
had been assigned to the Curragh: 'The Adjutant there, Captain Henchy,
said, "Where the hell have you been? I've got orders, I was looking for you.
You're taking a draft to France next week." So out I went with the draft.'[21]

The first wave of recruits was, of course, army veterans who were on
reserve lists. Having some sense of what they were about to embark upon,
many of these men were determined to enjoy their last hours of civilian life.
Colonel E.H.M de Stacpoole, then a lieutenant in the 2nd Leinsters, was in
barracks when news came, on 4 August 1914, of the mobilisation:

> Shortly afterwards men began arriving from the town (a lot of our men
> were townsmen) and when they opened their mobilisation orders they
> found a three and sixpenny postal order, and Guinness then was tup-
> pence a pint, so some of them were pretty muddled when they arrived
> for me to take down particulars of their families. They had large numbers
> of children, but most of them couldn't remember the names of them, and
> they could never remember their ages. This led to confusion later on
> because when the wives discovered there were allowances for the children
> and that they were not recorded as having the right number of children,
> the Paymaster was flooded out with complaints and had to settle that up
> in the end.[22]

This first batch of seasoned recruits was despatched quickly to France via
Cork and England. De Stacpoole followed them and joined the battalion in
the trenches at Armentieres.[23]

As many nationalists were keeping their options open pending the
conclusion of discussions on the role of the Volunteers, the second wave of
enlistments included many of the more ardent southern Protestants (and by
extension unionists). It is largely a myth that members of the Protestant
population of southern Ireland joined up in greater numbers than their
Catholic counterparts,[24] but they were likely to enlist more quickly, hence the

greater proportion of Protestants in the 10th Division than in the 16th. Southern Protestants and unionists tended to be far better disposed towards the British Empire, to have stronger family ties with the army or navy and to be somewhat more exposed to peer pressure to enlist.

Within a week of the start of the war F.H. Browning, the President of the Irish Rugby Football Union,[25] issued a circular to Dublin Rugby clubs asking them to encourage their members to join the forces. There was an immediate response which led to the inauguration of the IRFU Volunteer Corps. Col. Geoffrey Downing, the recently appointed CO of 7th Dublin Fusiliers, was persuaded to hold open a company (D Company) of the Battalion to all footballers who wished to join. In early September Downing published a very Kitchener-like call to arms in the Dublin newspapers.

To the Irish Rugby Football Union Volunteers,

I am keeping my Battalion open for you to join. Come in your platoons [fifty men]. 'Mess', 'drill', and work together, and, I hope, fight the common enemy together. The 1st City of Dublin Cadets are joining me as a body. I am waiting for YOU, but I cannot keep open long. Come at once, TO-DAY.[26]

This method of recruitment was familiar in Britain and in northern Ireland, where the famous 'Pals' battalions, consisting of men from particular localities or professions, were common. But the 'Footballers' or 'Pals' company of the 7th Royal Dublin Fusiliers was almost unique among southern Irish regiments,[27] where such commonality was discouraged by the War Office.

The response to Downing's call was excellent; nearly 200 men turned up to enlist at Lansdowne Road, as Henry Hanna records in his contemporary book, *The Pals at Suvla Bay*: 'What class of men were they? Barristers, doctors, solicitors, stockbrokers, bankers, medical students, engineering students, art students, business men who had responsible positions, civil servants, insurance agents, and many others of a similar class – the best that Dublin city could give, and nearly all of them well known in its public and social life.'[28] Though D Company was predominantly Protestant (and unionist) in its composition, it was not exclusively so. Many of those who enlisted in its ranks did so as privates but had an OTC background and might have obtained commissions elsewhere.[29] Some were prominent Dublin citizens. Poole Hickman (one of three brothers in D Company) was an eminent barrister, as was W.H. Atkinson, who started out as a private but rose to the rank of sergeant by the end of the war. The stately Lt. Ernest Julian was Reid Professor of Law at Trinity College. The thin, balding Charles Frederick Ball was Assistant Keeper of Royal Botanic Gardens, in Glasnevin. Harry Boyd was a member of the family firm of Boileau and Boyd. Ernest Coldwell was a winner of the

National Graceful Diving Championship in London in 1900. There are other familiar Dublin commercial names scattered through the ranks, such as Findlater and Elvery.

Edgar Poulter, older brother of Terence, was one of D Company's early recruits:

> I was with the North British and Mercantile Insurance Company and the call came along for volunteers and I decided to go and so with my brother I went down with a lot of the rest of our friends to Lansdowne Road. We were all packed along there, lined up, and Col. Downing, he was to be our commanding officer, walked along and had a chat with each of us and where we played and then he said, 'Are you willing to join up' and everybody said, 'Yes'. After that we were all told to run down to Brunswick Street and we were all stripped there and run through. There wasn't much formality. We were weighed, measured and given three and sixpence, our pay for the weekend, and told to go off and report to the Curragh on such a date.[30]

In contrast to the myth that only a few traitorous and renegade southerners fought with the British army during the Great War, many Irish nationalists of a fanatical or more moderate stripe also enlisted. Erskine Childers masterminded the Howth gun-running but spent the next period of his life in the British army. Former nationalist MP, barrister and poet Tom Kettle had distributed anti-recruiting literature during the Boer War but enlisted in 1914. Another MP, Arthur Lynch, had been sentenced to death for fighting with the Boers in South Africa but he became a committed recruiter for the Munster Fusiliers during the Great War. Tom Barry was to play a prominent part in the IRA campaign in Cork during the War of Independence but he acquired much of his military 'nous' in the British Army in Mesopotamia where he was involved in the unsuccessful attempt to rescue General Townsend's force from Kut. In *Guerilla Days in Ireland* he wrote:

> In June, 1915, in my seventeenth year I had decided to see what this Great War was like. I cannot plead I went on the advice of John Redmond or any other politician, that if we fought for the British we would secure Home Rule for Ireland, nor can I say I understood what Home Rule meant. I was not influenced by the lurid appeal to fight to save Belgium or small nations. I knew nothing about nations large or small. I went to the war for no other reason than that I wanted to see what war was like, to get a gun, to see new countries and to feel a grown man. Above all I went because I knew no Irish history and had no national consciousness.[31]

Emmet Dalton also played a prominent role in the War of Independence, particularly as an associate of Michael Collins. But while Collins was returning to Cork to avoid pressure in Britain to enlist, Dalton was volunteering his services:

> I actually became a young officer, it was a general move at the time, I was very young and I was imbued with the same feeling of patriotism that existed all round. An overwhelming majority of the Irish people at that time favoured the action being taken by the National Volunteers and I was the son of one of the people prominent in the encouraging of others so I naturally would, but apart from that there was the glamour of going to war. I mean, at eighteen years of age what do you know?[32]

Getting an accurate estimate of exactly how many Irishmen fought in the Great War is well nigh impossible. Upwards of 30,000 Irishmen were already part of the regular British army at the outbreak of war. A total of 30,268 Irish reservists went directly to their depots on the announcement of mobilisation. 140,460 enlisted in Ireland during the war itself, and as Patrick Callan, in a UCD PhD thesis, has pointed out, 'The response to the recruiting call by the Irish in Great Britain, and the introduction of conscription to Britain in 1916, took the total number of Irishmen who served in the combined services beyond the half million mark.'[33] More than a third of the 140,000 voluntary recruits in Ireland enlisted within six months of the declaration of war. By August 1915 more than 75,000 had joined up. Thereafter the drive to secure the services of more able-bodied Irishmen became more difficult, especially after the Easter Rising of 1916.[34]

The pattern of recruitment tended to reflect an urban-rural divide.[35] It appears that if Irish farmers left their land-holdings it was more likely to be to emigrate than to enlist. Thus it was left to the urban working classes (and the unemployed) to swell the ranks of the Irish regiments (and many British regiments to which drafts of Irish soldiers were often diverted). For example, the Royal Commission on the 1916 Rising heard from an Inspector Gelston of Clare that 'recruiting was very good in County Clare amongst the labouring class and in the towns but there was no recruiting at all from the farming class'. In Kerry Sir Morgan O'Connell observed that 'Almost since the outbreak of the war I have been doing the work of the local branch of the SSFA [Soldiers and Sailors Families Association] in Killarney and it has brought me into the lanes and byways of Killarney. It is from these lanes of the small towns that nearly all our gallant Irish soldiers are drawn.'[36] Work done by the Trinity College History Workshop on enlistment in Co. Wexford has shown the same pattern. Statistics have been produced to back up anecdotal testimony of one rural native to the effect that 'not many fellas from the country

joined up. It was mainly the poor people from the towns, who had nothing
much to lose anyway ... the labouring people were awful poor in those days.
I think most of them went for the excitement of it all. It was better than staying here.'[37] As is clear from one court case involving an attack by a farmer on
a soldier in a public house in Kilrush, Co. Clare, there was a feeling that 'it
was all the scruff and corner boys of Kilrush that were in the army and that
only for being rowdies they would not be in it at all'.[38]

What was true of Clare and Wexford was true of Leitrim. In April 1916,
in the County Court, Judge Brown had appealed to the people of the predominantly rural county for more recruits, pledging that 'Your sons will be well
kept, fed and paid and no longer pass lives of monotonous uselessness in the
country.' Clearly the young men of the county did not see their lives in quite
the same light as his Lordship, because the County High Sherrif called for
conscription as 'the only way to bring these laggards to the front'. Where
there were successes they were, once again, in the towns. The Leitrim nationalist MP Meehan told a meeting in May 1915 that 'Manorhamilton is only a
small town in North Leitrim with a population of 1,000 inhabitants and it has
sent 117 recruits to the army to do their part.'[39]

Experienced recruiters would try to convey an image of the army which
would impress the young, the unsophisticated and the ill-educated. Dubliner
Jimmy O'Brien had just reached military age (18 years) in December 1915:

> I was walking up Grafton Street one day and this recruiting sergeant came
> up to me and asked me would I like to join the army and I said, 'All
> right.' So I went in and joined. As simple as that. The recruiting officer
> had a badge of red, white and blue in his coat, a rosette. He brought me
> up to a place in Grafton Street, a recruiting office, a beautiful place with
> smoking rooms, a lounge and a canteen, which we didn't get in the army.

Despite his youth and the suddenness of his enlistment, O'Brien experienced
no opposition at home: 'My brother was in Gallipoli and I had an uncle who
was a regimental sergeant major; he was killed in France. I had a lot of my
relations in the Army.'[40]

A vigorous recruiting campaign was organised throughout the country in
the early months of the war. This occasionally took on a risible aspect. For
example, recruiting correspondence was sent to the males of a number of
counties. Ned Gilligan from Mullingar in Co. Westmeath was sent a letter
exhorting him to enlist. He was seven years old at the time! His two younger
brothers got them as well. The three letters were ceremonially burnt, along
with his own, by a father who was clearly out of sympathy with the cause
which he and his sons were being asked to serve.[41] This drive, however,
became increasingly ineffective as the war proceeded. In January 1916 Frank

Laird was pressed into service as a recruiter while attached to the Naas barracks of the Royal Dublin Fusiliers. The aim was to secure the services of the farmers of Wicklow and Kildare, whose rush to the colours up to that point had been anything but a blur.

> Our mode of operation was to arrive on a fair day or on Sunday after Mass. The band paraded a few times up and down and then the speaking began from a car or a couple of forms. The band got hold of likely converts and drank with them in adjacent publichouses to fire their martial ardour. In spite, however, of all the music, eloquence, and good liquor that was used in these weeks, the results were almost nil. The rustics of Kildare and Wicklow, who remained at home in January 1916, had apparently made up their minds to stay there for the duration.
>
> Our promoters returned from one meeting flushed with the acquisition of three recruits, but when they came to be examined by the doctor, one had been in the asylum, one had heart disease, and one was blind of one eye!
>
> At Lacken we addressed the congregation coming from Mass. A major, carried away with the torrent of his own eloquence, ordered out a half barrel of stout from an adjoining publichouse. It was rolled into the crowd and opened amid much interest. Then it was surrounded by a crowd of old farmers far past military age, who soon left nothing but the smell and all went home.[42]

'Pour encourager les autres' authentic Irish war heroes were used in the campaign. One such was the much vaunted Michael O'Leary, VC. O'Leary, an Irish Guard, had won his Victoria Cross at Cuinchy on 1 February 1915. The Coldstream Guards had lost a trench, and the Irish Guards were sent in to try and recapture it. O'Leary was off duty but decided to take part in the attack anyway. He opted to do things his own way. Instead of joining the frontal assault he slipped along a railway cutting. Re-emerging opposite a German barricade he shot and killed five of the defenders before ducking back down into the siding again and moving forward. He came back up in front of a German machine-gun which threatened to do serious damage to the Guards assault. He shot and killed the officer and two other members of the machine-gun section, and the remainder, five in all, surrendered to him.

O'Leary's action was courageous and effective in saving Irish lives, but was his subsequent fame (he is still the most celebrated southern Irish VC) engineered by the War Office, who needed heroes to help jog the Irish recruitment drive? Although a number of other VCs were listed on the same day he received his, the British media seem to seize on O'Leary's award. A tumultuous welcome was organised for O'Leary in London. The Redmondite

MP T.P. O'Connor brought him to speak, and be admired, in Hyde Park, on
10 July 1915. He had been promoted sergeant in the field by his CO, but the
War Office made him a lieutenant and assigned him to a Tyneside Irish
battalion. As Irish numbers dropped off, O'Leary was drafted into the recruitment effort, but to little obvious effect. Wallace Lyon of the 7th Leinsters
found himself in charge of the band accompanying the VC in the latter's native
Co. Cork. In his post-war memoir he wrote that 'On another occasion I took
the band down to Skibbereen in support of a recruiting tour by the famous
Michael O'Leary VC. We halted outside the chapel, and struck up as soon as
the people started to come out. I can't remember whether we got anyone to
join up. I rather fancy it was a flop.'[43]

Public recruiting meetings did not always go unopposed by Republican
elements. Disruption was more common in the months after the Easter Rising,
but the Republican, Ernie O'Malley, remembers:

> I attended recruiting meetings held in the streets. Recruiting officers
> were asked questions about the freedom of Ireland when they spoke of
> poor little Belgium. The interrupters were silenced by police or arrested.
> Sometimes a rival anti-recruiting meeting would begin; police and
> detectives would force their way through the crowd and attempt to
> arrest the speakers. Many were fined for answering the police in Irish.[44]

The 'terrible beauty' which William Butler Yeats wrote about in his poem
'Easter, 1916' cast a pall of its own over the frontline Irish. It fundamentally
changed the relationship between many nationalist servicemen and the army
for which they fought. It had a further dampening effect on a recruitment drive
which had long since begun to falter anyway. And, ultimately, its ramifica-
tions affected another vital relationship – that which existed between the men
who had gone to war between 1914 and 1916 and the society they had left
behind them. At the time it happened the Rising itself was an unwelcome
event to the bulk of Irish nationalist soldiers. It was a denial of the cause for
which many of them were fighting, almost a repudiation of their Irishness. A
story, probably apocryphal, illustrates the ambiguity which was soon to be
dispelled as the Republican course superseded that of the constitutional
nationalist. It tells of the Dublin woman who, on Easter Monday, got a letter
from an officer in her son's platoon to say that he had been killed at the front
but that 'He died for Ireland': that afternoon her other son came crashing
into the house mortally wounded, having fought for the Volunteers. His last
words were 'I'm dying for Ireland.'[45]

The actions of Pearse, Connolly and their associates were anathema to the
bulk of the civilian population of the city of Dublin. The people's feelings
were best summed up by a typical newspaper editorial: 'It would appear that

an armed conjunction of the Liberty Hall heroes, with some of the Sinn Fein
Volunteers, has made an attempt at some kind of miserable rising. The King's
troops and the police force have now got the Larkinites and the Sinn Feiners
well in hand, and the ridiculous "rising" has been crushed and broken.'[46]
Monk Gibbon was in Dublin when the fighting broke out: 'For the duration
of the rebellion it could be said that the sympathies of all parts of Dublin,
including the slums, were on our side. There were far too many Dubliners
fighting with Irish regiments, in France and elsewhere, for the population to feel
that this was the right moment to embarrass England. The insurrection had
little approval.'[47] Nevertheless, after the executions of the 1916 leaders,
Gibbon began to question who exactly was 'our side'.

Frank Laird was also in the capital city when the fighting began. He was
sent to Wellington barracks, where he remained for the next ten days 'listen-
ing to the roar of guns and the rattle of machine-guns and watching Dublin
burn'. An incident he recounts offers an illustration of the low regard in
which the Irish Volunteers were held by the general populace. A few days
into the fighting a ration party was sent out from Wellington barracks and
walked into a trap. One soldier was killed, one disappeared. The sergeant and
a third solider fought their way back to the barracks. 'The missing man turned
up later in civilian clothes and his uniform was afterwards handed in, made
up in a parcel, at the barrack gate.'[48] Within a year the civilian population of
Dublin would be offering the same sort of assistance to the rebels from whom
it was then protecting soldiers of the British army.

There was no more graphic illustration of the popular opposition to the
Rising than the removal of the prisoners through the streets of Dublin to be
transported to Frongoch and other prisons in Britain. Tim Pat Coogan offers
this description in his biography of Michael Collins:

> Here and there a man calls out a jeer or an oath. He might have a
> brother or a son at the front. Generally it is the woman who are most
> vituperative. These are 'separation women'. Their only income is the
> separation allowance they are paid by the British Government while
> their husbands are away fighting for the rights of small nations. Their
> comments express both their disgust at the destruction and killing caused
> by the week-long rebellion and their fears that the Government may
> react by cutting off their livelihood.
>
> 'Bleedin' bastards, my husband's out in the war fightin' for you bow-
> sies and yiz go and yiz stab them in the back.' 'Yiz are too cowardly to
> fight, and too lazy to work.' One lady with a shawl yells something
> about her two fine sons and runs along the line of soldiers guarding the
> prisoners to call out, 'Everyone of yiz should get a dose of capital
> punishment, and a bloody good kick up the arse after.'[49]

Reaction among southern unionists in the Forces was predictable. Noel Drury typefied it as he confided to his diary:

> We got the most astounding news on the 27th that a rebellion has broken out in Ireland. Isn't it awful? Goodness knows what they think they are going to gain by it. It's a regular stab in the back for our fellows out here, who don't know how their people at home are ... I don't know how we will be able to hold our heads up here as we are sure to be looked upon with suspicion. The men are mad about it all, but don't understand who is mixed up in the affair. I'm sure Germany is at the bottom of this somehow.[50]

German units sought to capitalise on the presence of Irish regiments facing them across the trenches. In the week of the Rising the Munster Fusiliers were in the line between Hulluch and Loos. The Saxon troops opposite nailed placards to two poles which they hoisted above their lines. The signs read 'Irishmen! In Ireland's revolution English guns are firing on your wives and children. The English Military Bill has been refused. Sir Roger Casement is being persecuted. Throw away your arms; we give you a hearty welcome. We are Saxons. If you don't fire, we won't.'[51] The Munsters responded by shooting up the signs, and that night, under cover of darkness, a party of about 25 stole them from the German trenches

New Zealand General Sir Alexander Godley (of whom more later) wrote to his Irish cousin Lord Kilbracken about the Rising. Godley, who was of Irish aristocratic stock, recalled that he knew Countess Markievicz when 'she was the most beautiful and attractive Miss Constance Gore-Booth of Lissadell ... We are of course much interested at "Pharaoh" (as Sir John Maxwell came to be called in this country) having been appointed Military Governor – he will do it well if he does not deal too leniently with the rebels.' He didn't and in not doing so probably changed the course of Irish history.

The revelation of the callous murder of the pacifist Sheehy Skeffington on the orders of a demented British army officer and the subsequent executions of the leaders of the Rising (especially the killing of a dying James Connolly) turned obloquy into support for the Volunteers and the Irish Citizen's Army. The Rising, and more particularly the executions of its leaders, led many nationalist soldiers to reassess their role and the cause for which they were fighting. In the wake of the passage of the Home Rule Bill, a trust had been built up between Irish servicemen and the British administration. The 1916 Rising was seen by many as a betrayal of that trust, but the aftermath of the rebellion was a far deeper betrayal. It placed the Irish serviceman in a 'no-man's-land' of his own. He could never again have the sort of faith in Britain that John Redmond had preached, and he could not be completely trusted by his own people as the dynamic of Irish history began to change.

Men like 2nd Lt. O'Connor Dunbar of the Army Service Corps began to question their loyalties. Dunbar was a colleague of Monk Gibbon's, who wrote that this convinced nationalist

> had taken part in the gun-running at Howth. Here was living proof there were plenty of hundred per cent Irishmen in France, and that Redmond had not been romancing when he offered the services of the National Volunteers to England at the beginning of the war. It had taken the Easter executions to make Dunbar begin to doubt the wisdom of the step he had taken.[52]

Tom Barry heard the news in Mesopotamia; he had already started on the road towards political consciousness, the Rising was his Damascene conversion:

> It was a rude awakening, guns being fired at the people of my own race by soldiers of the same army with which I was serving. The echo of these guns in Dublin was to drown into insignificance the clamour of all other guns during the remaining two and a half years of war ... Thus through the blood sacrifices of the men of 1916, had one Irish youth of eighteen been awakened to Irish Nationality.[53]

Barry saw out the war and joined the IRA after his demobilisation.

This questioning of loyalty was mutual. Anthony Brennan of the Royal Irish Regiment was stationed in a quiet French hamlet when news came through of the Rising: 'Although we were all mildly interested nobody took the thing very seriously. Apparently, as we now know, the Army authorities were of a different mind. Our sojourn in the country was prolonged for a few more weeks to guard against any possible sympathetic reactions to affairs in Dublin.'[54] Ernie O'Malley recounted how British officers in Irish regiments took the news:

> [They] were indignant at what they had misnamed the Sinn Fein Rebellion; but there was a half understanding; risings and attempted risings were part of the country. I heard an English officer say with dawning surprise: 'Why those people look upon us as the Belgians do the Germans.' He had been used to Ireland as a good hunting country in the same way that he had looked upon Northern Scotland as a fine place for grouse, deer, fish, and the wearing of kilts.[55]

At official level this distrust persisted as support for Sinn Fein grew at home, and it can be partially blamed for the drafting of many British soldiers into Irish regiments and the effective disappearance of the 16th Division after the German offensive of March 1918. At local level it led to Irish battalions being labelled 'Sinn Feiners' and to a growth in chauvinistic pettiness. The spirit of this mistrust was captured by Noel Drury (ironically himself a southern unionist) in his diary in September 1917. While in Ismailia he studied some grounded planes with the curiosity of one unused to such sights. But he was discouraged from asking questions and from continuing his examination when the pilots appeared: 'They were very chary of letting us see much of the machines. Suppose they thought the Irish couldn't be trusted.'[56]

Irish soldiers in non-Irish units were more exposed to British hostility than most of their fellow countrymen. Those in the officer class who happened to be of a nationalistic turn of mind (probably a minority) would have been subjected to the often chauvinistic and blinkered mentality which prevailed among the British officer corps. Monk Gibbon, who was in the Service Corps, made the mistake of getting involved in a discussion with a fellow officer about the Rising. The British officer argued that its leaders were 'traitors':

> It would have been useless to point out to him that a traitor is someone who, having subscribed to a certain loyalty, subsequently turns his back on it. You cannot betray what you have always opposed. I enraged my companion by pointing out this out to him. But his indignation soon passed. He refused to take me too seriously. The Irish were all mad. Supported by this premise, you did not allow yourself to be worried too much by any particular manifestation of their madness.[57]

Gibbon allowed himself to be patronised in that instance but later could not avoid the persistent questioning of his own CO, a Major Scarfe, who sought his opinion on one of John Redmond's speeches. Gibbon, only after much urging, launched forth in defence of Redmond and was told afterwards that Scarfe's reaction when he left the mess was, 'The buttons ought to be cut off his tunic and he ought to be drummed out of the British Army.'[58]

Many Irishmen simply shrugged their shoulders and carried on. Lt. Pat Farrelly of the Leinsters, when interviewed in 1973, didn't recall much interest in the 1916 Rising among members of his unit, though they were aware of it. Lt. Michael Fitzgerald of the Irish Guards has a similar recollection:

> Curiously enough, that was not talked about at all. On Easter Monday 1916 I was one of a battalion of Irish Guards marching near Worley in Essex. We passed by the newspaper shops as we marched along and, of course, saw what were the headlines on the billboards, 'Rebellion in Ireland – Heavy Casualties' or something like that. We looked at one another. When we got back to our rooms, of course, we discussed it briefly. We were angry, but we didn't know the whole story, so we got

on with our ordinary conversations until we could get the whole story. But I must say that we were not impressed with the whole thing. We were too preoccupied with what was in front of us and what we had to do, and we were committed to what we had to do, and whatever might happen in Ireland after we'd gone we could do nothing about that. That was our attitude.[59]

Denis Kelly, also of the Irish Guards, believed he had more important things to think about: 'Ah, you wouldn't be talking about things like that there, you hadn't time. You'd be thinking of where you were going to fall. There would nothing bother you like that.'[60]

The recollection of Emmet Dalton, given his subsequent history, is especially interesting:

I thought, and at that time remember I was very young, I had no preconceived notions about what was right or wrong. I did what I believed to be right, I thought the insurrection was a mistake, but then I think the rest of the world might have judged it to be a mistake at that time. I think that what changed the whole trend of the outlook of Irish people of that event was the execution of the leaders perpetrated by the British for no valid reason ...

I thought that the insurrection as such was a hopeless gamble because it had no earthly hope of succes as far as I could see. They were inadequate for that sort of event, and in fact I don't think the leaders themselves contemplated any measure of real success other than to make a blood sacrifice. I can't envision them believing in a military success ... I can only speak of the people that I met and associated with at that time, and they were my contemporaries in the war and they looked askance at the 1916 Rising. They didn't see it in the way one sees it now. Hindsight is a wonderful thing, but at that time to me and to my associates we thought it was crazy. I think it should never have happened. I think if it had not happened the Home Rule Bill ... could have been achieved, and I don't see that there was such a whale of a difference between the Home Rule Bill at that time and the Treaty as it subsequently was accepted.[61]

But Emmet Dalton, despite his misgivings over the Easter Rising, would play an active part in the War of Independence. On their return from the front many of those who had joined the British forces would be subjected to the sort of animosity previously reserved in Dublin for the Irish Volunteers, the IRB and the Irish Citizens Army. Some, like Tom Kettle, did not have the opportunity to explain their motivation. Most chose to remain neutral (in terms of active participation) in the conflict which followed in Ireland. But in the Ireland which grew out of the War of Independence it appeared that only those who swapped khaki for the battledress of the IRA could 'redeem' themselves. Suspicion plagued many of those who did not adopt that course of action..

The decline in recruitment into the army in the aftermath of the 1916 rising was apparent, but it would be a mistake to attribute it entirely to the growth in Republican sentiments brought on by the Rising. There had been a similar decline in British recruitment which was stemmed only by the introduction of conscription. Many Irishmen of military age were more attracted by jobs in the exempt munitions industry in Britain than they were by military service, so the available pool was depleted by temporary emigration. Nonetheless the fall in numbers was marked. The fall in recruitment between the first six-month period (August 1914–February 1915) and the second (February 1915–August 1915) was almost 50 per cent. That was to be expected after the initial rush had subsided. Enlistment in the first months of the war established the military complement which was then to be replenished by subsequent recruits. Between August 1915 and February 1916 there was a falling off of roughly 20 per cent but in the period which coincided with the Rising the drop-off was back to more than 50 per cent (only 9,323 men were recruited in the whole of Ireland during those six months). A year later the figure had almost halved again and the country was not producing enough new soldiers to replace casualties in Irish regiments. The threat of conscription in 1918 helped keep the figure low, and it was only when the war was obviously drawing to a successful conclusion for the Allies that the figure climbed once again towards 10,000 (from August to November 1918).[62]

Col. F.E. Whitton, later the historian of the Leinster regiment, observed that from the time of the introduction of the 16th Division to serious action in 1916 incessant fighting had greatly depleted the ranks. There was little time for training new recruits; some received as little as eleven weeks before being shipped off; men discharged from hospital were given little time to recuperate:

> At this time, too, the flow of recruits from our regimental recruiting area had practically dried up and though a few 'category' men, only fit for home service, were still joining, the class of recruits which the Battalion had received for the first eighteen months of the war was no longer forthcoming. Recruiting in Ireland had been confined very largely to two classes, the gentry and the town labourer; the farmer's sons and the shop-boy class were conspicuous by their scarcity. The result was that when the two former classes dried up it was with difficulty that the demands of the fighting battalions could be met, and men were often hurried back to France from hospital sooner than might have been the

case with English, Scottish or Welsh Regiments ... At this period, too, the first whispers of conscription were heard, and those who had poured cold water on the recruiting campaign in Ireland, became more openly hostile, and many who were waverers found an excuse for not joining up in the propaganda of the anti-conscriptionists.[63]

To many Irish officers it seemed that from 1916 onwards the military authorities were hell bent on reducing the 'Irishness' of Irish battalions. Drafts of newly trained Irish troops were, it seemed, being diverted with frustrating regularity to English units, while non-Irish drafts were 'diluting' Irish regiments. Frank Hitchcock of the 2nd Leinsters, in his diary, later published as *Stand To: A Diary of the Trenches*, catalogued some of these shifts. On 18 July 1916 he recorded that 'A Leinster draft of over fifty was sent to the Black Watch! Posting men of one Irish regiment to another was reasonable, but sending Leinsters to join any regiment but an Irish one gave cause for much legitimate grousing.'[64] In December 1916 the 2nd Leinsters were in trenches near Loos when a draft arrived from the Dorset Regiment instead of, as expected, the 5th Royal Irish Lancers; 160 men from that battalion had gone instead to the Middlesex regiment: 'This was an injustice to us, and to the Lancers. Of the Irish cavalry regiments, the 5th Lancers and the 6th Inniskilling Dragoons were particularly representative of our country. The 5th drew their recruits mainly from Dublin and the South of Ireland.'[65] Despite such a haphazard, or carefully contrived policy, Hitchcock was careful to note at the conclusion of the war that 'Racially the Battalion was still overwhelmingly Irish. I do know that the percentage of Englishmen serving with it was not more than 8 per cent. I record this especially, as I have heard it stated that at the end of the War the Irish Regiments were Irish only in name.'

How much of an influence the 1916 executions had on the decline in recruitment is open to debate. Patrick Callan, who has done more research into the subject than any other historian, tends to underplay its significance, as did contemporary recruiters. In his thesis he cites the revival in numbers in 1918 and points out that 'The radical improvement in the last period confirmed the view of seasoned recruiting officials that the success of their operations depended more on social and economic factors than on the political atmosphere.'[67] Factors such as the diminished size of the available pool of recruits, the reluctance of farmers (north and south) to join up and the unpopularity of the war *per se* must also be taken into account when assessing the reasons for the fall in numbers. It is interesting to compare the Irish situation with that of Canada. So unpopular had the war become there[68] that of the 331,934 Canadian men called up in 1917 only 21,568 reported for active service while 310,376 applied for exemptions, most of which were granted. In 1918 404,395 men were called up, of whom 380,510 sought exemptions.[69]

In evaluating the reasons for the decline in Irish recruiting, account must be taken of a number of factors. Some 40,000 potential soldiers went from Ireland to work in British munitions factories between October 1916 and June 1918. Without the contribution of these men the war effort would have been weakened. Many more went to work as agricultural labourers on farms in Britain. The impact of emigration must also be taken into consideration. The official army report on recruitment noted that six per cent of the total male population had joined the armed forces between 1914 and 1918 but added that 'The male population ... [was] composed chiefly of young men up to 18 years of age and men over 50, as a large proportion of the remainder emigrated.'[70] Ireland also had a higher proportion of landowners than Britain, and in both countries the rural population was notoriously reluctant to enlist. In his report on recruiting in Ireland, published in August 1915, Lord Wimborne, the Lord Lieutenant, cited a figure of 416,409 Irish unmarried males of military age. He then added the rider that 252,000 were engaged in agriculture. If one were to add in those unfit,[71] 'It would be surprising if, after all these deductions were made the balance of men available exceeded 100,000.'[72] Little had changed in this regard in the post-Rising period.

Whatever effect the Rising had on recruitment it had a polarising effect on attitudes towards Irish servicemen in the British Army. Some nationalists continued to support the war, others understood the reason why so many thousands of fellow Irish nationalists were involved, but a growing percentage viewed an Irishman in khaki in much the same light as the 'distributors of white feathers' would have viewed one in mufti at the beginning of the conflict. Such hostile attitudes were reinforced by events like the return on spurious leave of dozens of Clare members of the Munster Fusiliers to vote against de Valera in the East Clare by-election. Assaults on men in uniform increased. A memoir in the Imperial War Museum, allegedly written by an Irish soldier named only as 'Casey',[73] tells of meeting a girl in Cork and of walking out with her, in uniform, on Sunday afternoons: 'One night she failed to keep an appointment with me. Later I was told by her young Brother she had been set on by a gang of the local boys, and they had cut off her lovely hair because she was associating with a British soldier, I was most upset and my mates felt very sorry for me, and said if they knew who did the terrible job they would get what was coming to them.'[74] 'Casey' claims that, despite this warning the woman refused to give him up. As a result she was attacked a second time ... 'she was almost stripped again, they called her a British Soldier's Moll and Whore and said she did not heed the first lesson, and being a disgrace to her family and Ireland if she did not leave Cork more trouble was inevitable.'[75] She paid heed to this second admonition and left.

Ernie O'Malley was called upon to defend his own actions to his republican associates when he continued to fraternise with servicemen.

I got many a scowl from my Volunteer acquaintances when they met me walking with my brother or a friend in khaki. I tried to tell them that some of these soldiers honestly believed in the Party leader, Redmond; some thought they were fighting for Ireland when they fought abroad. In the Wicklow I had met a group of officers from the P.B.L.'s, Poor Bloody Leinsters. Two of them had been influenced by the Rising. They had followed Redmond; now they thought that by promising Irish help without getting a working measure of fredom in exchange, he had failed. No longer they believed in what they were fighting for; but, in honour felt bound to return to their battalion in France. 'When I come back next time,' one began, but did not finish as we shook hands. Both were dead within three weeks. When I spoke of these two men I did not find sympathy or understanding. Men in the company had relatives and friends at the Front; their creed was simple. They believed either in an uncompromising Ireland – or not at all.[76]

This indicates the hardening of attitudes that was to become even more common after the savagery of the War of Independence.

The other great disincentive to enlistment was, of course, the attempt by Lloyd George's government to introduce conscription in Ireland in 1918, much as had been done in Britain two years previously. This was resisted by all shades of nationalist political opinion. Emmet Dalton shares the belief of many historians that it was this botched effort which raised nationalist ire and self-consciousness to an even greater extent than had the Rising:

The entire atmosphere in Ireland towards Britain had changed not as a result of 1916 so much but as a result of the endeavour to impose conscription on the Irish people. I think at that time the Irish people stood solid against conscription and I can recall the signatures and protests outside the various churches on a Sunday. I think this had an extraordinary effect … an advantageous effect for the Volunteers because it created more recruits for them than anything could have done otherwise.[78]

The introduction of compulsory military service in Ireland (for all males between the ages of 18 and 51) would have led to a much earlier intensification of the IRA campaign and would probably have resulted in more recruits for that organisation than for the British army. The IRA had hatched plans of its own in response to any attempt to enforce conscription. Ernie O'Malley, on a visit to England in 1918, was surprised to run into Cathal Brugha: 'He was over on special work himself; if conscription was attempted in Ireland the first blow would be struck by shooting the British Cabinet. Men had come over from Ireland for the purpose and were waiting.'[78]

In April 1918 the poet W.B. Yeats tried to warn Lord Haldane of the impact of conscription on relations between Britain and nationalist Ireland. 'I read in the newspaper yesterday,' he wrote, 'that over 300,000 Americans have landed in France in a month, and it seems to me a strangely wanton thing that England, for the sake of 50,000 Irish soldiers, is prepared to hollow another trench between the countries and fill it with blood.' Yeats went on to quote Lady Gregory to Haldane: 'women and children will stand in front of their men and receive the bullets, rather than let them be taken to the front.'[79] Britain was eventually dissuaded from introducing compulsory military service in Ireland[80] simply because it was persuaded that it would require more troops to police conscription than its enforcement would produce. But the very threat of its application to Ireland further weakened the 'moral force' movement in Irish politics which reflected the philosophy of many of the Irish servicemen in the British army.

F.E. Whitton believed that the British government had missed the boat on conscription in the immediate aftermath of the Rising:

> In the opinion of most people who knew Ireland the crushing of the abortive rebellion in 1916 was the moment for extending to that country the universal liability for service which had been introduced into Great Britain. It has been asserted that the burden would have been accepted by the great mass of the people and certainly the 4th Battalion found that, after the rising, recruiting began to look up, it being not uncommon to enlist fifteen a week locally, or at the rate of nearly 800 a year.[81]

The anti-conscription campaign, the growing frequency of raids on army arsenals and the regularity with which servicemen handed over their guns to the IRA prompted the British government to remove Irish regiments from their traditional barracks around the country and install British regiments in their place. Terence Poulter was stationed in Longford in late 1917 and remembers that

> IRA fellows were joining up, getting their uniforms and rifles and hooking it into the countryside. It had been going on in Longford. Our old Colonel was very keen on Market Day on saying, 'You're a fine young fellow come in and join up.' He'd get his uniform and rifle and be gone the next day. He'd throw his rifle over the wall into the waste ground at the back of the barracks. The ass and cart would collect it, he'd go out on evening pass and that's the last you'd see of him.[82]

F.E. Whitton, in his history of the Leinsters, described the deterioration of discipline which ultimately led to the departure of the Irish regiments from their home bases: 'By the autumn of 1917 the Sinn Fein movement had become extremely active and the loyalty of the Irish soldier was subjected to a severe test. From some battalions came reports of the loss of rifles, Lewis guns, and ammunition.'[83] On 4 November the IRA brought a barge up to the perimeter of Wellington barracks in Dublin. Edgar Poulter recalled how 'They went in took every rifle out of the place handed it through the railings and loaded it onto the barge. The command decided they couldn't trust the Irish regiments, they brought over an English regiment to replace each Irish unit and we were put back on the boats that they came over on.'[84]

As early as 1917 men like Ernie O'Malley's brother felt it safer to walk around Dublin in mufti. A year previously they would have moved freely about the city in uniform. By 1918 they were potential targets for physical rather than mere verbal abuse. By the time the War of Independence got seriously underway in 1919 their former allegiance made them potential targets for assassination. West Cork in particular was not a very safe place to be an ex-serviceman. It was subjected to a reign of terror by the Black and Tans and Auxiliaries (themselves composed largely of British war veterans). Many former soldiers were shot in retaliation for the activities of the 'Tans' and the 'Auxies'. Some were probably still working for the British administration, some were not. But as Ernie O'Malley wrote of Sean Hegarty, one of the IRA leaders in the county, 'East Cork had shot many spies. Hegarty had the name of not being very particular about evidence, but that might be talk. All information connected with an espionage case had first to be sent to Dublin and the sentence confirmed by our HQ before an execution took place.'[85]

Another Cork IRA leader, Tom Barry, was even more ruthless with some of his former comrades. He wrote in *Guerilla Days in Ireland* that 'The remaining civilian prop on which British power rested in West Cork was a large group of retired British naval and militay officers. These lived in comfort, in groups, in the most beautiful parts of a lovely countryside. They, too, never considered themselves as Irish, and were soon to prove that their loyalty to British power was not simply a passive one.'[86] Barry claims that his West Cork Brigade of the IRA shot 12 'British' agents between 22 January and the end of February 1921 and four more in the months before the December truce. Some of those were ex-British army officers who

> were no less dangerous than the paid spy and unpaid informer. There was a large number of retired British military and naval officers resident in West Cork and some, while posing as civilians, worked feverishly to

destroy the IRA; nominally retired, they were back again in the active service of King and Country ... All the sixteen were not arrested and courtmartialled. Some could not be arrested as they were under enemy surveillance.[87]

Barry also contradicts O'Malley's contention that IRA Headquarters exercised ultimate control over such 'executions':

> Despite suggestions to the contrary, the Brigade never sought G.H.Q. sanction for any of those executions. How could it? We had no jails to hold these men and we dare not put all our evidence in writing because it might be captured en route or at G.H.Q. and expose to certain death our own informants. G.H.Q. during all the conflict never knew of the killing of an informer in West Cork until it read of it in a newspaper. How could those staff officers in Dublin offices judge better as to the guilt of an informer than the officers who had effectively to combat in the field the nefarious results of the traitor's activities?

Then, without naming names, Barry outlines three specific cases. One involved a retired lieutenant-colonel designated only as 'C'. The description of this man makes it quite clear that Barry is talking about Colonel W.J. Peacocke, who was decorated after leading the 9th Inniskillings into action on the first day of the Somme. The dates tally, Peacocke having been killed on 1 June 1920, aged about 37. Barry alleges that Peacocke personally guided raiding parties of the Essex Regiment. He claims the former lieutenant-colonel wore a mask during the raids but one day his mask slipped and he was recognised. From December 1920 he moved into barracks for his own safety:

> When, on occasions, he ventured back to Innishannon, he was invariably guarded by Black and Tans and his movements were most irregular. On the night of May 30 he went home to sleep at Innishannon, and on the following morning two of the Column went to shoot him. Stealthily approaching 'C's' house, they hid in the laurels until he came out of the hall door and crossed to his garage. One of the IRA then walked up to him, spoke and shot him three times as he tried to pull his gun ... The death of this 'retired' lieutenant-colonel was greatly welcomed. He had long been a menace to the IRA and the people of that locality.[88]

The fate of Lt.-Col. Peacocke was shared by many of his fellows as former affiliations rather than concrete evidence of collusion became sufficient grounds for assassination. The suspicion which led to the killing of many ex-servicemen (some by erstwhile comrades) lingered among the civilian population long after old scores had been settled. Only veterans who had 'purged' themselves of their former associations were above suspicion (men like Dalton and Barry – or Reginald Dunne and Joseph O'Sullivan, ex-soldiers executed for the murder of Field Marshal Sir Henry Wilson). Just as there was widespread political disillusionment in Britain among the demobilised soldiers who returned expecting the 'Homes fit for Heroes' they had been promised, there was a spiritual upheaval amongst Irish ex-servicemen who felt rejected by a society they had sought to protect, even create, a society which had moved on and left many of them behind. The miasma which afflicted US veterans of the Vietnam war returning to an uncaring, ungrateful and often hostile society provides a latter-day parallel. Stephen Gwynn asked, 'Was there anything more tragic than the position of men who had gone out by the thousands for the sake of Ireland to confront the greatest military power ever known in history, who had fought the war and won the war, and who now looked at each other with doubtful eyes?'[89]

At least some of the antipathy towards Irish veterans of 1914–18 is the responsibility of the British authorities because of the manner in which they prosecuted the War of Independence. The World War 1 'veteran' became indelibly associated in the mind of the Irish population with the Black and Tan and the Auxiliary, men who carried out atrocities on the civilian population. Commemoration and memory of the war became associated with support for the military campaign of the British administration in Ireland from 1919 to 1921. On occasions this took a concrete and visible form. For example, in November 1920 a notice was posted in Athlone, Co. Westmeath. It read: 'Shop keepers of Athlone are hereby ordered to close their premises on Armistice Day, November 11, in honour of the fallen heroes of the Great War and the police murdered in Ireland. This notice applies to all business houses and factories. Any failure to comply with this order renders the destruction of said premises inevitable. (signed) BLACK AND TANS'[90] (their capitals). The association made between Armistice Day and opposition to the IRA campaign against British occupation was the sort of negative reinforcement which caused many Irish ex-servicemen to be branded as in some way 'anti-Irish' and to consign most of them to silence and anonymity.

Patrick Callan has written that:

> The post war world neglected the victims of the conflict, and ignored the sense of loss among those who survived. Thomas Kettle wrote in 1916, 'while the mad guns curse overhead/And tired men sigh, with mud for couch and floor/Know that we fools, now with the foolish dead/Died not for flag, nor King, nor Emperor/But for a dream, born in a herdsman's shed'. Kettle did not live to taste the disillusionment of the peace and the idealistic dream which he had cherished soon faded.

Sean O'Casey believed that the ideals of the Irish soldiers who had gone out to fight for the humanity of the world had been swallowed up by the greed of eternity and were destined to lie motionless forever.[91]

Their ideals and their memory have also been swallowed up by the amnesia of Irish nationalism/republicanism.[92] By a nation anxious to forget one aspect of its past as it celebrated another. As Declan Kiberd has put it in a discussion of the 'confusion' caused by the 1916 Rising in the minds of Irish servicemen, 'Only a state which was anxious to repudiate its own origins could have failed – after a predictable period of post-independence purism – to evolve a joint ceremony which celebrated the men who served in either army.'[93]

A veil of silence surrounded the very existence of the huge cohort of Irish nationalists and southern unionists who fought for their ideals (rather than 'taking the shilling') on many Great War fronts. In terms of modern Irish popular culture it has been penetrated in the last decade by the likes of Frank McGuinness (with his play *Observe the Sons of Ulster Marching towards the Somme*) and Kevin Myers (often in his 'Irishman's Diary' column in the *Irish Times*).

It was this veil which smothered Sean O'Casey's *The Silver Tassie*, an honest attempt to depict the impact of the Great War on Dublin's working classes which foundered largely because it merely acknowledged the contribution of such people to the war effort and to the British army. It quickly strangled any attempt at a cohesive and effective Irish commemoration of the War on all but a few of the earliest Remembrance Days.[94] It allowed the Islandbridge Memorial to the Irish fallen of the Great War to crumble into a virtual ruin; indeed so many obstacles were put in its way that its construction was almost abandoned. It was this same veil which stifled all attempts by the Commonwealth War Graves Commission to erect the simple stones over the graves of Irish war dead in Glasnevin Cemetry in Dublin which dot the fields of Flanders and Picardy. It is the veil which has obscured the sacrifice and the legitimacy of service in the Great War from generations of teachers of Irish history.[95]

Granted, things have changed for the better. The Irish peace process has brought a recognition of the benefits which might accrue from a better understanding in the Republic of Ireland of the Great War legacy of nationalist and unionist forces. In November 1996 a 'Journey of Reconciliation' was undertaken by a contingent of prominent Irish citizens from North and South to the battlefields of France and Belgium on Remembrance Day. It was led by Donegal TD Paddy Harte and unionist politician Glen Barr. Acknowledgement was made of the contribution of each other's tradition to the defeat of Germany in the Great War. It was a small but significant step in the direction of mutual recognition. The Islandbridge Memorial has been beautifully restored and reopened on the instructions of the Irish government. A Sinn Fein representative (Tom Hartley) and an Ulster Unionist party MP (Ken Maginnis) attended the same commemoration there recently. The President now attends the Remembrance Day service in St Patrick's Cathedral on an annual basis. Scholars have begun to assess and examine the Irish war effort where before it was seen as an historical *cul de sac*. Societies have been formed devoted to the commemoration and study of the Dublin and Munster Fusiliers.

Mais plus ça change plus c'est la même chose. Where are the Commonwealth War Graves Commission crosses in Glasnevin cemetry? Despite the continued attempts by the Commission to erect its headstones almost eighty years after the end of the war, the Rainbow Coalition government (1994–7) which might have been expected to have adopted an enlightened or proactive approach expressed itself 'reluctant to intervene in this matter'.[96] And what of the political fate of Paddy Harte, the Donegal Fine Gael TD who invited his fellow politicians, in November 1996, to wear a Poppy in Leinster House to commemorate the Irish fallen of the Great War. In June 1997 he was defeated by Republican candidate Harry Blaney in the general election after serving his constituency with distinction in the Dáil since 1961!

At his funeral Major Bryan Cooper's coffin was draped in both the Tricolour and the Union Jack. He was sending a message about the duality of his Irishness. Tom Kettle's 'dream' was of a unified Ireland in a peaceful Europe. He knew before he died that his ideals would be superseded and misunderstood. A final end to amnesia and suspicion, an exploration of Cooper's duality and an attempt to truly understand Kettle's motivation, would serve us well today.

2   The Killing Machine

Many ghastly but appropriate metaphors have been used to convey some sense of the scale of mortality on the Western Front in the Great War. Images of the abbatoir or of the charnel house predominate. Or of a huge 'sausage machine' into which men, rather than pigs, were fed. Some were ground to a pulp, some got off lightly, but none escaped entirely. The Killing Machine was the huge gun which dominates the second, surreal act, of Sean O'Casey's *The Silver Tassie*. It was the pile of cadavers on which a cartoonist had a French general stand in order to get a better glimpse of Verdun.

The barrages and machine-gun bullets may have seemed anything but random to the troops as they picked off friends and comrades and as they waited in their subterreanean hovels for the bullet or the piece of shrapnel which would 'have their name on it'. But, at the outset of the war the killing was not well organised (just as the Nazis took months to perfect the reduction to order of the death camps). In war it is normally the civilian population that does without, but in 1915 there was rationing even within the Killing Machine. Capain Frank Hitchcock wrote in his diary on 7 June: 'There was a terrible shortage of shells, at this period each gun was rationed to three shells per day. When Algeo [Lt. N. Algeo, C Coy] rang up the gunners for retaliation, the answer he invariably got was: "Sorry, but we have expended our allowance, and if we fire any more shells off today we will be left with none to repulse attacks with tomorrow!" '[1]

Not that there ever seemed to be any shortage of shells coming in the opposite direction. Lt. J.F.B. O'Sullivan of the 6th Connaughts has left a highly literate and evocative account of a typically terrifying but oddly stimulating and strangely beautiful barrage: 'In a matter of seconds a hissing and shrieking pandemonium broke loose. The sky was splashed with light. Rockets, green, yellow, and red, darted in all directions; and simultaneously, a cyclone of bursting shells enveloped us. The intensity of the onslaught was stupefying and overwhelming.'[2] O'Sullivan was involved in a night-time raid and was forced to seek shelter in a bomb crater. There is an irony in the physical fruits of destruction providing sanctuary. As he watched the shells flying over and back like some prone spectator caught under the net at a deadly tennis match, he was struck, as never before, by the deafening noise all around him:

We could see well enough now – in a lunatic carnival way. Shell bursts made a continuous flickering that spasmodically flared with dazzling splashes, and gave a weird photo-negative effect to the surrounding liver-coloured earth. After twenty feverish minutes a Leinster major suddenly appeared. He came with mouth opening and shutting in soundless greeting, and I shouted back at the top of my lungs till he realised the futility of speech ... The hellish crashing and banging was at its very peak when a breathtaking and incredible lull occurred. Suddenly all noise stopped. The flickering light went out, and a black silence throbbed for three or four seconds. Everybody paused. One man in an awed voice said 'Christ!' and the witless profanity hung on the air like an invocation till the hurricane noise once more took over.[3]

And then there was the prospect of being killed by one's own artillery. Nowadays this is known, in a bizarre misuse of the English language, as 'friendly fire'. During the Great War shells that fell on one's own trenches were known as 'unders'. Any movement in no man's land involved the risk of being pulverised by a shell which spoke your own language. Peter McBride of the Inniskillings recalled in a radio interview an attack near St Quentin in April 1917 where German artillery was picking off the offensive force.

We had to move slowly, the whole Brigade, across a big plain with two batteries of German guns firing at us from the heights up above St Quentin. The killing thing was that we had to walk at a slow pace because if we went too fast our own artillery were putting down a barrage in front of us [a so-called 'creeping barrage' developed in the wake of the artillery débâcle of 1 July on the Somme] and if we went too fast we'd have walked into our own fire. My company was on the right, D Company, and the shells were skimming our heads all the time, and still we had to walk slowly and of course your whole inclination is to run for your life.[4]

The artisans directly responsible for wreaking this havoc 'could be a mile behind the trenches'. Ned Byrne was member of a well regulated team which 'could fire twenty rounds in five minutes'. Despite his distance from the lines, the danger was no less acute. German guns were always eager to 'take out' enemy artillery. 'You had the ammunition hid down in case it got hit.'[5] The work was physically tough, a fact to which infantryman Lt. John Staniforth of the 7th Leinsters attested: 'It was a lovely picture; the gunners stripped and sweating, each crew working like a machine, the swing and smack of the breech-block as clean and sweet as a kiss, and then a six-foot stream of crimson from the muzzle, a thunderclap of sound, and away tore the shell over the hills to Boche trenches 5,000 yards away.'[6] The physical effort involved in the work of an artilleryman can be gauged from the semi-nakedness of the gunners in the freezing cold winter of 1915.

Col. F.E. Whitton's history of the Leinster Regiment suggests the lengths to which gun crews went to conceal their positions in advance of a major bombardment. He described the barrage in advance of one of the many attacks on Guillemont: 'Thousands of tons of shells were crashing down on the enemy trenches on the skyline. Shells came from places unthought of and unseen, so excellently were they camouflaged; field guns in pits with only a covering of rabbit wire interlaced with grass and leaves to conceal them. Behind them again were rows of howitzers all staked to the ground so tremendous was their recoil every time they fired. ... We passed some of the gunners on our way up; they were all stripped to the waist, their dirt and sweat-begrimed bodies showed one the almost superhuman effort of endurance they were making under the blazing heat of an August sun at midday.'[7]

During a bombardment Whitton craved only two things (aside, presumably, from peace and quiet): 'water and a cigarette – inexhaustible quantities of both were required'.[8] Frank Hitchcock experienced the same urges: 'During a bombardment one developed a craze for two things: water and cigarettes. Few could ever eat under an intense bombardment, especially on the Somme, when every now and then a shell would blow pieces of mortality, or complete bodies, which had been putrefying in no man's land slap into one's trench.'[9]

Understandably, the average British infantryman harboured extreme feelings of hostility towards the German gunners who wreaked such havoc on his front-line trenches. But the cannier, more alert and agile soldiers could often manage to avoid the worst of it. Frank Laird, an officer in the 8th Dublin Fusiliers, endured a succession of mortar hits one day and became adept at avoiding the blast of the descending explosives:

> ... quick to hear the soft 'phut' which told that one was coming, and to spot it as it reached the highest point of its flight. A sharp eye could tell then the direction of descent, and thus diagnose the correct traverse to dodge round so as to put some feet of solid earth between the burst and its intended victims ... I could fully enter into the feelings of the Tommy who, on a trip over the top, entered a German trench and was met by a Boche with his hands up, who said, 'Me no fighting man, me Minninwerfer man.' 'Ah,' said old Bill, 'you are the bleeding man I am looking for', and put his bayonet through him.[10]

GAS

A more insidious killer was gas. It was introduced, by the Germans, on 22 April 1915, in an engagement near Langemarck. Although the British quickly responded in kind, the first use of this deadly, discreditable weapon lost the Germans any moral high ground they might have had left. Its psychological effect on troops was probably worse than any physical effects, as it was a crude weapon which often affected attacking troops as much and more than it did defenders. There are many recorded instances of gas (varieties included phosgene, mustard and chlorine) blowing back onto the trenches from which it had come or into the faces of troops launching an attack behind a cloud of gas.

Within days of the first German attack, the Allied forces issued the first crude gasmask, a respirator doused in chemical (or in a man's own urine if nothing better was available). This went some way towards reducing the number of horrendous deaths from the after-effects of an attack. These could include blindness and blistering of the skin and/or soldiers, quite literally, drowning as their lungs filled up with water ('the poor things burnt and blistered all over with great mustard-coloured suppurating blisters,' wrote Vera Brittain, then nursing at No. 24 General Hospital, 'with blind eyes – sometimes temporarily, sometimes permanently – all sticky and stuck together, and always fighting for breath, with voices a mere whisper, saying that their throats are closing and they know they will choke').[11] Even those exposed to only mild doses suffered greatly. During the massive German offensive of 21 March 1918 the dispirited and retreating British forces were subjected to gas bombardment on the opening day of the assault. Guy Nightingale of the Munster Fusiliers didn't feel the effects until a few days into the withdrawal. 'This gas business is rotten,' he wrote.

> We all have a nasty pain in our lungs and bad throats, but now the worst cases are getting blind. It's the rotten mustard and phosgene gas which they gave us on the first day of the offensive and it's like a red hot needle going through one's lungs everytime one breathes. It doesn't come on for four or five days and is aggravated by exercise, of which we've had a considerable amount.[12]

The gas was 'delivered' by shell, but the first indication of its presence was either the distinctive smell ('Beastly smell just like strong mustard and cress, and very irritating to the eyes,'[13] Eric Dorman-Smith wrote to his family on 24 April 1915) or a visible cloud: 'It came in the air like a fog,' according to Denis Kelly, an Irish Guard from Dysart, Co. Roscommon. 'You'd get the word and you'd see it coming. Then the order would come "Gas helmets on." You'd have it slung over your back like a hood. You'd put it on and take the tube in your mouth ... you'd be nearly smothered by it, you know. You'd get the all clear command and you'd take it off. And then you'd get your fans and you'd have to fan the trench out, blow it out for fear there was any gas in the trench.'[14]

The first defensive response to this deadly new weapon was understandably crude. Edward Byrne, then with the 72nd Royal Field Artillery, was issued with the most rudimentary protection days after the initial German attack: 'The Sergeant Major gave us a veil and a cloth to put around our necks and we had to keep it damp.' A month later Frank Hitchcock described how soldiers became acquainted with a barely more sophisticated device which was supposed to protect them from gas: 'The Company stood-to at about 4 a.m. The men were practised in gas-respirator drill. This consisted of putting a piece of gun-cotton between the teeth and tying a piece of crape round the mouth. This gear had proved fairly successful in a last gas attack at Ypres. Each man had, in addition, a bottle of hypo solution, with which he was to keep his mask moistened in a pukka gas attack.'

By the following year the masks were more sophisticated but inspired little confidence in Davy Starret, batman to Lt.-Col. Percy Crozier of the 9th Royal Irish Rifles, who wrote of a gas attack at Armentieres that

> The noise of the battle had lost its power to keep me awake, but one night Fritz certainly got me up, and a good job too, for gas was coming over and being stirred with shell of the same order. It took a lot to convince some of the boys, as it is always, for most get some way to coma before they're warned. But at last we were all staring at each other's ugly mugs made hideous by the War Office contraptions reckoned by the London staff to keep out gas. If they'd been forced to wear them in the conditions we did, they would not have been so cock-a-hoop about them.[15]

The use of gas could, quite literally, backfire on the aggressor. The unpredictability of wind conditions meant that an attack launched under cover of a gas barrage could quickly turn into an ignominious retreat and lead to a successful counter-attack. Frank Hitchcock's diary entry for 6 October 1916 illustrates what could, and often did, go wrong: 'We all knew by this time that our offensive at Loos had been written off as a failure, and our casualties had been colossal; as bad luck would have it, the gas used by us for the first time had been caught by a sudden change of wind and was blown back in the faces of our attacking troops.' The men around Hitchcock seemed to have about as much confidence in the efficacy of the weapon as they did in the means of protecting against it:

We had never expected gas to be used, and we were all greatly surprised owing to the following story, which was current throughout the BEF, to the effect that our attempts at gas had been so unsuccessful that when experimented on a flock of sheep, the animals had been seen grazing away contentedly after the gas cloud had passed over them! The Staff were reported to have witnessd this fiasco from a few fields distant, all smothered in gas helmets of every description![16]

It is one of the ironies of history that one of the worst gas attacks involving Irish troops was to come in the week of the Easter Rising. It was at Hulluch, near Loos. There Bill McMahon, of the Royal Irish Regiment, noticed an odd but not unpleasant smell: 'You didn't know it, it was too nice a smell to bother with, but by God the Irish Division went through it in that gas attack.'[17] It certainly did; the gas killed 338 men[18] and Wallace Lyon was given the awful task of disposing of the dead. He wrote:

one misty morning, when in support, we were greeted by an extra artillery barrage, and from the fog of battle in front of us it soon became evident that the Huns were attacking behind their barrage, and what was more, before long we began to smell chlorine gas. Luckily for us, with the rising sun the wind began to change and we immediately counter-attacked and drove the enemy off, but the Dublin Fusiliers had been caught unawares and their casualties were very heavy. When it was over, I had the sad job of collecting and burying the dead. They were in all sorts of tragic attitudes, some of them holding hands like children in the dark. They were nearly all gassed, and I buried about 60 of them in an enormous shell hole. For several days afterwards we picked up soldiers gushing out yellow green froth, and there were half poisoned rats by the hundreds which failed to get away in time.[19]

Many of those who were exposed to gas attacks escaped with their lives, but the long-term effects could be crippling and debilitating. Jack Campbell was the last of the 'Old Contemptibles' to die in Leopardstown Park Hospital in Dublin. One of five Dublin brothers who enlisted, he passed away in 1992 at the age of 94, having lived with a deposit of mustard gas in his lungs for more than seventy years. In March 1918 Campbell, of the 1st Royal Highlanders (the 'Black Watch') was stationed on the Somme. He went out with a working party detailed to heft equipment and barbed wire. Campbell had his gas mask over his shoulder and hanging down by his left hip: 'Old Jerry must have seen us because he put over a shell barrage. I got hit in the hip and got knocked into a shell hole. Right away I'd my pants down to see if I was wounded and if there was any blood. There was no blood. So I figured I must have been hit by a piece of broken trench board, or a piece of hard clay or something like that.' Campbell carried on working until later that evening when an officer of the Grenadier Guards came across the group having a smoke and sent them back out into no man's land to bring in wounded. He recalled:

> We'd just started when Jerry sent over a shell barrage, but they were gas shells. Of course as soon as you smelt it everyone roars, 'Put up your gas masks lads.' Up comes my gas mask, but I hadn't it on two minutes before I began to feel groggy and get sick into the gas mask. I had to pull it off or I'd have suffocated. I couldn't breathe. Anyway I staggered around for a while and went down. Luckily a lad came along, I couldn't see him because my eyes were streaming with water, they were burning out of my head, my chest and lungs were burning. I hate to think about it. This fellow asked me, 'Where are you hit mate?' I said, 'I'm not hit I'm gassed.' So when he bent down to help me he said, 'No wonder you're gassed there's a big piece of German shell in the metal container of your gas mask.' That was what had hit me earlier in the day. My hip would have been blown away if that had got through the metal container.

Campbell was removed to the Casualty Clearing Station and from then on to the Base Hospital. Having lived with varying degrees of discomfort and pain brought on by his exposure, he often wondered would he have been better off to have been allowed die: 'It would have been a humane thing to do, to let any of us die. I've seen poor buggers there saying, "Oh Jack, for Christ's sake put one through my head, put me out of my pain." I was often tempted to do it but I never did.'

RAIDING/PATROLS

So tedious was life on the Western Front that even certain types of terror offered relief from the *ennui* of the trenches. Because the advantage almost always seemed to lie with the defender in early trench warfare, major offensive activity, at army, division or corps level, was an irregular occurrence and one which, invariably, seemed to result in unconscionable casualties for precious little gain. For a number of reasons, chiefly to cultivate an aggressive spirit among troops who would otherwise have simply been active, and to energise defenders and passive recipients of tons of enemy ordnance, the practice of 'raiding' became widespread. Charles Miller of the 2nd Inniskilling Fusiliers captured the essence of the raid in his memoir:

your infantry, if they are good infantry, will want to do something to show that they are alive, and the only means of doing that is by tummy crawling at night in no man's land. Given a dark night, three or four men can crawl across to the enemy's wire, and, when they hear voices, lob a few bombs over, and then either bolt for it or dive into an adjacent shell hole and lie up. If you find a weak spot in his wire you may possibly crawl through or under it, and scupper a drowsy sentry, or even knock him out and get a prisoner. Of course the enemy adopts the same tactics, and two patrols crawling in no man's land may meet. Of course, all that kind of thing is immensely exciting. It is less exciting to be torn to pieces by a screaming piece of metal fired from several miles away.[20]

Raids were carried out at battalion level by small groups of selected troops against the trenches of the enemy. The principal avowed objective, and the chief prize, was to return with a prisoner or prisoners. The very least that this would accomplish would be the identification of the unit in the trenches opposite, and a capable intelligence officer might elicit much more than the very least from a co-operative prisoner. Raids also had an obvious effect on enemy morale. Some units were content to adopt the line of least resistance during their spells in the front line. Others were much more aggressive and liked to make their presence felt across no man's land as disagreeably as possible. The coincidence of two such units being rotated into the trenches opposite each other at the same time might have hazardous consequences. Essentially, raiding was a form of terrorism, a strange concept in a conventional war perhaps, but an apt description nonetheless. According to John King, a seven-year veteran of the 1st Royal Irish Regiment, 'You were always doing something to annoy them; even though you hadn't the strength, you were always making a try.'[21]

The training and planning which went into some of the more ambitious raids was, in microcosm, like the preparation for a much grander offensive, so it had practical benefits for the tacticians and logisticians. But raiding also had the effect of giving inexperienced junior officers an opportunity to assess themselves, and be assessed, in actions where dozens or hundreds of lives did not depend on their decisions. It offered a similar opportunity to the other ranks to gain experience under fire, and it satisifed the rear echelons that a sufficently belligerent spirit was being maintained amidst the stagnation into which the war had slid. Even without taking prisoners, information gleaned from a quick Cook's tour of the enemy's trenches could be extremely useful. The location of trench mortars and machine guns could be identified. The defensive strength of the enemy could be gauged and saps advancing into no man's land could be detected, as, vitally, could mining activity.

Sgt. de Margry of the 2nd Royal Irish Regiment found himself, in 1916, in a part of the front line near Ploegstreet known as the Bullring:

> the two front lines at this point almost merged, so near they were to each other (some few feet only at the very centre, which happened to be allocated to my platoon more often than not). One night in particular stands out in my memory, for we carried out several raids into the enemy trenches before we could capture the one prisoner we had been ordered to bring back – a practice often resorted to when we wanted to 'pump' some information or other out of Jerry. Unfortunately, the prisoner we caught at last created such a disturbance as we dragged him willy-nilly across the narrow strip separating the two trenches that we soon came under heavy rifle and machine-gun fire, and we had to leave him for dead half way across as we dived for shelter into the nearest shell hole to crawl into our trench at the first opportunity. For several nights in succession after this exciting misadventure we raided the German trenches at various points, but failed to contact the Germans, who had withdrawn some distance back probably as a precautionary or foiling measure. However, we made up for this in some measure by collecting a variety of souvenirs and piles of 'bunff' [*sic*] and private mail left by them in their dug-outs. The souvenirs we kept for ourselves, but the various papers and letters we handed over for subsequent examination by Intelligence Officers at their H.Q. behind the line.[22]

While this form of 'terrorism' did relieve the monotony of trench life, and did appeal to the sense of adventure of some of the gung-ho spirits who had not had such sentiments eroded by exposure to the squalor of the front, raiding soon fell into disrepute among those whose actual job it was to organise and participate in the practice. Raids could be wasteful of lives and, almost inevitably, invited retaliation in the form of counter-raids or, more usually, a prolonged bout of shelling directed at the trench positions of the offenders who had upset the comfortable status quo. (This was all the more galling for those in the line, as the raiders often retired to the reserve trenches or moved well away from the front parapets after the completion of their mission.) Wallace Lyon of the 7th Leinsters (later a colonel) described one typically disastrous and costly raid:

> The raiding party consisted of one officer with Harry Wilson [a sergeant and friend of Lyon's] and almost 20 bombers, and as soon as the barrage opened they went over the top. Immediately there was a hell of a din as the enemy reacted violently by strafing us with everything he had got, and after about 20 minutes the first of our raiders returned

with a prisoner. He was an expensive prize, for about half of our party never got back and among the missing was Harry, who we afterwards learned had died of wounds in the German trench.[23]

One of the cardinal objections to the 'raids' was that some units saw in them an opportunity to enhance the reputation of their platoon/company/battalion/regiment by being more daring, productive and destructive than had any of the other units engaged in similar operations in their section of the line. An element of competition crept in which was, quite literally, unhealthy. 'Raids' should not be confused with patrols, which were much more regular and mundane. Anthony Brennan of the 1st Royal Irish Regiment had not established the distinction when he went out on his first patrol, near Englebelmer, along a railway line which ran from the British to the German trenches: 'I remember waiting with a thrill to hear the first sign of conflict; not realising, as I was to later, that "patrols" had always a healthy respect for each other, and except where it was necessary to procure a prisoner for the benefit of the "Intelligence" branch of the Army, gave each other a wide berth.'[24]

One of the most audaciously successful German raids (which prompted a well planned British response) took place near Loos in January 1917. It is described (in a tone verging on approbation) by Capt. Frank Hitchcock in *Stand To*.[25] Reports came in to the GOC in the Loos area (at the time it was Major General Capper), picked up from German wireless transmissions, of a successful raid which had netted 50 British prisoners. Immediate situation reports were sought from all units but none indicated that any action of any kind had taken place that night. A tour by Headquarters staff of the 17th Brigade's sector, however, revealed a stretch of the line completely unmanned. The only sign of human habitation was that of a single corpse. Capper sought out the Battalion CO, who was totally nonplussed. Peering across no man's land, somebody spotted something. Flapping in the light southeast breeze was a large triumphal notice, in English, stuck in the middle of the British barbed wire entanglements. It read, 'Say, what about those 50 rations?'

Subsequent inquiries revealed what had happened. A regular German patrol had caught unawares the British occupants of an advanced post and had taken them prisoner. Deciding to take advantage of this opening, the German commander opposite had organised an immediate raiding party which was led back to the sap-head and filed into the communications trench one by one. They then quietly and efficiently marched down the front-line trench, accounting for each sentry as they passed. Lacking the resources, drive and ambition to continue this process until they wound up somewhere near the North Sea, they built up sandbag barricades at the limit of their triumphant procession and then turned their attention to the men in the dug-outs now at their mercy. They could have crudely tossed hand grenades into each one, thus announcing their presence, and sprinted back across no man's land. But this resourceful unit had too much style and panache for such a clumsy procedure. Instead they positioned themselves at the entrance to every dug-out, yelled 'Gas!' in English and grabbed the occupants as they emerged, drowsily, encumbered by their respirators. Their prisoners were then dragged across no man's land to become guests of the Fatherland for the rest of the war. For good measure they captured a party of Australian miners who had been expected to reach the German lines by the underground route! Astonishingly, so effective was the raid that neither of the companies on either side heard so much as an irregular footfall.

The British response was to send in the 2nd Leinsters to wreak a much more prosaic revenge for this embarrassment on the German lines in the Loos Triangle. Hitchcock was chosen to lead the raid, which would be conducted, in broad daylight, with four other officers and 80 men. The timing of the raid, the practice having heretofore been confined to the hours of darkness, was, doubtless, some staff officer's idea of a display of chutzpah similar to that of the recent German escapade. To assist the raiders and to avoid their being slaughtered while crossing to the German trenches, the element of surprise was essential. This was to be preserved by the absence of any preliminary bombardment. On the face of it the enterprise was an extremely hazardous one which defied the accepted 'rules' of trench combat: Do it in the dark or, if you don't, then plaster enemy lines with sufficient ordnance to dessicate his wire and ensure that he keeps his head down.

But the gamble paid off; the plan worked, with minimal British losses. This was partly down to the fact that the raiding party did not return to the line with the rest of the battalion but remained, far from the Loos cockpit, in Les Brebis. There they trained on mocked-up trenches, and, just as importantly, where they rested. The operation was also meticulously planned. The officers and men knew exactly what their function was, where they were to go and what was expected of them when they got there. It was like a well-rehearsed play, the difference being that the audience was likely to prove at best, imponderable, at worst assertively hostile.

During training, on 7 January 1917, Capper, still smarting from being a victim of one of the most outrageous German actions of the war, arrived to make the standard speech about the honour and glory of the Leinsters and how he knew they would get the job done.

The operation itself took place on 10 January.[26] Prior to moving off, each member of the party was blessed by the Padre and issued a tot of rum. Body and soul thus prepared, they moved carefully up to their jumping-off trenches which pushed out into no man's land. Had they been spotted, the mission might as well have been aborted, because they would have drawn fire from every artillery piece in the Loos Triangle. When a barrage began on their flanks, aimed at convincing the Germans that an attack might be coming to the right or left of the actual target, they moved off. Sappers armed with bangalore torpedoes (explosives encased in long metal strips) had left gaps in the German barbed wire, and the unit met no resistance as they headed towards these.

Hitchcock records the first moments of the raid in his diary: 'There is no doubt that we greatly surprised the enemy occupants at this point. I landed right on top of a Boche sentry standing by a periscope, occupied, not in recon-naissance, but in reading a newspaper. I never saw any man take off equipment with such rapidity as this sentry. He, a typical young Hun, stood with his hands up, livid with fright, yelling "Kamerad".'[27] The fact that he might have been trying to surrender loudly enough to alert his comrades doesn't seem to have occurred to the adrenalised Hitchcock.

The raiding party spent upwards of three quarters of an hour in the maze of German trenches of the Triangle, wreaking havoc. Prisoners were taken and dugouts were bombed. The whole affair lacked none of the audacity but most of the panache of the recent German operation. However, both its aims were achieved with deadly effect. Hitchcock, riding his luck, strode along the German parapet directing operations and presenting a ludicrously simple target. But no German sniper was able to summon the composure to take advantage. The raid produced eight German prisoners and at least 20 killed amongst the 9th Bavarian corps facing the Leinsters, as against five dead and 18 wounded for the Irish battalion. Predictably, the retaliatory barrage had already begun by the time the party returned to the British lines, but they passed on through and moved back to the reserve trenches. Hitchcock returned to an officer's mess bedecked with banners reading 'Vive les Irlandais'. He ate well, with an appetite he had not possessed that morning before the assault began.

Guy Nightingale, of the 1st Munsters, one of the few surviving veterans of V Beach, led a large scale raid involving 110 men at Tincourt Hamel on 18 February 1918. His unit was also taken out of the line for a week and allowed prepare over trenches which were dug to replicate those in the area they would be attacking. They performed the exercise nine times in daylight and 11 times at night. They too went into action fit and rested. Unlike Hitchcock's experience, however, this raid was more orthodox, it took place in darkness and was supported by a preliminary bombardment:

> At 4 a.m., which was zero hour, the barrage commenced with a roar all up the line. It was a fine old row and as we were firing gas shells and even liquid fire (thermite) it fairly frightened the Boshe [sic]. The moon had gone down but the light from the bursting shells was quite enough. Our men were splendid. The wire was all cut and they got five prisoners and killed a lot who showed fight and we came off with one man killed and about a dozen slightly wounded.[28]

For Nightingale, who had experienced unparalleled misery, danger and frustration at V Beach and Suvla, the success of the raid was heartening, 'though of course it was a very small show, it was ten times more to the point than anything we had in Gallipoli'.[29]

GOING OVER THE TOP

Most raids were 'small shows', destructive, wasteful of human life but not on a par with the full-frontal assault. In the Great War soldiers went 'over the top' much as they had been doing for hundreds of years, and with even more ruinous results. Between 1914 and 1918 the machine-gun made sure of that. It doled out death and injury at an unprecedented rate. It did so to troops who were hampered by the sheer weight of the accoutrements with which they went into battle. A man's most bulky items were his greatcoat, two blankets and a ground sheet. A lot of the weight would have been accounted for by the two hundred rounds of ammunition with which he was supplied. His rations consisted of three days' supply of the much loathed bully beef and biscuits, which were as hard and about as edible as dog biscuits. His water bottle was often the most essential item he carried, as, on occasions was his respirator. The main implement of his 'trade' was his rifle, but to afford him some cover in the open (on the rare occasions when he ever ventured onto truly 'open' ground) he carried a variety of entrenching tools.

Before venturing out into no man's land, troops had plenty of time to think about the prospect of being cut to pieces by machine-gun bullets or blown apart by a shell blast. As John Breen of the 2nd Royal Irish Regiment recalled, 'You stood there and tried to have a joke and a laugh. But you'd be thinking of your own people and would you ever see them again. Of course, there was always a chance you could be killed before you got over the top at all. Once you got over, you were all right, but it was the waiting. Waiting, waiting, waiting!'[30] Before going into action, soldiers would write letters home, pray, smoke, anything to take their minds off what lay ahead. Lt. John Staniforth of the 7th Leinsters had his own form of distraction: 'What does it feel like to go "up and over"? I don't know. I concentrated my thoughts on keeping my pipe alight. It seemed to be the most important thing at the moment, somehow.' Lt. J.F.B. O'Sullivan wrote to his mother about the sort of jitters which were typical of troops waiting for the whistle to blow:[31]

> We found ourselves at a spot, hidden from the enemy but with a good enfilade view of our assembly and support trenches; and there we prosaically chatted (if bellowing into each others ear could be called 'chatting') about lack of sleep and missing rations, till Fitz [Fitzgerald]

incautiously touched on the basic and taboo anxiety: our chances of surviving the looming day. He earnestly expounded his pet theory of 'probability ratio of five wounded to every one man killed – even in the fiercest battles'. A Job's comforter indeed; though whether the ratio prospect really raised his spirits was impossible to say, as his usual poker face and half closed eyes gave no flicker of emotion ... As a last warning to the men I shouted the grim Brigade orders against any falling-out to help wounded neighbours; a special RAMC group was supposed to be close behind us for that purpose, but as there was no sign of such a group the warning sounded cold-blooded and brutal. I took off my wrist watch, got the helmet strap fixed under my chin and waited fidgeting uneasily wishing for 12.03 to break the horrible apprehension. The crashing and deafening minutes dragged out endlessly and the forced inaction preyed on nerves and mind. Glancing at the waiting men it was hard to avoid a morbid wondering about their chances of surviving the coming hour. I was too tired to be very excited and the waves of sickening fear that had plagued me at various intervals during the morning had vanished – except for the odd sensation that my heart had been suspended on hair springs in the very middle of my stomach.[32]

Almost eighty years after he first went into action Dubliner Jack Campbell, talking to the author, could still recall and recreate the fear:

I never went over the top when I wasn't afraid. I was scared of my life every time I went over the top because I didn't think I was coming back ... Everybody seemed to shout. I suppose it was nerves or something like that. It came naturally to shout like hell. Of course the artillery had been in action before you went over and they'd smashed down the barbed wire entanglements and played merry hell with the Jerries but everyone shouted as they went over. Your whole thought was getting to the German trenches and getting cover, rather than be out in the open. I always prayed that if I did get hit I'd get hit in the body and not in the head because I figured if I got hit in the head there'd be no hope for me. But that was all wrong, because plenty of fellows got hit in the head and they lived. You were under fire all the time, from the time you were exposed. But you took your chances. When you do get through you say to yourself, 'How did I get through that lot? How did I manage?' You're thankful, of course but it's just luck in my opinion that you do get through, because the machine gunners are firing at you, every Jerry that can see you is firing at you.

As terrifying an experience as going 'over the top' was, some preferred it to the daily round of sniping and shelling. In June 1915 Eric Dorman-Smith wrote to his family: 'I wish they'd give us a show. It's really very easy to go on, once you've seen the enemy's trenches get shelled and got your blood up. The loss of whole platoons in an attack is not half so hard on the nerves as a few men shot through the head in trench work.'[33]

Once 'over the top', the tightness-inducing tension was replaced by a flood of adrenalin. Ivone Kirkpatrick, fighting against the Turks in Gallipoli, offered an interesting description of the emotions experienced by a man in a situation of extreme danger:

> My own state of mind is difficult to describe. My body and soul seemed to be entirely divorced, even to the extent that I felt that I no longer inhabited my body. My shell, at the bidding of purely automatic forces, over which I had no control, ran hither and thither collecting men, hacked its way through the scrub with a rifle, directed the fire of my platoon and in short struggled with all the duties which I had been taught to perform. But my mind was a distinct and separate entity. I seemed to hover at some height above my own body and to observe its doings and the doings of others with a sort of detached interest. I speculated idly on the possibility of my body being hit and thought it probably would be. I wondered if it would be in the head, round which so many bullets seemed to be flying; I felt no fear, only a mild sense of curiosity. Meanwhile my body strove and swore and sweated as we advanced.[34]

Death has as arbitrary a quality about it in war as it does in life. In the latter it is inevitable; in the former you can guard against it and it may still come, you can court it and it may not. That element of randomness, fortune, luck, call it what you will, played a determining role in the lives of many veterans of the war. Almost all who survived had at least one brush with death. Some, like Sgt. de Margry of the 2nd Royal Irish Regiment had more than his own allocation. Whatever 'things in heaven and earth' determined, whether he lived or died, his own 'philosophy' was one of conscious inaction:

> The curious aspect about the most dangerous moments is that one has not only to decide rightly, and in a flash, on the action to be taken, but that quite frequently the safest decision is to refrain from doing anything, since acting any other way might defeat the object – that is, saving one's skin. This has happened to me quite a few times when, if I hadn't stayed perfectly still just where I was I'd have been in much greater danger, as when trying to dodge falling and rapidly disintegrating or blazing aircraft shot down immediately above one's head during a dog fight. I actually saw two of our men crushed to death

against the trunk of a tree to which they had run for cover, by the engine from a falling aircraft, whereas by merely standing still where I was, with parts of the aircraft falling all round me, I didn't even have to duck once for safety – showing that luck, too, can play an important part at such times. I claim no merit for such action as I only wish to show that precipitate and instinctive moves at such times can be more dangerous than inactivity.[35]

Sometimes the soldier's good fortune could be ascribed to others. On one occasion de Margry had been involved in a raid, had flopped, exhausted, into a dug-out and had been dragged out again by an NCO who required him for fatigue work. Grumbling under his breath de Margry reluctantly marched off;

> Some few seconds later there was a blinding flash and a terrific explosion, and as we automatically turned round to see what had happened we were horrified to find that some heavy shell had completely obliterated the dug-out I'd only just left, and that all that could be seen of it was a huge crater about which some of the smoke and dust from the explosion could still be seen, but of the poor chaps I'd left sleeping there no sign of them could be seen anywhere. On realising I had had such a narrow and lucky escape, I somehow forgot my fatigue and went on my way feeling jolly thankful, specially towards the NCO, whom I'd been abusing *sotto voce* a minute or two before.[36]

The good fortune of the 'undeserving' often defied belief. In October 1915 Capt. Frank Hitchcock watched as

> A man of A company had one night gone out under the influence of drink. When this fact was discovered the NCO in charge tried to persuade him to go back, but nothing would induce him to. Instead he walked up and down in front of the enemy's wire entanglements to the left of Railway Wood, reviling the Huns in most awful language. He cursed them in the name of Cromwell and called on all his saints, including St Patrick, to come down and look at them! The Huns fired and machine-gunned him, but the darkness and the devil who looks after his own, saved him. He was eventually brought back by CSM Kerrigan, who had felled him with one blow, a dazed, hiccoughing lump of mortality, but absolutely unscathed![37]

But for every story of great good fortune there was always one of sheer and fatally bad luck. Anthony Brennan of the 2nd Royal Irish Regiment recounts in his memoirs the result of 'souvenir' hunting in German dugouts after the first day of fighting on the Somme: 'In the evening of the 2nd of July one of our men was down in a dug out when a RAMC orderly, of all people, bent on a similar treasure-hunt, threw a bomb down the shaft as a precautionary preliminary to his own descent. Our luckless comrade received it all to himself, and was thus our first loss in the Somme battle.'[38]

That was the nature of the Killing Machine of the Great War – random and brutal.

3   Irish Chaplains at the Front

In his book *The First Casualty* Phillip Knightley traces popular mistrust of newspaper stories to the trenches of the Great War. When soldiers went home on leave, they read accounts of life in the front lines which were often mere promotional propaganda. The credibility of the journalistic profession was severely dented by its supine and jingoistic coverage of the war. Much the same thing happened to the standing of the Church of England. Attendance at C of E services declined in the immediate post-war period, a dip which could not be totally explained by battlefront fatalities. Much of the decline was probably due to the disillusionment of ordinary soldiers with the quality of many of their Church of England chaplains. One of the most famous padres of the Great War was the Revd Geoffrey Studdert Kennedy, whose closeness to the troops earned him the nickname 'Woodbine Willie'. Kennedy's parents were Irish, and he himself had spent three years studying theology at Trinity College. His advice to all chaplains was simple: 'Work in the front line and they will listen to you.'[1] But it was advice which was not heeded by his own religious authorities. Anglican chaplains were not allowed to accompany troops to the front line; Roman Catholic chaplains were. The decline in Church of England attendances was accompanied by the alleged conversion of over 40,000 Church of England soldiers to Roman Catholicism.[2] Such was the influence of the chaplain in the Great War!

The inspirational figure of the chaplain, part-mediator with the Almighty, part-counsellor, part-consoler, part-entertainer, recurs in much of the material written from and about the front line soldier. Generally the references to 'the Padre' are glowing, or at the very least complimentary. Only occasionally do chaplains come in for criticism from troops, officers or contemporary writers. Research by Jane Leonard, then of Trinity College, tells us that 109 Church of Ireland clergymen were listed as wartime chaplains. Eight of these were killed or died of wounds, while three were decorated, receiving the Military Cross. A total of 25 Irish Presbyterian chaplains served with British Army units, while three more served with Colonial forces; four of them received the Military Cross. By far the biggest representation in proportion to the numbers of its congregation was the Methodist Church; 27 of its ministers became chaplains.[3] Estimates of the numbers of Irish Roman Catholic chaplains vary widely. The Irish Hierarchy was not over-zealous in its appointment of chaplains, partly because the Irish Catholic Church was not flush with priests in the initial years of the war. French and German Catholic missionaries had been withdrawn from parts of Africa when the war began, and many of them had been replaced by Irish Catholic missionaries, hence the shortage of priests. But when there were complaints that Irish Catholic soldiers were being sent into battle (for the protection, after all, of 'Little Catholic Belgium') without the ministrations of a priest the bishops issued a statement in 1915 indicating that 'We welcome applications from the zealous clergy for service as chaplains'.[4] A total of eight priests were appointed by the archbishop of Armagh, Cardinal Logue, as chaplains to the two Irish divisions, the 10th and the 16th. By the time of the armistice the *Irish Catholic Directory* claimed that over 500 Irish Catholic priests had served as chaplains during the war, an unlikely figure given that there were only 649 Roman Catholic chaplains in the entire armed services at the time of the armistice.

One of the principal functions of the chaplain in the Great War was also the most melancholy – the administering of the last rites. Some went to inordinate lengths to fulfill what they saw as a virtual covenant with their troops. As the war progressed, chaplains became conscious of the solace these ministrations brought to bereaved families and the effect they had on the morale of troops. Granted, some chaplians got no further than Casualty Clearing Stations, where they could minister to the dangerously ill, but others put themselves in the line of fire to get to dying men in no man's land. To a dying soldier in a simpler era the sight of a chaplain could be more consoling than the sight of stretcher bearers whom he knew could do nothing to save him. 'And his chaplain! The Irish battalion must have its chaplain as well as its colonel, and both must be of the best ... men like Father Finn, killed at V Beach, refusing to stay behind on the ship because, as he answered, "The place of the chaplain is with the dying soldier;" and like Father Gwynne, of the Irish Guards, killed at the French front.'[5]

The ambiguity of chaplains conducting religious services for men who were about to be sent out to kill will not be debated here. Few would have seen those particular ministrations in that light anyway. As far as they were concerned, they were preparing men for death. The consolation thus provided was important for the peace of mind of soldiers who did indeed stand a fair to middling chance of suffering a grotesque death.

Major Bryan Cooper's account of two chaplains in the 10th Brigade suggests how much solace was derived from the proximity of a 'sky pilot' (the affectionate nickname the troops had for their padres):

> Before dawn, each of the two chaplains attached to the Brigade held a service. The Church of England chaplain, the Revd J.W. Crozier, celebrated Holy Communion in the operating tent of the 30th Field

Ambulance, while Father O'Connor said Mass in the open air just outside the camp. It had been decided that the chaplains were not to come with the Brigade, but were to remain with the Field Ambulance. This decision caused much regret, not only to the chaplains themselves, but to all ranks in the Brigade. The Roman Catholics in particular disliked losing Father O'Connor even temporarily, for he was personally loved by the men, and in addition the Irish soldier faces death twice as cheerfully when fortified by the ministrations of his Church.[6]

But the presence of these men of the cloth undoubtedly had other consequences, intentional or fortuitous. In a era of elementary verities, religious rituals were also a reminder of one's cultural identity. By attending Mass or an Anglican service, the soldier was receiving a subliminal exhortation to kill the enemy in order to defend this cultural identity, to protect what he held sacred. In the case of the Eastern front, where the war was being prosecuted against an alien religion and culture whose troops often went into action chanting the name of 'Allah', the admonition could not have been more manifest. Writing about 7th Leinsters before their offensive at Guillemont on 3 September 1916 the Regimental historian, Lt.-Col. F.E. Whitton observed that 'The padre, Father Rafter MC, is spoken of with affection ... and there is a note of a service held by him the night before the Battalion "left for the line". Father Rafter held a service on the bare side of a hill, ankle deep in mud. It was a deeply impressive sight and sent the men into action with a burning faith in the justice of their cause.'[7] Some contemporary writers saw the chaplain as an essential constituent of the war machine. Not only did his presence give a spiritual and religious legitimacy to a dubious cause, but it helped in the practical attainment of ends: 'In order that the Catholic soldier may thus show himself at his best, it is necessary that he should have ready access to the rites of the Church ... Thus the Irish Catholic soldier goes into battle stimulated by the services of his chaplain ...'[8]

World War I padres had considerable rank and status. They were officers, but they were not subject to the constant danger and recurrent unpopularity of their peers. Chaplains came to visit the front-line troops, look after the sick and minister to the dying. They did not usually give orders which put soldiers in harm's way. As officers, chaplains were frequently called upon to censor the letters of troops. In many cases they would also become the custodians of the final letters home of men who had died. It was common for a soldier who was about to go over the top to entrust what could be his final message to his family to the hands of a padre. In his propagandistic work *The Irish at the Front* Michael McDonagh, who had read some of those letters, wrote that 'happily in none have I come upon any heroics about the nobility of the youth's self-sacrifice and the grandeur of the cause for which he died'.[9]

Attendance at courts martial was also another regular duty of the chaplain. They would often be asked to defend prisoners against charges up to the level of desertion or murder which carried the death penalty. A chaplain might also be expected to look after the morality of his troops, this meant discouraging them from frequenting brothels.

Church of Ireland clergy were better paid than their Catholic counterparts. (Many Anglican padres were better paid than curates who did not enlist and remained in Britain.) Odious comparisons were made between Roman Catholic and Anglican clergymen, both in terms of their physical courage and their workloads. The restrictions placed on the Anglican padres often led to their being unfairly branded as cowards. (Though with 88 Anglican chaplains killed, as against 30 Catholic, it is clear that many paid scant attention to the instruction to keep out of the firing line.) They also seemed to have far less work to do than their RC counterparts, though this was probably a function of the difference in rituals between the two churches. Some Anglican chaplains were remote from the needs of their co-religionists, preaching sermons on obscure topics to men whose minds were on the battle ahead. There is no evidence, however, that Irish Protestant chaplains were out of touch with their flocks in that way.

In the front lines, being a non-combatant (in theory at least – some chaplains actually wielded weapons when the humour took them) was no guarantee of security. Take Gallipoli, for example, where,

> With very few exceptions it was impossible to have a parade service near the firing line. Owing to the number of hostile aeroplanes that were continually scouting, the men on parade would be exposed to immediate shell-fire. The alternative was to take the men in the trenches by battalion and have celebrations of the Holy Communion. The officiating chaplain wore no vestments over his uniform, only a stole, as anything white would attract sniper's fire.[10]

A total of 172 padres were killed in the Great War, 16 of whom were Irish. Among the best known Irish chaplains to die were Fr Willie Doyle (who is discussed elsewhere) and Fr Finn, the first padre of the war to be killed, who died at Gallipoli after having ignored an order not to go ashore with the troops. He was a Tipperary man serving with the 1st Dublin Fusiliers. Before the V Beach landing he asked to be allowed to accompany the Dublins into what became an infamous massacre. He is reputed to have said, 'The priest's place is beside the dying soldier; I must go.'[11] He certainly spent a considerable part of the day beside dying soldiers as there was an abundance of them at V Beach. He attempted to save a number of drowning and wounded men before being hit himself, in the right arm. He managed to get ashore and crawled around the beach offering help or consolation to the wounded and dying Dublins and Munsters. In order to give absolution he had to hold up an injured right arm with his left. While he was blessing one of the men in this fashion, there was a shrapnel burst above him which blew part of his skull away. He was buried on the beach and his grave marked with a cross made out of an ammunition box 'To the Memory of the Revd Capt. Finn'.

The first chaplain to be wounded in action, at Cuinchy in February 1915, was also an Irishman, Fr John Gwynne from Galway, a Jesuit who served with the Irish Guards and who had volunteered for service as soon as the war broke out. He was hit by a blast of shellfire as he approached a German trench and was unconscious for a while.

'A Doctor bandaged me up,' he wrote, 'and I found I was not so bad – splinters of the shell just grazed my face, cutting it; a bit, too, struck me an inch or so above the knee and lodged inside, but in an hour's time, when everything was washed and bandaged, I was able to join and give Extreme Unction to a poor Irish Guardsman who had been badly hit.'[12] In the autumn of that year, at the Battle of Loos, Gwynne was in the thick of the fighting again. An Irish Guardsman described how he had watched the priest during an attack on an objective known as Hill 70:

> Once I thought he was buried alive, for a shell exploded within a few yards of where he was, and the next moment I saw nothing but a great heap of earth. The plight of the wounded concealed beneath was harrowing. Out of the ground came cries of 'Father, Father, Father' from those who were in their death agonies. Then, as if by a miracle Father Gwynne was seen to fight his way through the earth. He must have been severely injured, but he went on blessing the wounded and hearing their confessions. The last I saw of him was kneeling by the side of a German soldier. It was a scene to make you cry.[13]

A short time later Gwynne was in the HQ dugout when a German shell landed in the doorway. He received eight separate wounds. He died in hospital in Bethune the following morning

'Muscular' Christians, like Fathers Finn and Gwynne, abounded among the ranks of the serving clergy. These were men who abjured the passive, ministering role and opted for engagement. Stationed at Ypres in 1915, Frank Hitchcock of the 2nd Leinsters wrote in his diary on 1 July about a visit from the battalion chaplain, one who clearly disliked the quasi-observer status of his profession: 'The Padre came round to see us on his black Uhlan horse. Its previous owner had actually surrendered to him at Le Cateau, when he was Chaplain to the Cavalry Brigade.'[14] The Revd William Forrest, an Irish Roman Catholic chaplain, was in no doubt about the credentials required of the worthy padre: 'Priests between thirty and forty, not afraid of some rough and tumble, with, perhaps, an adventurous vein in their composition, and with plenty of zeal and sympathy, would be the most suitable – riders and good horse-masters rather than ponderous theologians and professors, though, indeed, these would have much to learn, and would greatly profit, by their experience.'[15] Tipperary priest Fr Francis Gleeson fitted Forrest's blueprint very well. Serving with the 2nd Munsters, he was adept at the mouth organ and brought one with him everywhere he went. He even supplied them to his troops![16] One Munster related how Gleeson, tending to wounded in a French village near the front line gave him absolution: 'It got so hot with stray bullets that he gave me absolution as I stood in the street of the ruined village. It was very dramatic, I covered with mud and standing bareheaded, and he blessing me. I'll never forget it.'[17] The courage of many Irish chaplains saw some of them decorated for bravery. Three priests with the 16th (Irish) Division at Guillemont and Ginchy were rewarded. Fr Maurice O'Connell received a DSO while Fr Willie Doyle SJ and Fr Rafter SJ got the Military Cross. Two MCs had also gone to chaplains with the 36th (Ulster) Division after the carnage of 1 July 1916 on the Somme; the Revd J. Jackson Wright, a Presbyterian minister from Ballyshannon, Co. Donegal, and the Revd Joseph Henry McKew, a Church of Ireland clergyman from Clones in Co. Monaghan, were the recipients.

In the novel/memoir of his service in the Great War, *The Great Push*, Patrick MacGill recounts an act of courage by a Roman Catholic chaplain at Loos. MacGill and his comrades in the 1st London Irish Rifles had watched as a mule-driven supply-wagon took a wrong turning and came under fire in an exposed position from a German machine-gun. One of the two drivers was killed immediately, but the second managed to find some cover after being hit. As MacGill looked on, a distant figure emerged from cover, ran for fifty yards and disappeared into a shell hole. A few moments later he was up again, sprinting, before he dived face forward to avoid a hail of bullets. His third effort got him to the wagon, and that was the last any of the London Irish saw of him. Later that day MacGill heard that the battalion's Roman Catholic chaplain, Fr Lane-Fox, had brought the wounded wagon driver into a dressing station shortly after dusk. MacGill wrote:

> The London-Irish love Father Lane-Fox; he visited the men in the trenches daily, and all felt better for his coming. Often at night the sentry on watch can see a dark form between the lines working with a shovel and spade burying the dead. The bullets whistle by, hissing of death and terror; now and then a bomb whirls in the air and bursts

loudly; a shell screeches like a bird of prey; the hounds of war rend the earth with frenzied fangs; but indifferent to all the clamour and tumult the solitary digger bends over his work burying the dead. 'It's old Father Lane-Fox,' the sentry will mutter. 'He'll be killed one of these fine days'.

Some war-time clergy were capable of egregiously un-Christian deeds. A Dublin Fusiliers chaplain, Fr Murphy, was on Suvla beach near a medical station during an offensive. As he tended to the needs of the wounded and dying, elements of the 33rd Brigade abandoned an attack on 9 August on Hill 70 and 112 and returned to the beach. Some approached the station for treatment and got short shrift from the irate cleric. As McDonagh relates, 'Father Murphy tells us it was the only time he was ever in a rage – "God forgive me, I hit some of them".'[18]

By far the best known and revered Irish chaplain of the Great War was the Jesuit Fr Willie Doyle, winner of a Military Cross on the Somme in 1916 and recommended for a posthumous Victoria Cross in 1917. Doyle possessed the sort of physical bravery of which war heroes are made, but it was a courage which was used exclusively in helping the troops to whom he ministered. Doyle was 41 years old when hostilities began. A spare man with a high-domed forehead and slightly aquiline features, he led such a charmed life in the front line that myths grew up among the troops of the 16th Division about his invulnerability. Once when he crawled into a dugout along with half a dozen men, one of them remarked, 'We're safe now, anyhow.' And on another, similar occasion it was, 'Isn't the priest of God with us, what more do you want?'[19] In his letters to his father, Doyle's tremendous humanity comes across; his physical courage was left to others to describe.

He took huge risks for the living but did not discriminate against the dead when it came to using up his quota of luck. Once, not long after becoming chaplain to two battalions of the 49th Brigade, he organised a burial party in an exposed position. It was his first war burial.

> As soon as it was dark, [he wrote] we carried the poor fellow out on a stretcher, just as he had fallen, and as quietly as we could began to dig the grave. It was weird. We were standing in front of the German trenches on two sides, though a fair distance away, and every now and then a star-shell went up which we felt certain would reveal our presence to the enemy. I put my ritual in the bottom of my hat and with the aid of an electric torch read the burial service, while the men screened the light with their caps, for a single flash would have turned the machine-guns on us. I cannot say if we were seen or not, but all the time bullets came whizzing by; ... somehow I felt quite safe, as if the dead soldier's guardian angel was sheltering us from all danger, till the poor dust was laid to rest.[20]

That experience persuaded Doyle that he should dispense with the torch and learn the burial service off by heart for the future.

Frank Laird, serving with the 8th Dublin Fusiliers, often came across Doyle and was a frequent witness to his acts of bravery.

> When shells dropped round, [he recalled] ordinary mortals took cover or an opposite direction. Father Doyle made for them to see was he wanted. One morning in the line I was standing watching the communication trench a short way down getting a very nasty shelling. In a few minutes Father Doyle arrived smiling, having just come through it on his usual visit to the front line, without his tin hat, which he could not be induced to wear ... Is it any wonder that he was welcome in every mess, that the men worshipped the ground he trod on, and that he was worth several officers in any hot spot where endurance was tested to its height?'[21]

At Messines, in 1917, the 48th Brigade, to which Doyle was then attached, was in reserve, assembled along a sandbag parapet known as 'Chinese Wall'. Their position was under heavy shell-fire. One shell exploded right on the parapet blowing three men fifty yards away and burying five more. Laird recalled how.

> Fr Doyle ran out at once and gave absolution to the three dying men. Then he ran back to the wall where the men seemed paralysed into inaction, except one sergeant who was tearing away the sandbags and cursing volubly. The Padre came to his assistance and, his presence having the usual effect, the others plucked up heart to give a hand so that they dug out three of the five men alive, the other two having been killed by the explosion. After this, as some of the troops were getting unsteady under the heavy fire in their exposed position, the good Padre restored their confidence by walking along the line without his tin hat or gas mask, which, as frequently happened him, he had forgotten.[22]

At one point (probably before the Battle of Messines) Doyle became a sort of front line 'anchorite', living in a dugout within sight of German gun batteries. 'I loved my tiny sand-bag hut, even though the roof was wondrous low and you had almost to put your legs outside the door if you wanted to stretch them. It would have given about as much protection as a cardboard box, had a shell hit it plump.' After a few close calls the 16th Division staff ceased to approve of his domestic arrangements, however, as 'the General [presumably Hickie CO of the 16th Division] came along and seeing the state of affairs, told the Padre to get him gone out of the danger zone, which I am sorry to say the disobedient Padre did not do; and then gave orders for the house to be pulled down, even though he had to admit that not a penny of rent was due.' (Doyle was recommended for a DSO at Messines/Wytschaete.)

The inspirational Jesuit chaplain had so many brushes with death that he almost began to believe in the myth of his own invulnerability. The last letter he wrote to his father, on 14 August 1917, read: 'I have told you all my escapes, dearest Father, because I think what I have written will give you the same confidence which I feel that my old armchair up in Heaven is not ready yet and I do not want you to be uneasy about me.'[24] But Doyle was to die, as were so many of the men of his 48th Brigade, in the mud of Third Ypres, sold short by the incompetent and careless staff work of the 5th Army, led by an Irishman, General Gough. The circumstances of his death are disputed and are dealt with in more detail in *Irish Voices from the Great War*.[25] He was killed, on 16 August 1917 on Frezenberg Ridge, and his body was never found. One Dublin Fusilier, Jimmy O'Brien, interviewed by Kieran Sheedy of RTE, claimed that

> Fr Willie Doyle was shot down beside me I can't remember where Doyle was killed. In a thing like that it was all for yourself. You see, you were trained, if your own brother was shot down, you mustn't stop, you must go on. There's people coming behind to look after him. I saw Fr Doyle being wounded but I didn't realise that he was killed. I just saw him falling down.

The reaction to Doyle's death was one of universal dismay, best encapsulated by the generous tribute of a Belfast Orangeman in the *Glasgow Weekly News* on 1 September 1917 who wrote that

> Fr Doyle was a good deal among us. We couldn't possibly agree with his religious opinions, but we simply worshipped him for other things. He didn't know the meaning of fear, and he didn't know what bigotry was. He was as ready to risk his life to take a drop of water to a wounded Ulsterman, as to assist men of his own faith and regiment. If he risked his life in looking after Ulster Protestant soldiers once, he did it a hundred times in the last few days.[26]

There was a bizarre tribute, by way of postscript, to the work and the spirit of Fr Doyle five years after his death. The story may be apocryphal but still gives an indication of the man's reputation. A burglar is supposed to have broken into the house of the priest's father, in Dalkey, and made the old man get up and unlock every drawer in the house. In one drawer he came across a photograph of the Jesuit and asked, 'Who's that?' Mr Doyle told him and the burglar responded, 'That was a holy priest, he saved many souls.' Whereupon he abandoned everything else he had intended stealing and left, taking only the photograph!

Chaplains were, officially, supposed to be under 45 years of age. Two men, who always seemed to hunt as a pair, were far from that vintage. Fr Murphy and Canon McClean of the 10th (Irish) Division were 48 and 60 respectively when they landed at Gallipoli. Despite the appalling conditions in which they operated, they never let their mature years get the better of them or interfere with their calling. McClean was the rector of the parish of Rathkeale and was a white-haired sharp-featured individual. Murphy was noted for his handsome smiling face and jovial disposition. Each was as fond of the other as the troops were fond of them. McClean wrote of Murphy, 'We occupied the same tents, we lived in the same dug-outs, and we held services in the trenches side by side. He was my constant adviser and friend in health and in sickness and was always looking after me. The affection I had for him was shared by officers and men of all ranks in the brigade.'[27] On 18 August 1915, Murphy wrote in his diary of the Church of Ireland padre, 'He is a splendid colleague.'

In his own diary account of the Suvla campaign Lt. Noel Drury wrote glowingly of the pair: 'Canon McClean and Father Murphy came round about 13.00 and insisted on going round and chatting to the men in spite of the risk. I don't know what we would do if anything happened either of them. They are the only two Padres we ever see near the line and the men are delighted to see them.'[28] Drury, as befitted his religion, was more partial towards McClean, rationalising that

> Father Murphy is a regular and it is his job to be up here, but the dear old Canon just does it because he thinks he ought to. He is really too old for this climate and rough life, and we notice a considerable change in him since he came out, but he is as cheery as ever and loves going along the line and chatting to the men. He hardly ever comes up without some little thing in his haversack for the men. I hear he goes off to the hospital ships and spins such terrible yarns about the hardships of the men that he seldom, if ever, goes away empty-handed.[29]

Major Bryan Cooper described McClean as 'the jewel of the Protestant chaplains'. He surmised that the padre was the oldest man in the Division but observed that

> No dangers or hardships were too great for him to endure, and his one regret was that his cloth did not permit him to lead his Brigade in a

charge. He had, too, the more valuable form of courage, the power of patient endurance, for, though seriously ill with dysentery, he absolutely refused to go sick and leave his men. There were many brave fellows in the Division, but none gained a greater reputation for courage than Canon McLean.[30]

Murphy and McClean were clearly great personal friends but theirs was by no means a typical relationship. There was often considerable rivalry between Irish chaplains of the country's two main religions. In addition it was frequently alleged that Catholic chaplains received a raw deal from the authorities, though some of the blame for this attaches to the Roman Catholic hierarchy. The archbishop of Westminster, Cardinal Bourne, was directly responsible for recruiting Roman Catholic clergy, into the British Army. Embarrassed by drunken incidents during the Boer war involving Catholic clergy Bourne liked to select chaplains personally. He was also of the opinion that they should be engaged on the basis of temporary commisions only (he felt that officially commissioned chaplains were overpaid).[31] Bourne's attitude tallied nicely with the approach of the War Office. The Irish hierarchy, as has been pointed out, initially showed no great enthusiasm for persuading Irish Roman Catholic priests to sign up for war service.

This led to a perception that Roman Catholic clergy were not well treated *vis á vis* their Protestant colleagues. The chaplain to the Connaught Rangers, Fr James MacRory, certainly felt this to be the case and devoted large tracts of his diary to fulminations against the authorities for perceived slights. Catholic chaplains, he pointed out, received half the pay and none of the allowances of other denominations but had far more onerous duties to perform. The worst treatment, according to MacRory, was meted out to Irish Catholic clergy. They were often posted to non-Irish regiments or to units with few Catholic soldiers. He claimed that 'the Catholic chaplain in the army is a doormat for the Protestant minister'.[32] MacRory wanted chaplains to be chosen by their own bishops and given official commissions. MacRory's complaints, though often bigotted and coming from a man who suffered greatly from shell-shock, were supported by the archbishop of Armagh, Cardinal Logue, who noted, in June 1915, that 'Catholic priests are not recognised … they have no official position.'[33]

Religious tolerance and mutual accomodation were the norms of the grisly Great War conflict. *In extremis* few questions were asked about the religious faith of men upon whom one's life might depend. The Revd H.C. Foster, who served in Gallipoli, wrote of 'the lack of sectarian hostility between Irish Protestant and Catholic soldiers'.[34] But bigotry or sheer ignorance could often be close to the surface. Take, for example, the indefatigable diarist Lt. Noel Drury, a Protestant and unionist member of the 6th Royal Dublin Fusiliers.

He made his feelings towards a particular Roman Catholic chaplain (and others of that ilk) quite plain in a diary entry during the period his battalion was stationed at Alexandria in Egypt in 1917. 'Father W.J. O'Carroll, the R.C. Chaplin [*sic*],' he wrote, 'seemed surprised that the Egyptians wore any clothes, as he said he thought " 'Natives' never wore clothes." He is a perfect specimen of the Maynooth-trained young priest – bigotted, narrow-minded and (from a worldly point of view) absolutely uneducated.'[35] Later that year, as the 10th Division neared Jerusalem, he pronounced, with considerable glee that 'Padre O'Carroll held an R.C. service in the gulley this morning and there was not a single person there, but he seemed to be quite oblivious of the fact as he kept his back turned to where they should have been, all the time of the service.'[36]

Chaplains themselves could be selective about whom they ministered to. Francis Ledwidge, wounded in Salonika while serving with the 10th Division, wrote home about one incident which occurred to him. While in hospital in Cairo, a Church of England clergyman 'seemed to be taking a great interest in me and promised me a book of poetry, but suddenly he saw on my chart that I was an RC and hurried from me as if I were possessed. He never came over to me since, although he has been in the ward many times. I wonder if God asked our poor chaps were they RCs or C of Es when they went to Him on August 15th.'[37] The date to which he referred was the day on which the 10th Division had suffered huge losses in the attack on Kiretch Tepe Sert overlooking Suvla Bay.

A friend of Frank Laird, during the Suvla campaign, was wounded in the stomach. Though stretcher-bearers managed to get him back to the beach alive, he was expected to die. Ten years after the event Laird wrote of how confusion and ignorance had prevented his friend from receiving the ministrations of a chaplain: 'Our friend was duly deposited on the beach, where divers chaplains examined his identification disc, and seeing C of I on it, the RC, C of E and others decided he could not belong to any of them, and so he failed to get the spiritual consolation they might have supplied.'[38] As it turned out, he didn't need it anyway as he managed somehow to survive his wounds.

The fact that Anglican chaplains were not supposed to accompany the troops up to the firing-line until 1916 told against them. Many troops, as a result, formed a low opinion of the Anglican chaplain. In his *Memoir of an Infantry Officer* Siegfried Sassoon satirised the Church of England chaplain's final injunction to his troops before battle thus: 'And now go with God. I shall go with you as far as the clearing station.'[39] Roman Catholic chaplains seemed to be far more in touch with the needs of their men and with the mentality of the man about to go into battle. Their Anglican counterparts tended to be more rigid and doctrinaire in their approach. Their sermons were often about obscure subjects which held little interest for the working class troops in their care. Meanwhile Catholic priests, like Fr Francis Gleeson of the Royal Munster Fusiliers (the man who used to order mouth organs for the entertainment of his men), delivered fiery and uplifting talks in which nationality and religiosity played a huge part. In 1914, writing about the flags carried by each company of the 2nd Munsters he observed: 'We are "Les Irlandais" and not "Les Anglais". Our flags have done that ... On all sides the Munsters are being congratulated for their magnificent behaviour. This is due to the men's faith! They are the best conducted battalion of all the Armies engaged in this world war, because they are the most Irish, the most Catholic, and the most pure.'[40] (The association of 'Irish' 'Catholic' and 'pure' is also a significant one.)

IRISH CHAPLAINS IN THE AUSTRALIAN ARMY

Most World War I chaplains knew very little about the army when they joined up, and were forced to adapt to life in the raw. This was especially true of padres in the Australian army, a largely volunteer force with less inhibitions than their British counterparts. One Anglican chaplain waited on a troopship in dock in Australia to greet his men as they filed on board. Most staggered up the boardwalk in a state of intoxication and ignored his proffered greeting. Some were so drunk they had to be carried on board. He spent most of the initial journey locked in his cabin, appalled at the obscene language (a normal part of Anzac argot) which floated in through his open porthole.[41]

Had he been a native-born Australian he might not have been so horrified. But Anglican chaplains of Australian birth were a rarity in the Anzac forces. There had been an initial rush of clerical volunteers, and most of those chosen for service were English. One Tasmanian clergyman noted that

> when there are hard and difficult posts to be filled, with no honour and glory attached, there is need for a native ministry, but when there is a position of honour and glory, although perhaps dangerous the motto is 'No Australians Need Apply.' I am full of admiration for the chaplains who have gone, but I am sorry that in an Australian force no room was found for Australian clergy.[42]

At least one Irish born cleric was an exception to this; Everett Digges La Touche didn't procure a chaplaincy when he applied, so he simply joined the Army anyway.[43]

The situation was entirely different among Roman Catholic clergy. There were few applicants and the chaplain-general, Archbishop Carr, found it hard to get Roman Catholic priests to accompany the AIF to Gallipoli. Fr John

Fahey was one who did volunteer. He had been born in Tipperary in 1883, ordained in 1907 and posted to Australia almost immediately. Fahey was an outdoor priest. He worked among the timbermen of Western Australia and enjoyed sharing their life. He was teak-tough, a fine sportsman and a good shot. All attributes which gave him far more status among his community than did any intricate knowledge of theological niceties. Fahey joined the Australian Imperial Force in September 1914, was assigned to the 11th Battalion (mostly recruited in Western Australia) and sailed with the first contingent of the AIF to Gallipoli.

He was the first chaplain ashore there because he flouted orders to remain on board ship when the Gallipoli landings took place in April 1915. For the first few days of the Gallipoli campaign he remained the only priest at the beachhead. He worked himself incessantly until he became ill in November and was evacuated. He rejoined his battalion in March 1916 and was with them in France until November, 1917. By the time he returned to Australia he had already become one of the longest serving front line chaplains in the AIF.

Fahey's attitude to war was strangely ambiguous. He enjoyed working with soldiers in extreme situations and reflected in a letter to his bishop, Archbishop Clune of Perth, that 'the war is not altogether an unmixed evil. It has brought men to the Sacraments who have not been to confession for years, and perhaps never intended to go had it not been for the war. Even men who had only been baptised, but had never been to a Catholic church, have been to confession. They are very good lads indeed; and I am delighted with the results of my work.'[44] This sentiment is echoed by another Irish Catholic chaplain with the AIF, Fr Edward McAuliffe. He once wrote to the archbishop of Sydney, Michael Kelly, ' ... very few *escape* [my italics] without the Sacraments. Parents who have careless sons will be glad to know this, for the War and uncertainty of life are excellent aids to amendment.'[45] Fahey's work, as he described it, often offered surreal moments such as this description of an unusual confession: 'It is all so strange and uncanny. Passing along the trenches, a soldier with his rifle through a loophole and one eye on the enemy may call me to hear his confession; while it is being done the bullets are plopping into the sandbags of the parapet a few inches away. It is consoling and satisfactory work, if a little dangerous.'[46]

Fahey claimed not to have been aware of the order restraining chaplains from going ashore in the initial attack wave, which is why he was crammed into a troop transport as it made its way with 50 men on board, towards Anzac cove; '... it was the longest and most painful journey I ever made,' he wrote to Archbishop Clune.

> It seemed ages while we were getting there. The sailor in the stern was
> hit first, then another fell across me; then an oarsman dropped his oar

and fell to the bottom of the boat, his place being immediately taken by another. It was horrible. You could see no enemy. You could not return the fire. You could not take cover ... you just had to sit there and wait for your bullet ... there was only one wish and that was to reach the shore.[47]

Fahey's luck held, both off and on shore. As he used an entrenching tool to dig some cover for himself on the beach, the men on either side of him were shot and killed. He rode his luck well in the days which followed the establishment by the Anzac forces of their inadequate beachhead:

> I have had four bullets in my pack, one through a jam tin out of which I was eating, which spoiled the jam and made me very wild. One through my water-bottle; one through a tobacco tin in my pocket; one took the epaulette off my tunic, and once I had nineteen shrapnel bullets through a waterproof sheet on which I was lying only a few minutes previously. I have lost count of the shells that nearly accounted for me; I hardly expect to get through the business alive, but seeing that I have been lucky so far I may.[48]

(In fact only one Australian chaplain was killed at Gallipoli though many others were psychologically traumatised by their experiences.)

Fahey's courage was well known among the Australian troops (he once led an attack against the Turks when all the officers in the 11th Battalion had been immobilised). One officer wrote to the archbishop of Perth thanking Clune for having appointed Fahey: 'The Padre fills in his spare time carrying up provisions to the men at the front, and helps the wounded back, and I can tell you he is not afraid to go where the bullets fall pretty thickly.'[49] Not all Australian chaplains were quite so courageous. George G. Allardyce, a Dublin-born stretcher-bearer with the 4th Field Ambulance of the AIF, wrote to his father about Australian Anglican chaplains after the AIF's transfer to the Western Front:

> I do not know who that parson was who was telling you about his experiences over here, but I would like to have a few words with him. They have no room to talk; the officer's mess at the Main Dressing Station is about as far as they get. I think if some of them heard a shell explode they would drop dead. I have seen a few of them run for their lives before today when the shells lobbed nearby.[50]

Ironically Fahey expressed the belief once that chaplains should not risk life and limb by spending too much time in the front line (a stricture he frequently ignored himself). He argued that a chaplain was hard to replace and served an important function, especially in raising the morale of the families of those who died of their wounds, by ensuring they knew their loved ones had not died without the ministrations of a priest. In a letter to Archbishop Clune from France, he wrote that

> The chaplain going about among the wounded in the battlefield, or going over the parapets to administer to one dying man, reads very well in books, but it is impracticable and unwise in battles as they are fought here. A dead chaplain is of no use to anybody. They are not easily replaced, as they cannot be drawn from the ranks. Needless exposure is therefore unwise, and Heaven knows there are dangers enough without it.[51]

His place, according to Fahey, was at the Casualty Clearing Station where the wounded and dying were brought. (However, he also noted that there was not a single square yard of the defensive positions at Anzac Cove which was not within range of the Turkish guns. In that sense the Casualty Clearing Stations were, in effect, in the front line anyway.)

Fr John Fahey survived the Great War. Not so fortunate was his compatriot, a Jesuit, Fr Michael Bergin. A Tipperary man, like Fahey, Fr Bergin was unusual in that, although he served as a chaplain in the AIF, he never set foot in Australia. He had been born in Roscrea in 1879, the son of a mill owner, and had worked mostly in the Middle East from the time of his ordination in August 1910. He was an indomitably cheerful and charming individual who does not appear to have had the sort of intellect one often associates with membership of the Jesuit Order. He was based in Damascus when the war broke out and was immediately interned by the Turkish government there. Later he was expelled from Syria and made his way to Cairo, arriving in January 1915. Here he met up with the Australian soldiers who had arrived in Egypt just a month before him. As Roman Catholic chaplains in the AIF were thin on the ground, he assisted with masses and confessions but was prohibited, as a civilian priest, from travelling with the Anzac forces to Gallipoli – until, that is, the ingenuity of the Aussies overcame the technicality by having him embark for the war zone with the Light Horse Brigade (by now an infantry unit) as Trooper Bergin.

Once he had enlisted, his commission as chaplain came through quickly, and it was in this capacity that he served at Gallipoli until his health broke down in October 1915. He served as priest, comforter and stretcher-bearer until he was invalided back to England with enteric fever. Not allowing himself sufficient time for recuperation, he tried to return to the front before Christmas but got no further than Lemnos, where he remained as a hospital chaplain before he was evacuated to Alexandria in January 1916.

In July 1916 he travelled with the 13th Australian Infantry Brigade to France. Like Fr John Fahey, Bergin appears to have viewed the conflict in the Western Front as a far more deadly affair than the murderous sideshow in Gallipoli. His letters, which previously had dealt with the hardships faced by others, now spoke of his own discomforts and difficulties. His final letter home was written on 6 October 1917, and he was killed five days later while moving into the front line with the 13th Brigade. As he stood at the entrance to an Aid Post near Zonnebike, a few miles north-east of Ypres, a German shell burst a few yards away from him and killed him instantly. He was 38 years of age when he died. Bergin, who was described by his senior chaplain as 'tall, spare, gaunt; he looked the typical Jesuit of anti-Catholic literature', was a popular figure among the Australian soldiers. In July 1916 his battalion Commanding Officer had written, 'I am sure no man was, or could be, more popular and loved, not only by members of his own flock, but by all others.' His effect on the morale of the troops with whom he served was acknowledged in a note opposite his name in the records of the 51st Battalion, among those cited for conspicuous merit. It read: 'For ready attention to the wounded, indomitable energy and cheerfulness to all ... '[52]

4 'Shell Shocked': The Psychological Effects of the Great War

We can speculate that the great 'sporting' army which went to war weighed down by the values of the playing field and brimming over with adolescent innocence was always more prone to disillusionment when confronted by the sordid and obscene reality of the Western Front than the soldiers of the more 'martial' nations whose ancient conflicts had brought the carnage about in the first place. But we do not know if the shock of the trenches was any more traumatic for those first raw, idealistic volunteer British soldiers (conscription was not introduced until 1916) than it was for the inexperienced French and German conscripts who were renewing an old quarrel in a new generation.

Soldiers from both sides were asked to tolerate conditions that flesh and blood could not be expected to endure. And yet endure it most of them did! Wounds healed, heat and cold were tolerated, hunger was borne with and without complaint. The physical discomforts and scars may have come and passed, but the psychological effects were incalculable. In his own Second World War memoirs Sam McAughtry writes about some of the Great War psychic 'wrecks' who populated his childhood in Tigers Bay in Belfast,[1] veterans of the 36th Ulster Division and its appointment with destiny on the first day of the Battle of the Somme. Sean O'Casey's Harry Hegan, proud bearer of 'The Silver Tassie' as a pre-war sportsman, returns from the conflict an embittered paraplegic. Irish literature and modern folklore abounds with similar examples of the 'Great Undead' from the conflict, wounded veterans who see out their days in physical or psychological torment, men who remain silent about their experiences throughout their lives.

It is hardly surprising that war should have such an effect. It is especially unsurprising in the case of the 'Great War' which was great only in compass and scope, not in its innate morality. Indeed, what is surprising is that far more men were not permanently crippled emotionally by what they saw and experienced. It is clear from memoirs and even from correspondence that soldiers quickly became desensitised at the front. The word 'callous', with its connotations of the growth of a hard protective flesh, is an appropriate description. Callousness became a defence mechanism, black humour in the face of death a necessary refuge. The extra layer of flesh allowed one to ignore what was happening and move on. Denis Kelly from Dysart in Co. Roscommon, an Irish Guard, told RTE's Jim Fahy about watching four men cleaning their rifles: 'A shell came over and it blew the four of them up, up in the air, no trace of them hardly. But you take no notice, not a bit. You hadn't time to be looking at them. You had to keep going.'[2] It helped if one could also dehumanise the enemy, though it must have been difficult to retain a sense of one's own humanity at the same time. Captain Paddy Tobin was a Trinity College medical student who died at Kiretch Tepe Sert in August 1915. Shortly after landing at Suvla Bay, he wrote to his father: 'Thursday 12th saw us trying to snipe Turks and I thought of you and me trying to snipe rabbits at Aughavanagh. There is some difference between the two forms of sport; and the bigger the game, the finer the excitement.'[3]

There might be sympathy for the anonymous dead, but there was also pragmatism. Anthony Brennan of the Royal Irish Regiment still retained a certain amount of his native sentimentality when viewing the bodies of dead Welsh troops lying untended in a wood in the wake of the Somme catastrophe:

> the men available to bury them [were] so few that large numbers of them remained lying about all around us throughout the time we were there. Rigor mortis had set in, and the intense heat served to expedite the ghastly process. Anyone who had to witness the ghastly sight of decomposing bodies lying neglected and uncared for and who realised that each body represented all that was left of someone's loved one could have little illusion left as to the romance of war.

But Brennan's compassion stopped short of offering any practical assistance: 'We could easily have buried the poor fellows but it was somebody else's job.'[4]

Eric Dorman-Smith achieved the rank of general by the renewal of activities in 1939 but for years a single image rarely left his dreams. 'Chink', as he was known, was a junior officer in the Northumberland Fusiliers in 1915. On 15 June he was involved in an attack by three regiments in the St Eloi sector near Ypres. At one point in the action a number of dead were lying in front of a flimsy trench which he commanded. Then one of the 'dead' was seen to move. 'The man did not call out', he recalled:

> He seemed like a curious bystander, propping himself up on his elbow to watch a sporting event. Suddenly I saw two of our Fusiliers leave their digging and run back to him. I watched them stoop to lift him. They looked towards the trench, crowded and shallow. I wanted to say 'Bring him over' but my brain was working mechanically. The trench

could hold no more and we had to have some freedom of movement to
use our weapons. I heard myself shout 'Come back to the trench – put
him down' and I could feel his eyes staring at me.[5]

In the trenches or out in no man's land the body of the Unknown Soldier
had as much standing as a carcass in a charnel house. Sergeant de Margry,
serving with the 2nd Royal Irish Regiment, noted that 'one of our fellows
came upon an officer's trench boots sticking out right by the German wire,
and, in trying to drag the officer clear by tugging at these boots, he suddenly
found the decomposed legs inside these boots parting company from the officer's body which must have been lying there for quite a time. As the fellow
concerned brought these foul and macabre boots back with him to our own
trench after we had located and carried our wounded officer to safety, we
were able to examine them more closely and found that they were obviously
of French pattern and origin, from which we concluded that the officer concerned must have been killed in the early days when French troops were
holding that sector. To complete this gruesome story, the finder insisted on
wearing these boots which he thought still serviceable enough to be well worth
the unsavoury trouble of cleaning for further wear, specially after risking his
life to get them.[6]

Some depredations were even more calculated and deliberate. Frank
Hitchcock, of the Leinster Regiment, in his diary of the trenches, *Stand To*,
recalls a visit to his sector by a brigadier general. The inspection ended with
almost everything passing muster:

> he, however, objected to a German's leg which was protruding out of
> the parapet, and I was told to have it buried forthwith by the CO. I
> called Finnegan, and told him to remove the offending limb. As it
> would have meant pulling down the whole parapet to bury it, he took
> up a shovel and slashed at it with the sharp edge of the tool. After
> some hard bangs, he managed to sever the limb. I had turned away and
> was standing in the next fire bay, when I overheard Finnegan remarking
> to another man: 'And what the bloody hell will I hang me equipment
> on now?[7]

A similar grisly sense of humour was displayed by a hospital orderly in
Gallipoli. After being shot and wounded, Dubliner Frank Laird, then of the
7th Dublin Fusiliers, was waiting in a hospital tent for treatment. An
Australian amputee was placed beside him. He was far too ill to be moved to
a hospital ship and, predictably, died within a few hours. Laird watched,
eating his dinner, as an orderly washed down the man's body. 'Having
completed the ablutions, the orderly returned to tie the feet together. Then

he burst out laughing, highly tickled at his mistake, and called out, 'Look here, boys, here I am trying to tie this chap's feet together and he has only got one!'[8]

An account of an average day in Delville Wood during the Somme offensive by Lt.-Col. F.E. Whitton amply demonstrates that soldiers often did not discriminate between the death of the anonymous and of the more familiar:

> There were grim incidents in that day of shells [1 September 1916]. Once, a corpse's legs were hit and its boots blown sky-high to come hurtling down near the trench, to the boisterous delight of the men. At another time a machine-gunner was sitting at the bottom of the trench; a small shell struck just above his head and burst into black smoke and powder. He made no movement and it was thought that he had had a narrow escape. A sergeant moved along and turned the body over with his foot. The man was dead. Not a scratch or wound, but his face was just slightly begrimed by the explosion. The shock or the blast must have killed him. 'Ah! sure, he was always a dirty sweep anyhow', said the sergeant philosophically. Funeral orations in war do not run on the lines of Periclean oratory or Lincoln's prose at Gettysburg.

It was, presumably, all part of a process of rationalisation!

Most such incidents are graphically recounted in subsequent private or public memoirs, but some are, surprisingly, recorded in contemporary letters. The element of surprise is in the 'need' to communicate such gory details in the first place and the fact that they escaped the attentions of official censors. In the case of two officers with Irish battalions telling descriptions of hideous scenes and events are actually communicated to their mothers! Lt. J.F.B. O'Sullivan of the 6th Connaughts uses the medium of a letter home to deal with some of his own ghosts. His mother had clearly been eager for information about the Somme offensive. She probably got more than she bargained for! As O'Sullivan explains,

> The truth of the matter is that the following long description has been for my personal benefit as much as to answer all your queries. Sitting here in the hospital bed, my mind is obsessed by the shocks and sights and the sudden deaths of so many friends during those last awful days. By writing down all the details I hoped to exorcise some of the mental migraine.[9]

He might, perhaps have spared her at least one supreme example of utterly malevolent callousness. After the attack on Guillemont, O'Sullivan, wounded in the assault, was walking into what was left of the French village:

No sooner had I laboriously started off than a little man came running out of a corpse-strewn trench. His hands were holding something cupped in one of those round German fatigue caps, and grinning like a maniac, apparently wanted to share the joke. He came up and showed me the cap – filled and quivering with its owner's brains. Only complete emptiness of stomach spared me further disgust as I retched convulsively and strained to hurry forward.[10]

Lt. Guy Nightingale, of the 1st Munsters, a veteran of V Beach, had written to his own mother in grisly detail about that first Gallipoli débâcle. One of the few survivors of that ill-fated landing, he was still not sparing her any details more than three years later. On 8 October 1918, he wrote of his battalion's entry into the town of Cambrai, with the Germans already beaten and in retreat: 'We found a few Boche in the cellars & killed them all. One old fellow came out waving a white flag & shouting "Kamarad" [*sic*] but as he came out of a hospital, & was fully dressed, we shot him in the stomach & he died. We took a topping photo of him shouting for mercy.'[11]

T.S. Eliot did not even have the Great War in mind when he wrote that 'humankind cannot take very much reality'. In the face of the horrible reality of the trenches of the Western Front, the brittle cracked and the solid crumbled. Erratic, uncontrollable behaviour and irrational actions were regular occurrences in the front lines. There was no shortage of negative stimuli to spark off an attack of what came to be known as 'shellshock' (later 'battle fatigue' and latterly in our own era of elaborate labelling, 'post-traumatic stress disorder').

Ned Gilligan from Mullingar in Co. Westmeath was seven years old when two young men in khaki came to his parents house to say goodbye before going off to war. One of them never came back. When the second did, he was a much altered man: 'The one who came back was so changed that the neighbours feared his strange ways. One Saturday night he burst into my parent's home in a drunken rage as we were polishing the boots for Sunday morning. He caught our pet dog sleeping by the fire and sat on the lower steps of the stairs holding it on his knee, and then choked it to death.'[12]

The response of most soldiers to the overwhelming awfulness of the trenches was to grow that extra layer of skin and get on with whatever was required of them. Some were unable to do so. They sought other forms of escape. Some took their own lives, others succumbed to temporary or permanent insanity. Others were proactive in ensuring their own removal from the trauma; they indulged in self-wounding. The bizarre ambition of many Great War soldiers was to suffer a mild wound, a 'Blighty', an injury which would not incapacitate but which would require the victim's removal from the front line. Those not thus 'fortunate' occasionally took matters into their own hands Their actions can be seen as a form of temporary insanity or as the only legitimate response of the sane in an insane world. In Joseph Heller's blackly humorous novel of World War II, *Catch-22*, the 'catch' in question is based on a syllogism. Roughly paraphrased it goes: 'The only way out of the war is to be declared insane! You have to be mad to fight! But if you do not want to fight, you cannot be insane and must, therefore, continue to do so.' There are all sorts of inherent flaws in the syllogism, but there is also a poetic logicality to it. A logic which makes it almost illogical to talk about self-wounding as an irrational response to the horrors of trench warfare.

There are many recorded instances of self wounding. In his memoir of the war *Goodbye to All That*, Robert Graves, scion of an old Irish family and former resident of Limerick, recounts one example of an attempt which failed, with fatal consequences; the story was told to him by his Welsh servant Fry:

> A bloke in the Munsters once wanted a cushy [another name for a 'Blighty'], so he waves his hand above the parapet to catch Fritz's attention. Nothing doing. He waves his arms about for a couple of minutes. Nothing doing, not a shot. He puts his elbows on the fire-step, hoists his body upside-down and waves his legs about till he gets blood to the head. Not a shot did old Fritz fire. 'Oh,' says the Munster man, 'I don't believe there's a damned square-head there. Where's the German army got to?' He has a peek over the top – crack! he gets it in the head. Finee [as in *finis*].[13]

Suicide was, on the face of it, a much less rational response, even in such destructive circumstances. Why go to the trouble of killing oneself, went the argument, when there were thousands employed to do the job for you. This fails to take into account the ever-present fear of an incapacitating injury, and the nature of depression itself. The 'Black Dog' will not wait patiently in its kennel to be obliterated by coincidence. At the outset of the war, the incidence of suicide among members of the 'sporting army' was as likely to be a result of honour as pathology. In a letter home on 13 September Lt. Neville Woodroffe of the 1st Irish Guards described how one officer took his own life in true *samurai* fashion: 'John Manners, whom you know by name, shot himself, when he saw that the alternative was to surrender to superior numbers of Germans.'[14]

Before long the taking of one's own life was more likely to be for entirely different motives. Those of an anonymous Munster Fusilier, for example, as recounted by Robert Graves:

Going towards company headquarters to wake the officers I saw a man
lying on his face in a machine-gun shelter. I stopped and said: 'Stand-to,
there!' I flashed my torch on him and saw that one of his feet was bare.
The machine-gunner beside him said: 'No good talking to him, sir.'

I asked: 'What's wrong? Why has he taken his boot and sock off?'

'Look for yourself, sir!'

I shook the sleeper by the arm and noticed suddenly the hole in the
back of his head. He had taken off the boot and sock to pull the trigger
of his rifle with one toe; the muzzle was in his mouth.

'Why did he do it?' I asked.

'He went through the last push, sir, and that sent him a bit queer;
on top of that he got bad news from Limerick about his girl and
another chap.'

Graves expresses not even the vaguest sense of shock at the story. And, as he
discovered when two officers of the Munsters arrived on the scene a little
later, this was by no means the first such suicide in the battalion. For reasons
of morale and/or common decency, the incident would never be reported for
what it was. As one officer said to the other: 'While I remember, Callaghan,
don't forget to write to his next-of-kin. Usual sort of letter; tell them he died
a soldier's death, anything you like. I'm not going to report it as suicide.'[15]

While not casting any doubts on most of the many acts of heroism which
punctuated the Great War, the state of mind of some decorated soldiers at
the time of their acts must be questioned. Many were characterised by an
obvious 'death-wish'.[16] Perhaps some were performed by men who were at
the end of their tether. This, for example, was the reaction of a Sergeant
O'Neill of the 2nd Leinsters, to the news of his brother's death during the
final push against the Germans in 1918. O'Neill's brother had been killed
while fighting with the 36th Division (by then no longer a Loyalist unit).

Not only did he swear 'red' but he saw red. When the attack opened,
he dashed ahead and soon was in advance of our own barrage which,
luckily, was on the thin side. He was the first man into any village or
hamlet on the Battalion's front. At the village of Staceghem he appeared
to have picked up with a Worcester Sergeant – the latter evidently had
appropriated more than one good bottle of 'du vin' *en route*. Seeing
sergeant O'Neill leave the village on his own, he thought it was his duty
to follow so long as his legs were capable, and, what with the two of
them bearing charmed lives, they cleared several houses on their own,
O'Neill giving no quarter and asking for none.[17]

O'Neill was subsequently awarded the Victoria Cross. There is a fine line
indeed between flight towards and flight away from the enemy!

'Shell-shock' is a wonderfully evocative and descriptive phrase for the psychological trauma which it represents. The sanitised 'battle fatigue' is the sort of neutral application much beloved of the military authorities. Contemporary accounts are filled with literal examples of 'shellshock', as in a trauma induced by the impact and consequences of a heavy barrage. In the midst of all the numbing violence of his long letter to his mother, J.F.B. O'Sullivan writes about a dugout which took a direct hit during the preparations, in September 1916, for the attack on Guillemont. The shell brought an end to a tactical briefing and to the life of one of O'Sullivan's fellow officers:

> Feeling very shaken and upset I stepped over poor Crowley's remains and, turning into the sap found myself surrounded by a group of maniacs. The same explosion had shocked the four runners into a state of utter delirium, and they sprawled about as if in the throes of tetany. How serious, or even genuine, such manifestations were God alone knows – they were horrible and degrading to see. I hurried past like one walking through a nightmare, and painfully deepened that illusion when meeting near A Company a racing and screaming MO [medical officer]. He came rushing towards me with his hands clutching his jaw, tore past, and on down the communication trench. Even above the surrounding bedlam his shrieks fading in the distance could be heard for several minutes. The men told me the grisly story of his collapse. Whilst binding up a man's leg, a shell suddenly smashed the man to pieces and, fantastically, left Doc unscathed except that a hunk of dirt struck his jaw with terrific force; the dead man's face had been sliced off and stuck like a rubber mask on the side of the trench. Doc caught sight of this suspended face, gazed at it with bulging eyes, put up his hands to his own face, 'started making noises like a bloody steam engine and took off'.[18]

On the first day of the Battle of the Somme W.V.C. Lake of the 1st Royal Irish Rifles waited, with his platoon, for the signal to attack. The Rifles, a Regular Army battalion, had been directed at the Ovillers Spur, on the left flank of the 3rd Corps attack. The trench in which his battalion waited was under constant bombardment. Lake's account of some of the sights he saw reads like an extract from a slow-motion nightmare. As he recalled it,

> Captain Ross, our Company commander came crawling along the trench quite oblivious of the groaning bodies that were under him. There was a glazed look on his face which was streaming with blood and in his mouth was a cigarette that would never light because of the blood on it. I said something as he passed, but he made no answer; he just

continued on his way on all fours like a wounded animal. I never saw him again and don't know how far he got.'

A short time later 'I became conscious then of a man who was making horrid noises like a trapped animal and with his mouth wide open. My platoon sergeant was standing next to him and fearing lest panic should spread, I said to him: "Dump him on the law, Sergeant." He was a heavy man with big biceps, and he dealt that man a punch that would have knocked out any boxer in the ring. But it made no difference, so stepping over to the man, I pointed down the trench and shouted in his face: "Go". He turned and fled and we never saw him again.'[19] Presumably neither captain nor enlisted man were among the 17 officers and 429 men lost by the 1st RIR on the opening day of the Somme offensive.

Lake might have felt entitled to have shot either man out of hand for desertion or cowardice. He chose not to do so. Colonel (later Brigadier) Percy Crozier, commanding officer of the 9th Royal Irish Rifles, had no such compunctions. On that very same day he watched as a group of stragglers approached, obviously intent on leaving the fighting to others: 'A young sprinting subaltern heads them off. They push by him. He draws his revolver and threatens them. They take no notice. He fires. Down drops a British soldier at his feet. The effect is instantaneous. They turn back to the assistance of their comrades in distress.'[20] Crozier himself, in April 1918, ordered that machine-guns be turned on retreating allied Portugese soldiers, 'in order to stem the tide. Had a complaint been lodged against me and had I been tried for murder, would Sir Douglas Haig have ordered my execution?'[21] On the same morning he had personally shot dead a young subaltern who was running from a German officer.

Crozier's batman, a working-class Belfastman named Davy Starret, was far more sympathetic towards the terror of others. His empathy probably had a lot to do with his rank and was, hopefully, a more typical response than that of his brigadier. In his personal memoir he writes about the Battle of Cambrai, in which Crozier led a Welsh Brigade:

> Some time during that battle I saw one of the Ulsters trying to get away. I knew somehow that was what he was after. He was a stranger to me ... I hung on to him for a bit, he being young, for I did not like the thought of him being shot by a wall for running away when he could go and get quite as much lead by going the other way. After a bit he did buck up, and I told him to get back. Told him to say he was a runner and had been to us with a message. He brightened considerably at that, and presently started off, and as I did not see him again I expect he got a grip on himself and had another go at doing his duty.[22]

Crozier would not have been very sympathetically disposed towards the notion of shell-shock. He, like many in the military establishment, was suspicious of what appeared to many of them to be simple, rank cowardice. There was an impression abroad that many of those exhibiting signs of trauma were simply malingering. But then many senior officers never got close enough to exploding shells to suffer the consequences (in fairness this was not true of Crozier). Jack Campbell, a Dubliner with the 1st Battalion, the Royal Highlanders and the last of the 'Old Contemptibles' to die in the Republic of Ireland, spent four years in the firing line and saw many men crumble:

> People have said that a lot of the fellows that were suffering from shell-shock were only kidding on that they were suffering to get away from the trenches. That's all wrong, because I had to help many a poor fellow that had shell-shock. They were insane, let's face it. As a matter of fact I don't think anyone who came through the '14–18 war was really mentally steady.[23]

However, as the war went on the results of 'shell-shock' could not continue to be ignored. It was not just young, inexperienced conscripts and volunteers who succumbed but experienced Regulars. Lt. Noel Drury recounts how 'Capt. P.T.L. Thompson (79th Carnatic Rifles) attached to 6th R. Dublin Fusiliers went off to hospital today. He was quite off his head and had to be restrained. He was the last I thought would have broken down under the strain.' Thompson was an old Indian army veteran described elsewhere in his diaries by Drury as 'very nice and very capable'.[24] The phenomenon became so widespread that 'By the end of the war, as many as 80,000 officers and men had been unable to continue in the trenches, and many had been invalided out of the army altogether for nervous disorders.'[25] Special centres were set up in 1917 to deal with 'shell-shock' victims. They were known as NYDN centres, it stood for 'Not Yet Diagnosed (Nervous)'.

'Shell-shock' was by no means the preserve of the faint-hearted or psychologically brittle. The 'warrior' was just as susceptible. After being hospitalised three times with wounds and surviving an ill-advised action in the Ypres sector in which his entire platoon was wiped out, Lt. Eric Dorman-Smith began to crack. He had seen his battalion lose almost all its officers and 486 out of 645 of its other ranks in an attack which had gained him a Military Cross and lost him many dear friends. As his biographer Lavinia Greacen has put it,

> His strong compassion for victims everywhere was magnified by his sensitivity to atmosphere, and where another man would have been able to switch off and busy himself in trivia or daydreams, Chink had no

escape route. His mind was the busy centre of the world, never in low gear, and he masked strain by a wit that was too sardonic to be humorous any more.[26]

Dorman-Smith's commanding officer, detecting the signs of a man who had succumbed to what we now know as post-traumatic stress disorder, pulled him out of the line. He was diagnosed as suffering from nervous exhaustion caused by the stress of his service and of his wounds and was hospitalised in August 1915. Less than a week after being admitted to the Fourth London General Hospital, he disappeared. His father found him sitting on a bench in the garden of their deserted and shuttered house in Maidenhead staring at the Thames. He went back to the trenches but was to finish the war in the relative backwater of the Italian front.

SHOT AT DAWN

For some, the consequence of their traumatic reaction to combat was fatal. Between 4 August 1914 and 31 March 1920 268 men were executed for desertion; 18 more were shot at dawn having been found guilty of cowardice. Many were distraught, confused men who paid the ultimate price for become victims of 'shell-shock'. All but three were enlisted men; many were in their teens or early twenties. Twenty-one were serving with Irish regiments at the time of their executions. More than 3,000 British soldiers were sentenced to death during the Great War. Fewer than ten per cent of the sentences were ever actually carried out. This suggests that the 10 per cent who were executed were, in some way, deserving of their punishment. Nothing could be further from the truth. Analysis done by His Honour Judge Anthony Babington in 1983 of court-martial transcripts to which he was given access, and further work undertaken by researchers Julian Putkowski and Julian Sykes, shows that many of those executed had distinguished service records, had not been defended when court-martialled and were the victims of a military establishment which clung to the belief that their executions would serve *pour encourager les autres*.

Most sentences of death were handed down by a field general court martial, a 'fast-track' system designed for maximum expediency. It consisted of a minimum of three officers, one acting as president (who, in theory, could not be below the rank of captain). A sentence of death could not be passed without the unanimous agreement of all those on the panel. Each prisoner was entitled to a 'prisoner's friend', normally an officer who would represent the accused, although one in ten of those executed between 1914 and 1920 were not represented at their court martial. Although the Army was not short of barristers (726 were serving by December 1914), few were ever asked to defend an accused deserter. Many defending officers were incompetent advocates. Often the court martial did not receive crucial information which might have persuaded them toward leniency.

In *Stand To* Lt. Frank Hitchcock of the 2nd Leinsters tells of how, in September 1918, he might well have saved someone from execution. He came across a man from B Company in a guard room awaiting a court martial for cowardice:

> He told me he thought he would be shot ... He said he had been a certain company commander's runner at Hooge '15, and that if he could only get in touch with him he would no doubt speak on his behalf for his work in that action. I promised to write to the officer, who answered my letter by return of post. He enclosed a good chit for the accused, and said that the man had performed a brave act at Hooge as a runner, coming through a hail of machine-gun fire and shrapnel with a message.[27]

It was not unusual for many of those 'shot at dawn' to have distinguished themselves in previous engagements. A Canadian soldier who was executed was the holder of a Military Medal.

Many of those executed were young working-class soldiers. They were not tried by their peers but by men of a different social class imbued with the prejudices of the military sub-culture of which they were now a part. According to Putkowski and Sykes, cases were 'characterised by flawed judgements, inconsistent decisions and class bias'.[28] As in peacetime magistrates courts, so in wartime courts martial did the Edwardian middle and upper classes pass judgement on the behaviour of the lower orders. Even in the case of more enlightened officers there was pressure to be stringent: 'To do otherwise was to solicit censure for lacking appropriate disciplinary zeal, and occasionally provoked a dressing-down from a superior officer. A number of junior officers made mention of this pressure.'[29]

Once sentence had been passed, a soldier's commanding officer had the option of recommending leniency. The ultimate decision lay with the supreme commander (Haig from 1915 onwards) and that decision might have little enough to do with the merits of a particular case but might, according to Percy Crozier, 'depend on circumstances viewed from afar in a survey covering the whole army ... Was desertion rampant, or was it on the increase? Was any division worse than another? ... These questions could alone be decided by one man, the supreme commander.'[30] But the runes had usually been read long before it came to Haig's turn to make the final decision: 'In the lottery of death that accompanied court-martial sentences and subsequent reviews, there seems to have been little consistency. An arbitrary decision coupled with an offence committed at an inopportune moment could send a man to his death with sudden ferocity.'[31]

Desertion was the most common crime which led to the ultimate sanction, but some were sentenced to death for offences such as falling asleep on guard duty or striking a superior officer. Noel Drury of the 6th Dublin Fusiliers wrote in his diary in 1915 'Had to prosecute no.10693 Pte. Gatercole 6 R.D.F. at a field general court martial at the 6 R.M.F. H.Q. for sleeping at his post. Poor devil; I know how hard it is to keep awake, but it has to be done or you would let all the others down some night. He was sentenced to death but the GOC commuted it to 10 years' penal servitude.'[32] Two incidents where soldiers were shot for killing superior officers probably involved considerable provocation. Robert Graves offers an account of two Welsh soldiers (both miners) who reported and announced that they were very sorry but that they had shot their company sergeant-major:

> The adjutant said: 'Good Heavens, how did that happen?'
> 'It was an accident, sir.'
> 'What do you mean, you damn fools? Did you mistake him for a spy?'
> 'No, sir, we mistook him for our platoon sergeant.'[33]

An Irish provost sergeant, Sergeant Walsh, assisted at the execution of an Indian named only as Yadram, in 1916. The convicted man had been a Delhi policeman and had shot and killed a native adjutant in the 29th Lancers. The officer was described by the assistant provost marshal of the 1st Indian Cavalry Division, Captain T.H. Westmacott, as 'an absolute rotter [who] goaded the wretched fellow to desperation'. As Walsh tied the unfortunate soldier to a chair, he shouted in Hindustani, 'I did this deed because I was abused. Those of you who have been abused as I was, go and do the same, but eat your own bullet and do not be shot as I shall be.'[34]

The first Irish soldiers to be executed were both men in their twenties serving with the 1st Irish Guards. Both Pte. Thomas Cummings and Pte. Albert Smythe had been pre-war regulars in action continually since the despatch of the BEF to France. The two men deserted in November 1914 while their unit was serving in the Ypres salient in weather described by Kipling in his history of the Irish Guards as 'a cold that froze the water in men's bottles'[35] and were harboured by a local Frenchwoman before being caught by the military police during a raid on a barn. They were tried for desertion and sentenced to be shot. Their battalion commander J.F.H Trefusis attached a rider to the court verdict, pointing out that Cummings had shown excellent service up to the time of his desertion but that Smythe had not. In the event both sentences were confirmed and both men were shot at dawn on 28 January 1915.[36] Kipling makes no reference to either the initial desertion or the carrying out of the sentence in his two-volume history of the Irish Guards in the war.[37] There is no reference to Cummings in his Appendix of NCOs and other ranks killed in action while serving with the Guards, but there is an entry for an Albert Smythe which claims that he was killed in action on 1 November 1914.[38] Neither man's body was found after the war, but the names of both are now commemorated on the war memorial at Le Touret.

The inappropriately named Private Thomas Hope was the next Irishman to be executed. He had joined the 2nd Leinster Regiment in September 1914. He deserted on 23 December when he was sent to fetch rations from a dump to the rear of trenches at L'Epinette and was arrested six weeks later at Armentieres a short distance away. He was disguised as a lance-corporal in the military police when captured and had aroused suspicion by refusing to give his name. He claimed that he had been taken prisoner but had escaped and was making his way back to his unit. Later he confessed to his court martial that he had gone absent after hearing that his two brothers had been killed in action. Hope did not have the benefit of defence counsel at his trial.

His commanding officer, Major Bullen Smith, does not appear to have had a very high opinion of Hope and this was to tell against him. The young private had already gone AWOL twice before, once in Cambridge and again on route march in France. Bullen Smith appended an opinon to the judgement of the court which claimed that Hope 'had made his mind up not to serve creditably and avoided all military duty'. In the face of that sort of indictment Sir John French did not opt for clemency and Hope was shot on 2 March 1915. He was 20 years of age.[39]

Twenty-one year old Pte. Thomas Davis was serving with the 1st Munster Fusiliers at Gallipoli when, on 21 June, he deserted his post as a sentry at battalion HQ. He was found after a three-hour search and was charged with quitting his post, a crime punishable by death. According to a diary entry of Lt. Guy Nightingale, Davis's court-martial was rapidly convened. His entry for 22 June reads: 'Had a court martial on all the afternoon.'[40] Davis told his trial that he had left his post because of a bowel complaint and had gone to the latrines. Dysentery was rampant at the time, so this would not have been an unreasonable excuse. But this was not the first time Davis had appeared before a court martial. On the night of 1/2 May the Munsters' positions had been attacked by the Turks. Nightingale recorded in his diary that 'they had crept up through the gorse and bayonetted most of the men in their sleep and swept on. Whatever remained of our coy [sic] retired. I ran up the line shouting to them to get back.'[41] The position was held by the remnants of the 1st Dublin Fusiliers which had been joined with the Munsters (as the 'Dubsters') after the enormous casualties of V Beach the previous week.

According to Nightingale the Munsters who had 'retired' were imme-diately court-martialled: 'They all got ten years but continued to serve to the end of the war.'[42] The initial sentence on Davis, however, appears to have been one of death. Ironically this was then commuted to ten years' penal servitude the day after he was shot for quitting his post. On 1 July 1915, Nightingale had the task of relaying the court-martial verdict on Davis to the rest of the battalion. At 5.00 a.m. on 2 July the young private was taken to Gully Beach. Nightinagle's diary entry for that day reads: 'Davis was shot at dawn this morning. I did not have to be there, I am glad to say; only the padre was there at the last moment.' Davis had survived the terror and carnage of the River Clyde landing and the subsequent horrors only to die before a firing squad; composed of his peers. Lieutenant Guy Nightingale became his own firing squad. The veteran of V Beach was a belated victim of the Great War: he shot himself on the 20th anniversary of the Sed el Bahr landing.

Thus far, all the cases referred to are of regular soldiers. But dozens of volunteers convicted of cowardice or desertion did not escape execution, and from 1916 onwards all the Irish victims fell into this category. It is interesting that the Australian Army refused to allow any of its soldiers to be executed for any crime (including at least two men who were accused of murder), as it was felt that the ultimate sanction was inconsistent with their status as volunteers. This status did not save the only 10th (Irish) Division soldier to be shot by firing squad, 20-year-old Private Patrick Downey, of the 6th Leinsters. The circumstances of his 'crime' are unclear, and his death 'provoked uproar in the ranks of his division'.[43] It appears that he was ordered by an officer to put on his cap, and disobeyed that order. To this offence he pleaded guilty. But his commanding officer, Col. F.W.S. Jourdain, who promulgated the charges, claimed that Downey had refused to enter the trenches. Downey was found guilty of 'disobedience' and was ordered to be shot. On hearing the verdict, Downey allegedly laughed and shouted, 'That is a good joke. You let me enlist and then bring me out here and shoot me.' Sentence was carried out on 27 December 1915. Downey was one of only five soldiers to be shot for 'disobedience'.

Many of the executions carried out during the war are shrouded in mystery. Relatives were often not informed that their loved ones had been shot, and the graves of the victims of firing squads are often difficult to locate. But one of the most poignant and best documented judicial slayings was of another young Irish soldier, 18-year-old James Crozier from Belfast. Ironically he was with the 9th Irish Rifles, which meant that in 1916 his commanding officer was his namesake, Lt.-Col. Percy Crozier, which is why his execution is so well documented.

Crozier had been an apprentice in the shipyards. He enlisted in September 1914 with all the enthusiasm of youth and inexperience. He was under age and his mother came as far as the recruiting office to persuade him not to join. In Crozier's account of the brief military career of James Crozier, *The Men I Killed*, he becomes 'Johnny Crockett'. 'Don't go, Johnny. Don't leave me, Johnny. You're all I have …' are the words Crozier puts into the mouth of the young recruit's mother. She threatens to tell the recruiting officer that he is under age. 'You can't do that, mother,' he responds. 'If you do, you'll be a coward. No Crockett was ever a coward.'

Crozier (senior!) stepped in at this point: 'While Johnny was taking the King's shilling; ... I spoke to his mother. "Don't worry," I said. "I'll look after him. I'll see no harm comes to him".'[44] The commanding officer of the 9th Royal Irish Rifles was hardly as good as his word. The 36th (Ulster) Division spent the winter of 1915/16 in dreadful conditions on the Somme. It was a miserably cold and drearily wet winter. In February 1916, 'the most trying week of that trying winter', the 9th Rifles were in trenches close to Serre. James Crozier went missing from his sentry post. A fortnight later he was returned to his unit. According to the account in *Shot at Dawn*, which is derived from Babington's study of the court-martial evidence, the young Rifleman had 'walked a considerable distance before being admitted to a Royal Army Medical Corps field hospital. The court were later to hear the private say that he had not known what he was doing when he made off, being in a daze at the time and suffering from pains throughout his body.'[45] However, the doctor who examined him pronounced him fit for active service (in mind and body), and he was returned to his unit to face the consequences of his desertion.

Lt.-Col. Percy Crozier's account is radically different and much more self-serving. His picture is not of a confused and disoriented young man who left his post to check into an RAMC field hospital, but of a cunning deserter. He writes that 'Crockett, fed-up, cold, wet to the skin and despondent, had sneaked off from the line under cover of darkness, throwing away his rifle, ammunition and equipment (a legal ground for a second charge, the maximum punishment for which was also death) and, obtaining civilian clothes from somewhere, had made his way to the coast where he was caught.' Crozier is vague about the circumstances of his namesake's 'capture': 'they are of no material moment. Probably he was given away by some civilian while in search of food – perhaps by some mother whose son had been killed or was still standing up to the strain.'[46]

Percy Crozier's distortion of the facts makes it easier for him to explain away his subsequent actions. The young Rifleman was court-martialled and found guilty of desertion. Despite his promise to the boy's mother the CO of the 9th Rifles had no hesitation in recommending to higher authority that the sentence be carried out. He justified his stand by saying that

> when it fell to my lot to recommend the carrying out or the remitting of the death sentence, I invariably recommended the carrying out of the extreme penalty – because I expected to be shot myself if I ran away ... And I invariably warned everybody connected with my command,

whatever size it happened to be, that from me they might expect no
mercy in matters relating to the safety of the line.[47]

However, Crozier also attempts to lay off some of the blame for his namesake's
execution. 'Young Johnny Crockett,' he wrote, 'died by order of Sir Douglas
Haig, whose signature I saw on the proceedings read out on parade the day
before sentence was carried out.' The carrying out of the sentence itself often
verged on black farce. According to Crozier he plied the young Rifleman with
drink in order 'to ease his living misery' before his execution. He may also
have had as a motive the desire to ensure that 'Crockett' went to his death in
a state of sufficient oblivion to avoid any embarrassing scenes. Crozier was
conscious that feelings against the execution were running high in the battalion. The military police and the assistant provost-marshal were convinced
that the firing party would deliberately miss. They even feared a mutiny by
the troops.

As he was getting 'Crockett' drunk, Crozier was making sure that the
officer in charge of the firing squad was stone cold sober and ready to apply
the coup de grace in the event of any dereliction of duty by the firing squad.
Just before dawn on the morning of 27 February 1916 the battalion was
paraded in the village of Mailly-Maillet. The execution was to take place in a
walled garden so the Riflemen could hear, but could not see, what happened.
According to Crozier, the 'windy' assistant provost-marshal was locked up
and not allowed witness the execution. Not unexpectedly, the firing squad
failed to kill their target, and the unnamed officer in charge was obliged to
step forward and put a bullet through young Crozier's head.

Percy Crozier, presumably in deference to his promise back in September
1914, attempted to have Rifleman Crozier's name added to the list of field
casualties. He failed. Mrs Crozier was duly notified that her only son had
been shot for desertion, and she was denied the normal allowance payable on
the death of next-of-kin. For his part Crozier 'did not regret his death at the
time, nor even the circumstances surrounding it, for intuitively I felt that it
would be the first and the last of its kind in my regiment.'[48] He was right,
but only just. At around the same time as the Crozier case, an officer was
court-martialled for desertion. Second Lieutenant A.J. Annandale was, however, more fortunate than Rifleman Crozier. Annandale was also convicted,
but managed to get off when 'influential friends' queried the legality of his
conviction. Unlike the subaltern, Rifleman Crozier did not have any 'influential friends'. Percy Crozier's attitude towards the latter case is typically
ambiguous: 'The least said about this the better,' he observes enigmatically,
'except to remark that had justice been done according to our code regrets
would have been fewer than in the case of Crockett'. However, he is quite
philosophical about the fact that justice was not done in the case of the officer.

Will justice ever be done in the case of those executed soldiers clearly damaged by post traumatic stress disorder before committing the 'crimes' for which they died. It now appears likely, in the wake of the election in Britain of a new Labour government in 1997. Over the years, attempts had been made to rehabilitate some or all of the men 'shot at dawn'. In 1988 then Labour backbench MP Andrew Mackinlay began a campaign to have these cases reopened. In 1996 he attempted to amend the Armed Forces Bill so that the executed men could be pardoned. His attempt was defeated but, in a free vote, was supported by a third of those who now compose the Labour cabinet. In May 1997 Mackinlay tabled another House of Commons motion calling for pardons. The new Armed Forces Minister, John Reid, has indicated his sympathy for the motion. The feeling is that, rather than issue a blank pardon, each case will be examined separately and an individual judgement made on its merits.

If that happens, hundreds of families will have the reputation of their loved ones restored, and government policy will finally catch up with public understanding, which has already pardoned most of the unfortunates who were 'shot at dawn'.

5   Irishmen in the Anzac Forces

The Irish are supposed to share many of the charactertistics of the Australian and the New Zealander – at least according to the stereotypes designed for each nationality by mainly British observers. Thus, the Irishman and the Antipodean are loud, brash and undisciplined men (and the stereotype is usually male) with a penchant for over-indulgent drinking. On the positive side these rude Colonials are physically courageous, although the unspoken implication is that their bravery often stems from a lack of intelligence or imagination. It is a comforting stereotype for the British (and one in which the Irish and Antipodeans have often colluded), and it helps account for the frequent antipathy between those same 'rude Colonials' and the Empire which they were defending during the Great War.

In an era in which Republicanism is growing in popularity in Australia, it is difficult to envisage the enthusiasm with which the governments of Australia and New Zealand came to the assistance of Britain when hostilities began in 1914. A large volunteer force (the Australian Imperial Force) was raised in Australia, and it became the basis for the Australian and New Zealand Army Corps (the Anzacs), which served on the Eastern front in 1915 and was transferred to the Western front in 1916, with some elements of that force remaining in the Middle East under the command of Allenby.

Thousands of Irishmen, many of whom had arrived in Australia courtesy of an assisted passage scheme, had their passage back to Europe assisted when they joined the AIF. They had expected to be fighting in France, but the acceptance by the war cabinet of Winston Churchill's plans for the opening of a second front resulted in their being diverted to Egypt and from there to take on the Turkish forces at Gallipoli. A sample of 350 of these Irishmen has been studied by Australian military historian John Connor. His research shows that the bulk of the Irish-Australian volunteers were Roman Catholic (60 per cent, as against 20 per cent Church of Ireland) and 65 per cent of them had emigrated to the southern hemisphere after 1909. That date coincides with the peak year of the assisted passage scheme which encouraged poor and unemployed British and Irish labourers to emigrate and suggests that many of those who joined up in 1914 were assisted migrants.

Connor's sample (which is weighted in favour of the professional classes, on whom more information was available) is still overwhelmingly composed of manual labourers. Just under half of the 350 men he studied, were labourers or farm labourers. Fifteen per cent were professional men and 10 per cent were members of the clergy. The latter figures, he believes, are disproportionate because it was easier to find information on officers. Clergy and professional men tended to become officers. Many of those enlisting would have been timber workers, men like Pte. Martin O'Meara, aged 30 when he joined up (Connor also discovered that the bulk of Irishmen 'were not enlisting as fresh-faced boys').[1] O'Meara was from Birr in Co. Offaly. While serving with the Anzacs in France in 1916, over a four-day period of heavy fighting he repeatedly went out into no man's land and brought back wounded men. O'Meara was awarded the Victoria Cross for his bravery. Two weeks after being honoured he was due home. His family had prepared a huge welcome for him, but O'Meara modestly arrived home unannounced and without any fuss. He had walked the five miles home from the local railway station.[2]

Why would Irishmen, such as O'Meara, who had been unable to obtain decent employment at home or in Britain, join the AIF in large numbers? The answer probably lies in the generous daily rate of pay offered to enlisted men. The Anzac soldier often sang a song to the tune of 'The Church's One Foundation' which went

> We are the Anzac Army,
> The A.N.Z.A.C.,
> We cannot shoot, we don't salute,
> What bloody good are we
> And when we get to Ber-lin
> The Kaiser he will say
> 'Hoch, Hoch! Mein Gott, what a bloody lot'
> To get six bob a day!'[3]

The six shillings a day paid to the Anzac soldier was two to three times the normal labouring wage and was a powerful incentive to Irish labourers to enlist, as, presumably, was the promise of paid leave back home in Ireland at some point during the war and the prospect of being able to find employment at home at the cessation of hostilities.

The members of the Anzac force were expecting to fight on the Western Front, in defence of an Empire to which many of its members still felt an allegiance. Thanks to Churchill's Turkish sideshow, carried through as though few lives depended upon it, the Aussies and New Zealanders (along with all the other nationalities which made up that force) ended up in Gallipoli, perched on precipitous slopes overlooking a stretch of narrow crescent-shaped beach which became known as Anzac Cove. The Anzac force landed at the same time as the Dublin and Munster Fusiliers of the 29th Division were being cut to pieces on V Beach further to the south. As the days and weeks wore on, the raw Antipodean recruits would become familiar with already extant names like Ari Burnu and Sari Bair. They would also coin a few of their own, names like Lone Pine and Shrapnel Gully – places with the sort of significance in Australian lore, history and popular culture which V Beach and Suvla Bay do not have in Irish memory. Anzac Cove was as much a benchmark in the growth of Australian disillusionment with the British Empire as the 1916 executions were with the Irish.[4]

The Irish and the Australians could hardly avoid each other on the tight, arid Gallipoli peninsula. In addition to the many Irish troops in the Australian force, one Irish Brigade, the 29th (a brigade of the 10th (Irish) Division), fought with their Australian allies at Anzac Cove. The Australians were also supposed to be the immediate beneficiaries of the landing, in August 1915, of the 10th Division at Suvla Bay. The two forces were near-neighbours, and from some points occupied by the Anzacs it was possible to see the activities of the 10th and 11th Divisions in the Suvla Bay area. So, quite a lot has been written by members of each force about the other.

Major Bryan Cooper in his book on the 10th at Suvla offers a revealing stereotype of the physical attributes and appearance of the Australian soldier:

> one could not help admiring their splendid physique and the practical way in which they had adapted their costume to the conditions prevailing on the Peninsula. Some were stripped to the waist, and few wore more clothing than boots, a slouch hat, a sleeveless shirt, open at the breast, and a pair of the shortest shorts that ever occurred to the imagination of a tailor. As a result of this primitive costume, they were burnt to a rich brown by the Gallipoli sun. They were splendid men, but quite different in physique from the European, for their sloping shoulders, looseknit limbs, and long thin legs suggested an apparent reversion to the kangaroo type as the result of climatic conditions. Above all, they seemed absolutely devoid of nerves; three months of constant shelling, which had left its mark even on the veterans of the 29th Division, appeared to have no effect of any kind on the Australians: Clearly, they were very good men to fight side by side with.[5]

It was a description with which Lt. Noel Drury of the 6th Dublins would probably have concurred in the early days of the 10th Division's Gallipoli experience. He wrote: 'Some Australian bushmen have arrived for special sniping stunts, and one of them arrived in our lines having been right behind the Turks. He was a hardy looking case with skin burned the colour of chocolate.'[6]

But the first mutually favourable impressions formed by many troops and their officers did not last. Rivalry between soldiers of different nationalities fighting for the same cause is not unusual and probably accounts for much of this. Certainly there was no measurable antipathy between the Irish and the Australians. But by 1917, for example, Noel Drury was writing from Palestine, as Allenby's army neared Jerusalem that 'The Australians have the wind up and allow the Turk to do just as he likes. They let old Johnny Turk stroll up to their sangars [stone breastworks] and lob bombs over the top on to their heads. They bitterly complain of not having their horses here.'[7]

However, most of the adverse comments seem to come from the other direction. Cecil Malthus, in his own diary of Gallipoli, doesn't cast any aspersions at the fighting qualities of the Irish, but he faults them on the grounds of hygiene and honesty. His entry for 8 May 1915, contains the following reference: 'At last we reached, with little hostile fire, a line of trenches occupied by the Munster and Dublin Fusiliers, who had made a gallant advance the day before. They had had such heavy losses that they were now a composite unit christened 'the Dubsters'. Hardly encouraging for us. Their trench was already closely occupied, but we managed to squeeze in amongst them. They looked worn and dirty, and being mostly close cropped they would have passed for a gang of convicts.' Unexceptionable so far, after all the 'Dubsters' had been through their own private and public Hell and the Anzac forces were not noted for their spruceness either. But Malthus goes on: 'Hastily we threw off our packs and piled them in heaps – which were promptly looted by the Irishmen ...'[8]

An Irishman in the Australian Light Horse, Trooper Brennan, wrote from Anzac Cove to his father in Kilkenny about V Beach: 'I tried to get some particulars from a few of the Dublins and Munsters themselves, and I failed miserably. They were all talking of poor Johnny this and that who got shot, and Paddy something-or-other, or the bad water, or the failure of the rum issue, so I came to the conclusion that an Irishman's fighting is somewhat like his temper or dislikes – no sooner dispensed with than forgotten.'

The Suvla débâcle of August 1915 was allied to an Australian push which proved very costly. The relative failure of the New Army forces of the 10th and 11th Divisions is largely attributable to the mediocrity and incompetence of their leaders, but among the Anzacs there was no great admiration for the performance of the troops, either. The New Zealand-Irish General Alexander Godley might have been expected to have had some sympathy for the men of his ancestral home, but he wrote to his cousin in 1915 about the August offensive, 'You can imagine my feelings when I watched my men fighting like Tigers doing practically the impossible, and at the same time could watch within three miles the 10th and 11th divisions loafing and bathing.'[9] He was not inclined to lay all the blame at the feet of his own peers, either:

Sir F. Stopford and Generals Mahon (who relieved us at Mafeking) and
Lindley have been made the scapegoats, but they had a very difficult task,
and I am afraid the quality of the troops (New Army and Territorial) that
they had at their command had something to do with it ... Some of the
K [Kitchener's volunteer army] battalions did well, but it was really too
high a trial for their baptism of fire, and it is unfortunate that they should
have had to be plunged into such desperate fighting from straight off
their ships.[10]

Godley became aware of rumours that Irish troops had run away during the
early Suvla fighting. He went on to draw the following conclusion which
reflected badly on the Irish volunteers of the 10th but rather better on the
regulars of the 1st Dublins and the 1st Munsters: 'A crucial result of the
Suvla campaign was the establishment of a firm belief that the soldiers from
the antipodes were better than those from Britain. At the April landings
Australians had felt honoured to be compared on roughly equal terms with the
29th Division, whose heroism was widely acknowledged in the Mediterranean
Expeditionary Force.'[11]

Godley, a senior officer with the Anzacs throughout the Great War, was
the cousin of the Cavan-based peer, Lord Kilbracken. He had served with the
Dublin Fusiliers after leaving Sandhurst, transferred to the Mounted Infantry
in 1894, and then joined the Irish Guards in 1901 when they were formed.
His Irish-born father had emigrated to New Zealand in 1860s, where Godley
was born, and Godley considered himself to be Irish. In 1917, for example,
he wrote of his position in the New Zealand army, 'I have now been commanding *their* [my italics] forces for over seven years and it is really too long
for an outsider to be at the head of affairs ...'[12] For more than thirty years he
kept up a regular correspondence with his cousin, Kilbracken. Both men were
conservative (with a small and large 'C') and committed to the vigorous
prosecution of the war. Given his seniority, Godley's political and military
insights are valuable.

His assessment of the task confronting his forces at Anzac Cove was, in
retrospect, accurate and realistic. He wrote:

Our Australians are fit and well and will I believe go for them properly
if they are once able to get ashore, and if we get ashore and if we can
once get out of the shore trenches, and on the move – I don't believe
the Turk will stand up against them for long. But it all depends on
what luck we have as regards getting our first footing.[13]

His comments in the aftermath of the operation reflect the antipathy towards
the British authorities which was to become innate in so many members of
that Anzac force:

I do not suppose, in history, that anything so utterly mismanaged by the British Government will ever be recorded [he wrote to Kilbracken]. All reports on the Dardanelles have always said that to force them would require a good fleet backed up by 150,000 regular troops. Our politicians, or rather that one of them who is First Lord of the Admiralty [Churchill], sends a Fleet to do the job entirely unsupported by the Army. This having naturally failed, and ample time having been given for all the resources of the Turkish Empire to be poured into this Peninsula (to say nothing of large reinforcements which have come from Asia), this politician then scrapes together a heterogeneous force consisting of (1) an indifferent French division (only 16,000 strong and part of that number cavalry which are of course useless here), commanded by a man who is said to have been 'stellenbosched' in the early days of the War; (2) an incomplete Army Corps (very short of artillery and of one infantry brigade) of irregular Colonials, who enlisted to go to the Continent to fight the Germans, and who are not well adapted for a sideshow of this nature; (3) a Naval Division, practically untrained as soldiers, and consisting either of raw boys who are terrified out of their lives, or of old time-expired warriors who are worthless for the Fleet, and who (as they say themselves) have done their service and had hoped to end their days in peace; and (4) one first-rate British division. A total of 60,000 at the outside, of whom a large proportion are being more highly tried than their training warrants.[14]

Despite his biting political and military comments, his letter was not subjected to censorship. (In a further letter on 3 July he had probably calmed down somewhat because he wrote, 'I was quite relieved to hear that my letter of May 9th reached you uncensored!')

Godley was, of course, the most senior 'Irish' soldier in the Anzac forces, but there were many more far less exalted than the blue-blooded New Zealander. Michael O'Callaghan, for example, could hardly have had less blue blood coursing through his veins. He was born in Co. Cork in 1889 in a humble, mud-walled hut, one of ten children of Ellen and Cornelius O'Callaghan. He began work as a farm labourer (his father's source of income as well) at the age of eleven, and in 1910 became an assisted emigrant to Australia. He worked as an itinerant labourer in Queensland, and at the end of the cane-cutting season, in September 1914, he enlisted in the AIF with the promise of higher wages and the possibility of an occasional return home from the front on leave. He never made it, however. He was killed during the 8 August Anzac offensive at Gallipoli.[15]

The O'Donnell twins, Jack and Tom, were born into a middle-class family in Tullow, Co. Carlow, in 1890. Their father was the local bank manager, and one of their uncles, Patrick McMahon Glynn, had made a name for himself in Australia. He had a successful solicitor's practice but had also helped write the Australian Constitution and became the country's attorney general in 1910. A year later Glynn paid for the the passage of the O'Donnell brothers (a middle-class variant of assisted emigration!) and they took up employment as bank clerks in Australia.[16] At the outbreak of the war, both brothers joined up in Angaston, South Australia, in August 1914.

Both survived Gallipoli, but Tom didn't make it through the war. He was killed at Anzac Ridge, Westhoek, near Ypres in September 1917 while with the 50th Battalion, AIF. A friend, Private Syd Robinson, wrote to O'Donnell's mother and organised to visit her in Ireland during one of his leaves. She had been concerned about her son's grave, but Robinson was unable to provide much consolation. He wrote that 'the people who look after the graves will be able to do nothing for you now, as the portion of the battlefield that we held at the time of poor Tom's death is now in enemy hands'.[17] On the anniversary of his twin's death, Jack O'Donnell wrote a poem to his lost brother. It begins:

> Now comes the cruel winter blighting every bloom
> That decked the little mounds in far-off France,
> Which plenteous Nature, so profuse alway,
> No more enhance.
> In yonder thicket by the old French mill,
> Where rose and tulips may no longer grow;
> He sleeps – and softly through the gathering mist
> The North Winds blow.[18]

Jack O'Donnell himself was also one of the fortunate survivors of Gallipoli. He lived to return to Ireland on leave and while in Dublin in early 1916 he met and fell in love with a young woman named Esther Dunn. Before he left for the Western Front he told her he would be back. He was as good as his word, after the Armistice he returned and began courting her. The young woman's parents, however, didn't approve of her moving to Australia, and they withheld their permission for a marriage. O'Donnell made determined efforts to persuade Esther to marry him anyway. He even went to the extent of going AWOL in March 1919 when his battalion was due to be shipped back to Australia. He returned to Dublin and tried one last time, unsuccessfully as it turned out. Back in Australia, Jack's influential uncle Patrick Glynn helped him purchase a farm. He hoped he would be able to use this to entice Esther to Australia, but to no avail. Finally he sold his farm and returned to Ireland in 1925. Romance blossomed on his return and in 1926 he persuaded Esther to marry him, a full decade after he had first met and fallen in love with her.[19]

O'Donnell, who was wounded twice and was consistently refused a commission, will not be remembered as one of the classic poets of the war, but he did have a volume of poems published in Dublin in 1918 under the title *Songs of an Anzac*. Much of it is uninspiring doggerel, but occasionally the 'songs' strike a chord, as in the case of 'The Sunken Road', where O'Donnell has just described the death of a young Australian soldier while on a tedious night fatigue. He writes ...

> Some poor mother in God's own land,
> Back where the almond and wattle bloom,
> Wakes in the night in the darkened room;
> Whispers a prayer to the unseen Hand,
> Whispers a prayer for her boyish son
> Over there where the angry night
> Hugs the secret she'll know too soon.[20]

John O'Connor, was a 44-year-old Limerick-born veteran of the British Army when he joined the AIF on 25 August 1914. His military pedigree was an impressive one. He had joined the British forces as a teenager and had served for eighteen years, service which brought him to the Sudan and the Battle of Omdurman (with the 2nd Lancashire Fusiliers) and then to the Boer War. He left the army in 1908 and emigrated to Australia, where he got work as a signwriter in Maitland, New South Wales. His previous experience meant that he was quickly promoted to sergeant. But the good fortune of this veteran of the Sudanese and South African campaigns gave out at Gallipoli. He was killed a few days after the Anzac landing. On 30 April 1915 he was shot dead trying to winkle out Turkish snipers who had been picking off Australian officers.[21] In his Australian War Memorial entry O'Connor is described as a 'prominent Irish Nationalist and Roman Catholic'. Both of those facts, allied to his humble origins, place him at some remove from his compatriot and fellow-soldier Everard Digges La Touche.

Had circumstances been different, the elegantly named Digges La Touche would have been dealt with in a different chapter. As an Anglican clergyman he should have been a chaplain, but he saw so many other volunteers for the chaplaincy appointed ahead of him that he enlisted in the AIF as a private. Digges La Touche was born in Burrendale, Newcastle, Co. Down, on 14 March 1883. His father had been a major in the Bengal Lancers, and his brother Averill would be killed serving with the 1st Royal Irish Rifles (a Regular Army battalion) at Loos in 1915, so he was no stranger to the martial spirit. But Everard's instincts were more bent in a theological than military direction. In 1910 his first book was published (*Christian Certitude: Its Intellectual Basis*), and the following year he became the youngest man ever to give the Donnellan Lectures at Trinity College. His subject for this series of theological discourses was the possibility of reconciling science and Christianity.

Digges La Touche's health had never been strong and in 1912 he was forced to emigrate to the more convivial Australian climate. (A biographer, Nigel Hubbard presents anecdotal evidence that he may also have been experiencing marital difficulties at the time.) In Australia he began a brief career of rubbing people the wrong way. He was of the evangelical persuasion and a strict conservative and was prepared to defend his principles volubly. This made him a number of prominent enemies among his fellow clergy, including his local bishop, Archbishop John Wright. Digges La Touche was also a committed unionist and a distant opponent of Home Rule. Consequently, when the Great War began he was anxious to be involved. He applied for a chaplaincy, but others were appointed ahead of him. Much to the annoyance of Archbishop Wright, Digges La Touche simply enlisted, on 27 August 1914, as a private. The following month he attended the Church Synod in military uniform and proposed the motion

> That this Synod, believing the Empire's cause to be just and, therefore the cause of Christ, commends the Officers and men of the Australian Imperial Expeditionary Force to the care of Him who alone has builded and preserved the British Empire; that it prays our Father, God, to give each Officer and man the ever-present consciousness that the Risen Lord is his Comrade and Friend, and to prosper their arms exceeding abundantly in the days of battle.[22]

By October 1914, Digges La Touche had been made a sergeant of the 13th Battalion but also acted as an unofficial chaplain. One soldier wrote of his training camp services:

> He's a wonderful chap – enlisted as a private and yet he is one of the brainiest men in the Church. He is now a sergeant. Ten years hence – if he lives, but his sort get killed early – he will be the most commanding figure in the Church of England in Australia. Already he is the most picturesque. He's a brilliant, fiery debater, a fervid Evangelist, a versatile scholar and a rabid partisan all in one. In fact he's Irish ... [23]

Unfortunately the clergyman's committment to and enthusiasm for the cause had no bearing on his fitness to serve and, on 22 November 1914, he was discharged as medically unfit. His mother claimed this was because of an ear infection,[24] but the official Australian History of the war insists that it was because of his varicose veins.[25] Such trifling matters were never likely to deflect the purpose of one as determined as Digges La Touche. One successful operation later and he was back in the army. His physical recovery only served to convince the clergyman of the rightness of his personal cause, which had been questioned by some who disagreed with 'a priest taking the sword'. The Irishman took the restoration of his health as 'the seal of divine sanction upon my service in this holy war'.[26] A further seal came in the form of induction into Officer School and promotion to second lieutenant.

Digges La Touche didn't arrive at Gallipoli until 5 August 1915, the day before the infamous attack on Lone Pine. C.E.W. Bean writes that Digges La Touche 'begged leave to join the attack'[27] and was mortally wounded near Owen's Gully. He was hit in the intestines and, although it was likely to prove fatal, insisted on being moved. A colleague, Captain Jacobs, knew enough about such injuries to have decided to leave him where he was, but Digges La Touche insisted, 'It's not me you must consider but the position.' His sometime antagonist, Archbishop John Wright, eulogised him in the following terms in September 1915: 'Some of us can never forget him, of commanding ability, brimful of enthusiasm, with that gentle charm of his Celtic temperament which endeared him to us, even when often though we differed most, but above all with a transparent soul, white-hot with devotion to his Divine Master, for whom he was ready to spend himself with almost a martyr's fire.'[28]

One of the most extensive collections of the letters of an Irish-Australian soldier in the Australian War Memorial are those of a young lieutenant, George G. Allardyce. He was born in Suffolk Street in Dublin in 1894, was educated at Trinity College (this included a stint in the Trinity Officer Training Corps) and emigrated to Australia in 1913. He enlisted in the Australian Expeditionary Force in November 1914 and was posted to the 4th Field Ambulance as a stretcher-bearer.

His letters have a wonderful guilelessness to them. They were clearly not written for posterity or as an *aide memoire* for some future narrative effort. They deal with the minutiae of the war (food, dirt, discomfort, leave, heat, exhaustion, bullets and shells) and of family life (his brother's education, his much younger brother's Junior Cup exploits). As one reads through them, one becomes drawn to the ebullient personality of this dedicated correspondent who manages successfully to shield his family from the real awfulness of what is happening around him on a daily basis. He makes no secret of the fact that he is already profoundly sick of the insanity of war by the time the collected portion of the correspondence begins, but he sinks this disillusionment down a well of sane personal detail.

Many of his letters come during his own period as a casualty. He had been wounded during the Anzac attack which coincided with the landings of the 10th (Irish) and 11th Divisions at Suvla Bay on 7 August 1915. During a night-time advance Allardyce had been hit in the knee while carrying wounded as a stretcher-bearer. His recovery was slow: 'I am afraid that I won't be able to stand another campaign stretcher bearing as it is about the hardest part to play in warfare ... at the present I do not seem to have any staying power at all. A quick march of a couple of miles and I am done.'[29]

His letters are striking for the faith they show in the establishment figures prosecuting the war. Early on in the correspondence he expresses his confidence in the entire *raison d'etre* of the Gallipoli campaign while still expressing a desire to be far away from Turkey: 'I wish it was all over here, as I am sure it will help greatly to shorten the war.'[30] Such faith is touching, if woefully misplaced. As Robin Prior has observed in his contribution on the campaign to the *Oxford Companion of Australian Military History*, 'Gallipoli had no influence on the course of the war as a whole. More depressing still, even if the expedition had succeeded in its aims, it is doubtful if the war would have been shortened by a single day.' Allardyce was profoundly affected by the death of Kitchener, the man responsible for short-changing the Gallipoli operation (which was Churchill's brainchild and not his). 'We have ... heard [he wrote to his father] that 150,000 Germans, including von Kluck and the Crown Prince, have been surrounded at Verdun. However, even if this were true it would not make up for the loss of Lord Kitchener.'

After the withdrawal from Gallipoli it took over a year for his unit to be posted from Egypt to France – a fortunate reprieve. The immensity of the casualties on the Western Front became apparent to him shortly after he arrived. In a letter dated 27 July, less than four weeks after the commencement of the Somme offensive, he wrote: 'It is simply slaughter wholesale over here; our division made what they call a small raid a few days ago and had 7,800 casualties out of 12,000 men; that isn't bad going. I am afraid these raids will not want to occur very often or they will have no Australs. left.'[31]

In common with many other soldiers, Allardyce had to bear the loss of one of his own. His brother was accepted into the Royal Navy in 1916 but within a few months was dead. His letter of condolence to his father underlines the difficulty of finding the words to console someone on the death of their son:

> It is simply terrible about poor Billie; however, we must live in hopes of meeting him and my poor mother in a better world than this ... it seems very hard luck that he should be taken away from us so soon. This last year has been one of many misfortunes, but I hope the present one will bring you all better luck.[32]

Despite the discouragement of the death of his brother Allardyce continued with a process which he had begun some months before, seeking a transfer to an infantry unit. On 31 May he joined the 4th Infantry battalion with the rank of private and a promise of admission to cadet training. The penultimate letter in the collection, written to his brother Jim (also, by now serving in the British army), tells us when he began his officer training (in the middle of July 1915). There is then an enormous gap, of nine months to the final, lengthy letter, written to his father on 19 April 1918. By then Allardyce was a lieutenant in the 4th Infantry battalion. The letter is detailed and breezy. Written from No. 3 Southern General Hospital, Oxford, it begins with the line, 'I am feeling a good deal better this morning, the wounds still ache a little, but that is only to be expected.' He then goes on to describe how he came by his wounds. While on patrol he was shelled by 'a salvo of 5.9's'. Allardyce was hit in the head and lost a lot of blood from a severed artery, but he also appears to have sustained a leg injury. The wound was a 'Blighty', deemed serious enough to have him removed to England. Ironically, a friend who had moved with him from the Ambulance Corps, had also been hit, and both were now together in the same ward. He concludes his letter with a breezy 'Well, I am afraid I cannot go on to detail the hospital now, but will do that in my next letter.'[33]

But there are no more letters in the collection. Allardyce may never have written another. Within less than a month he was dead. There is no indication as to the cause of death, other than the normal 'died of wounds'. Whether the young lieutenant was concealing the extent of his wounds from his father or whether he went into some sort of delayed shock from which he did not recover, is uncertain. Reading his letters, with all their innocence and high-spiritedness, one cannot but come to like the man. Like a well-written novel, one turns the pages wondering what will happen to him. As the number of letters left in the pile begins to dwindle and there are clearly not enough left to get us to 11 November 1918, one experiences a sinking feeling that here is another unfortunate young man who was fated not to make it through the first great crisis of his life. And so it proves with that one bald statement, 'Died of Wounds, Oxford, 18/5/1918.'

THE PHONEY WAR OF DAVID FALLON

Amid the raft of post-war memoirs was one entitled *The Big Fight* in which an Irishman, Captain David Fallon, wrote about his part in the Gallipoli campaign with the Australian Expeditionary Force, his subsequent transfer to the Oxfordshire and Buckinghamshire Regiment, and his involvement in the Battle of the Somme. Fallon was born in Co. Mayo to an Irish father (a naturalist) and a French mother. His parents had met after his father 'rushed away from gentle scientific pursuits in 1870 to bear arms for France against the Prussians'.[34]

Inspired by his father's recounting of incidents from the Franco-Prussian war, Fallon Jr. enlisted in the British Army in 1904, joining the

Northumberland Regiment. He saw service in China and India before being detailed to the Royal Military Academy in Dunstroon, New South Wales, as an instructor with the rank of sergeant major. When war broke out in Europe, he became a recruiting officer and had his application to join the Australian Expeditionary Force denied. He was to be kept at Dunstroon to train the rookie soldiers being turned out in their thousands by Australia (400,000 out of a population of five million, Fallon notes proudly). Unhappy with this decision, he appealed to the Australian Defence Minister, Senator George Pearce, and was allowed to join General Birdwood's Gallipoli force.

His account of his experiences is colourful and wildly propagandistic, though his treatment of the reality of war and of the Gallipoli campaign means his chronicle is not a glorified recruiting pamphlet. His narrative is larded with anecdotes (including the discovery on board the troop transport ship of a woman 'little Betty Grainger' disguised as a soldier)[35] and commentary ('Australia had come to know how tremendous and frightful a war Germany had planned, how viciously and hatefully Germany had resolved to strike at the very life of the British Empire, and Australia began to realise that if the British Empire went under, she herself would eventually have the Hun at her own throat')[36] and is florid in its presentation of the details of the Gallipoli landing and its aftermath.

However, there is something about the over-descriptive nature of the early part of the book which doesn't quite ring true. Events are described in elaborate detail but in a style more suited to fiction than personal narrative. Fallon is oddly vague about the unit with which he served, saying nothing other than that he was part of the 1st Division of the Australian Expeditionary Force. There is no identification of any officers, fellow NCOs or other ranks with whom he served. Only once is there a specific reference to his own command: ' "Fall in Number Nine platoon!" came the growled order. That was my command.' However, in a force the size of the AEF there would have been a 'Number Nine platoon' in each battalion. The events which Fallon describes have a ring of authenticity about them, but it is a verisimilitude which might easily derive from the experience of being under fire (which Fallon had been in India), a modicum of research and an imaginative prose style.

Sad to say, there is no evidence that Fallon ever actually fought in Gallipoli. His biographical card in the Australian War Memorial tells us that he served as a physical training instructor from July 1913 until September 1914. On 16 September he was transferred to the Second Military District, New South Wales, and was discharged from the Australian Military Forces on 25 January 1916. The British Army List of 1916 has a David Fallon becoming a lieutenant in the Oxs and Bucks on 11 June 1916. As a member of the Australian Military Forces, Fallon would have been detailed to training duties or to the defence of Australia itself. If AMF members wanted to fight against the

Turks or the Germans, they had to join the Australian Imperial Force or enlist in another army altogether. This is clearly what Fallon did between January and June of 1916.

The few details offered by Fallon only serve to trip him up. He writes about embarking for the Eastern Front with the first wave of Anzac troops, travelling from Australia to Egypt on board the *Themistocles*,[37] a converted White Star liner of 13,000 tons which had formerly travelled between Australia and Scotland. The *Themistocles* was indeed a familiar ship to those who, in the words of the Eric Bogle song, 'sailed off to Gallipoli',[38] and would have been a logical choice of transport for someone wishing to pretend that they had made such a trip. But the *Themistocles* was not in the first convoy which ferried Australian soldiers to Egypt. Fallon also claims to have been on board the *Euripides* in a convoy of twenty ships which took 10,000 men from Egypt to Lemnos Island, the final staging point before the ill-fated Gallipoli landing. The *Euripides* was also a familar ship to many Australian servicemen, but it too was not, at that point anyway, involved in the transport of troops on the Eastern Front.[39]

Fallon's service on the Western Front (where he won a Military Cross) is recorded in the second part of his book, which is far more generous in its detail of times, places, and names and clarifies the reason for the probable deception of the first part. It appears to have been aimed at an Australian audience increasingly embittered by the Eastern front experiences of its Anzac force and less enthusiastic about enlistment. Fallon seeks to revive this enthusiasm by disinterring tales of German atrocities, warmed-over propaganda reminiscent of that from the 1914 period but given added authenticity by having been 'witnessed' by himself. 'We had heard these stories and believed them', he wrote:

On March 16 [a full three months before he joined the Oxs and Bucks] when we entered the village of St Elois, I saw with my own eyes that these stories which had come to Australia were not lies. My first confrontation with the shocking facts was when in this village. We came upon a shattered convent. I cannot tell you its name because whatever inscription had been on the building was smashed in the general wreck. But the ancient archway of the entrance still stood, and on it was the Mother Superior. The villagers so identified her. She had been nailed to the door. She had been crucified. In the ruins we brought out the bodies of four nuns, unspeakably mutilated. Their bodies had been stabbed and slashed each more than one hundred times. They had gone to martyrdom resisting incredible brutes. They had fought hard, the blond hair of their assassins clutched in their dead hands.[40]

The blond hair is a nice macabre touch in what is otherwise the journalese of the unsubtle zealot, unoriginally perpetuating the rampant 'crucifixion' myth of the trenches. The style of the narrative casts considerable doubt on the provenance of the writing. It seems likely that Fallon, who definitely did exist, simply lent his name to a crude piece of propaganda which he saw as merely an extension of his duty. It is likely that *The Big Fight* was a 'ghosted' work, based on information from Fallon and from veterans who *had* gone through the Gallipoli campaign. Fallon, a former recruiting sergeant, was simply continuing his duties in that area by means of outrageous propaganda.

THE BEESTON PAPERS

One tends to take for granted the professionalism of doctors in war situations. It is an avocation which is not for the squeamish, and in the normal course of events members of the profession must harden themselves to the reality of death (or else treat each death as a personal failure). The assumption is made, therefore, that in war, where horrible violent death and injury is commonplace, the medical practitioner would be inured to the suffering and the pain of others. However, the diary of an Irish doctor in the Australian Army hints at the vulnerabilty behind the facade of the professional. Joseph Livesley Beeston was colonel commanding the 4th Field Ambulance, the unit to which George Allardyce was attached as a stretcher bearer. A graduate of the Royal College of Surgeons of Ireland, he was 56 years old when he travelled to Gallipoli, landing, with the rest of the Australian and New Zealand forces at Anzac Cove, and bringing with him for company his dog, Paddy.

On Monday 3 May he assisted at a Casualty Clearing Station close to the front line trenches. He records the experience in the following terms:

> Great amount of operating, chiefly amputations, and serious abdominal cases. Some of these are very ghastly. A shell will carry the whole of the intestines away, others half of the abdomen. Nothing can be done for these unfortunate fellows, but fill them up with morphia, and await the end. The contents of the man's pocket are frequently in the abdominal cavity, sometimes clips of cartridges, and once the cap of a shell.
>
> It was a dreadful experience, to see all these men, just coming into vigorous manhood mangled and maimed with in many cases wounds that must prove fatal. Yet with all they were so cheerful, not a groan out of one of them but each waiting his turn to be operated upon, and this, not in the calm atmosphere of a hospital but laid out along a beach in the open and shrapnel falling at intervals, frequently contrasted in my mind the fuss that would be made were there even three of these

cases at the one time in any town, and here there [were] that many hundreds. However, it is not the time to allow the sentimental side of one's nature to predominate or one would never get through the work.[41]

Casualties in Beeston's unit were heavy. Doctors, medical orderlies and stretcher-bearers were often expected to put themselves in harm's way when regular soldiers could (and would) keep their heads down. In the aftermath of an Anzac offensive on 8 May 1915, Beeston and other members of 4th Field Ambulance were sheltering from some withering shell and machine-gun fire. A runner arrived from a forward unit looking for a doctor urgently. Beeston, although CO, would not give the order to one of his junior officers to make the hazardous journey and set off himself to offer whatever help he could to a man he assumed was at death's door: 'I certainly thought that my last hour had come,' he wrote,'so thick were the bullets hitting the ground. It is remarkable how one can get through without getting hit. I made the blighter who came for me go ahead to show me the way, but I could not keep up with him. I subsequently found that the man complained of had a pain in the stomach.'

The following week Beeston recorded a similar incident involving two of his bearers: 'A man in hospital in the gully was to be sent to Hospital ship with colitis. He was not bad, but desired to be carried down. While the bearers had him on a stretcher, a shell came over and caught them. One of the bearers lost his leg, and the other was wounded. The blighter who insisted on being carried, got up and ran for his miserable life, and has not been seen since.'

Beeston survived Gallipoli and even made a return trip to Dublin (to which he devotes a significant portion of his diary). He was just one of hundreds of Irishmen, from all stratas of the societies of the 'Colonial' countries[42] who were part of the Irish 'diaspora' which volunteered to come to the assistance of their adopted lands.

6 'The Foolish Dead': Three Irish Writers of the Great War

Know that we fools, now with the foolish dead,
Died not for flag, nor King, nor Emperor
But for a dream, born in a herdsman's shed,
And the secret Scripture of the poor.

(Closing quatrain from Tom Kettle's sonnet
'To My Daughter Betty, the Gift of God')

Name a single poet who established his reputation writing about his experiences in World War II? Name a single poem about that war? They do exist but are overshadowed by the outpouring of literature from the previous great global conflict. The 1914–18 war may simply have inspired great poetry because it included great poets in the ranks of its armed forces. It was the first conflict in which civilians enlisted en masse and in which well-educated young men were able to turn their experiences into poetry. But that was also true of the Second World War! The difference was that the generation which fought World War II (and which included many survivors of the Great War) did not enter in to it with quite the same innocent heroic, self-sacrificial vision which prompted some of the more zealous and romanticised output of the '14–18' conflict from poets like Rupert Brooke. Neither did that generation become as angry and disillusioned with the motivation for and the conduct of the war as did the young men of the 'teens'. This revulsion was reflected in some of the later poetry of men like Wilfred Owen and Siegfried Sassoon.

Ask any Irish schoolchild to name an Irish poet who fought in and wrote about the Great War and the answer will invariably be 'Francis Ledwidge'. This information will probably not have been gleaned from reading any of his war poetry but from knowledge gained about the poet as a result of studying his most famous work, 'Thomas McDonagh'. It is highly probable that any mention of the name 'Thomas Kettle' will be greeted with blank looks. This is despite the fact that at least one poem by Kettle invariably finds its way into any anthology of World War I poetry. In a very real sense Ledwidge 'redeemed' himself in the eyes of nationalist Ireland. He might have 'sold out' to King and Empire (which of course he never did) but had the decency to be appalled by the reprisals for the 1916 Rising and wrote his most memorable poem in honour of one of the leaders of that insurrection. Tom Kettle did not 'redeem' himself. He actually asked to go to front in the aftermath of the Rising and never used his writing skills to celebrate or even commemorate the sacrifice of those who died in 1916. This has been the logic and the received wisdom of two generations.

In fact, as we shall see, Tom Kettle had just as much reason to be revolted and traumatised by the 1916 Rising. He was in Dublin when it broke out, and his brother-in-law, Francis Sheehy Skeffington, an innocent pacifist, was brutally murdered by the British armed forces in the city. His departure for France was, ironically, dictated by his distaste for the cause in which he now served and by his desire to be with a group of men who at least made adherence to that cause more bearable, the Dublin Fusiliers.

What follows is an attempt to synopsise the lives of three significant Irish writers, Francis Ledwidge, Tom Kettle and working-class Donegal novelist and poet Patrick MacGill, who used their abilities, in different literary forms, to express their feelings about the Great War and to convey some of the truth of the war to people who could not experience the sights, sounds, terror and tragedy of that conflict.

FRANCIS LEDWIDGE

In December 1914 the Irish poet Katherine Tynan, in keeping with the romanticism of the likes of Rupert Brooke,[1] published a poem in the *Spectator* which read:

> Lest heaven be thronged with grey-beads hoary,
> God, who made boys for His delight,
> Stoops in a day of grief and glory
> And calls them in, in from the night.

Three years later the God about whom she wrote would 'call in' a man and a poet who had become her friend and her protégé, the rural working class poet from Co. Meath, Francis Ledwidge.

Almost every Irish school child knows at least one line of verse written by one of the country's 'war poets'. The line goes, 'He shall not hear the bittern cry'. Ironically, it was written by a man who was seriously disillusioned with the cause for which he fought and was written about a man to whom that cause was utterly alien. Francis Ledwidge wrote 'Thomas McDonagh' in response to the brutal execution, after the 1916 Rising, of a fellow poet, after a sentence passed in the very barracks where he himself had trained prior to leaving for Gallipoli with the 5th Inniskilling Fusiliers.

Ledwidge was, in almost all respects, an unlikely poet. He was the son of a farm labourer, born, in 1887, into a large family in a tiny rural district council cottage in Slane, Co. Meath. Before he was five years of age, his father died, leaving his mother Alice and her family virtually destitute. Rather than see the family broken up, which logic and circumstances dictated, she undertook tough physical labour to support her children. Ledwidge himself would work as a farm labourer, copper miner and a road worker. His experience of the hardships inherent in all such employments prompted his commitment to the Labour movement. He became a trade union organiser.

He also began to write, falteringly at first and then with increasing confidence. He cherished hopes of making a career for himself in journalism and began to write his first poetry, verse which reflected the lush, luxuriant countryside surrounding him. Ever the activist, he became involved with the Irish Volunteers in the Slane area, as did his brother Joe. In 1914 he was elected to the Navan rural district council and board of guardians. His first poems came to the attention of the writer (and slightly eccentric) Lord Dunsany, and he also fell in love. Things looked promising for the 'peasant' (Dunsany's later description) son of an impoverished widow.

One by one, however, the supports which underpinned his life, shattered. The woman he loved, Ellie Vaughey, married another man. The onset of the Great War led to the split in the Volunteers and the severing of relations between Ledwidge and the dominant Redmondite faction in the local Slane organisation. Finally he found himself at odds with the other members of the Navan rural district council. He flew in the face of the *zeitgeist* and was shot down by the bluff, moralising followers of the Redmond line. Ledwidge saw the Volunteers as a force, or a catalyst at least, for political change in Ireland. His antagonism toward Redmond's National Volunteers made him a target for the majority faction on the council. Some of Ledwidge's sentiments about the war, such as those expressed on 19 October 1914, were guaranteed to draw fire, all the more so because they lacked the self-serving romanticism and self-delusion of the earliest Irish war zealots.

'In the north of Ireland,' he proclaimed at that time, 'the recruiting sergeants have been saying to the men, "Go out and fight with anti-Papal France." In the south of Ireland they will say, "Go out and fight for Catholic Belgium." The people around Liege and Namur are the greatest Walloons and anti-clerics in the world and they have shown their brutality by their treatment of German prisoners.' (He did not address himself to the reasons for such 'brutality'.) Challenged by an opponent to respond to a question on his allegiances, which implied that he was pro-German, he replied, 'I am an anti-German and an Irishman.'[2] He found himself in that most uncomfortable of minority positions – total isolation.

He didn't attend any more council meetings. Instead, he shocked his fellow members by doing something they themselves showed little inclination to do:

he joined the Army. He had been driven to it by the taunting of the council-
lors, by his own sense of duty, by an innate abhorrence of naked Imperialism
(German) and by Ellie Vaughey's rejection of him. As Seamus Heaney has
put it, 'He very deliberately chose not to bury his head in local sand and, as a
consequence, faced the choices and moral challenges of his time with solitude,
honesty and rare courage.'[3]

His enlistment makes Ledwidge a somewhat inconvenient figure for
Republicans, who otherwise admire the sentiments expressed in 'Thomas
McDonagh'. His later political 'reconversion' (or enlightenment!) renders him
acceptable to that school, while his earlier ambivalence could cast him in the
role of a revisionist icon. But no political theorising can stifle or disguise
Ledwidge's often tortured humanity. In order to complete the full circle from
which the inconvenient chunk is missing, some have demonised Dunsany and
his role in Ledwidge's decision. Because the poem 'Thomas McDonagh' testified to his spiritual enlistment in the cause of militant nationalism, how
otherwise could one explain his service in the uniform of the state which had
executed McDonagh. For those who like their history uncomplicated, the
figure of Lord Dunsany becomes a Loyalist ogre who suborns the youthful
and impressionable republican Ledwidge into joining the forces of the Crown.
But, as the poet's biographer, Alice Curtayne, has shown, Ledwidge was no
Trilby to Dunsany's Svengali. True, he did join the older man's battalion but
given the latter's patronage of him that is hardly surprising.

Ledwidge represented his own motives as being very different from the
romantic notions frequently ascribed to those with the status 'Poet': 'Some of
the people who know me least imagine that I joined the Army because I knew
men were struggling for higher ideals and great empires, and I could not sit
idle and watch them make for me a more beautiful world. They are mistaken.
I joined the British Army because she stood between Ireland and an enemy
common to our civilisation and I would not have her say that she defended
us while we did nothing at home but pass resolutions.'[4]

Essentially Ledwidge carried within him the seeds of that innate moral
certainty which sent thousands of Irish nationalists to the trenches, despite
considerable scepticism and reservations about the sincerity of the fight 'for
small nations'. Seamus Heaney has commented that 'to see him as the
uncomplicated voice of romantic nationalism misrepresents the agonized
consciousness which held in balance and ultimately decided between the
command to act upon the dictates of a morality he took to be both objective
and universally applicable, and the desire to keep faith with a politically
resistant and particularly contentious Irish line'.[5]

Army life appeared to suit Ledwidge. He was fit and used to hard labour,
fussy about his appearance, and his involvement with the Volunteers meant
that he was no stranger to military discipline and rituals. But from the outset

he was pragmatic about the odds against returning alive from the Front. On 9 March 1915 he wrote to his friend Mattie McGoona about his arrival at training camp in England: 'I flew in here on Pegasus Matt. He brought me here and then left me but I think he will come back for me when peace unfurls her flag of truce. But I may not be anywhere in the world when he calls again. If you do not hear me singing after the war, you will know that I have gone across the tide to Keats and the rest of them.'[6] Posted with his battalion to Gallipoli, his baptism of fire came on the infamous 15th of August at Kiretch Tepe Sert. The 5th and 6th Inniskillings were given the responsibility of attacking the coastal heights from the landward side. Forced to advance across uneven ground in the face of determined oppostion, they failed to take or even reach their objectives. 'In broken scrub-covered ground, the stubborn, courageous Turk showed his best qualities. Manning positions which gave perfect observation of the advance, the Turkish machine-gunners stopped every attack with a withering hail of bullets.'[7] The Inniskillings lost most of their officers and took 350 casualties.

For Ledwidge, seeing death and human misery on such a scale should have been an intimidating and unnerving experience. Instead, he described feeling something bordering on elation in a letter to Dunsany,[8] back in Derry training recruits: 'By Heavens you should know the bravery of these men, Cassidy standing on a hill with his cap on top of his rifle, shouting at the Turks to come out; stretcher-bearers taking in friend and enemy alike. It was a horrible and a great day. I would not have missed it for worlds.'[9]

The daily grind of Gallipoli followed the stark terror and adrenalin of Kiretch Tepe Sert until the 10th Division was pulled out of that lost cause and despatched to Salonika to participate in another, this time against Bulgaria. Here Ledwidge became one of the stoical defenders of a reeling Serbia in a war which I have described in *Irish Voices from the Great War*. In a subsequent letter to his friend Robert Christie he complained that 'no words could describe the cold, the blizzards, the frost and the hunger. We did not fear the Bulgars even though we were outnumbered; we only thought it unfair of England to send us, a broken division, up there where so many had failed.'[10] By December 1915 the 10th were being forced to abandon Serbia and retire to neutral Greece, hoping that the advancing Bulgarians would show more respect for Greek neutrality than had the Entente forces. The retreat was exhausting, tedious, dangerous, freezing cold and bitterly contested.

'It poured rain on us all the ninety miles we had to march,' he wrote to a friend, '... Shall I ever forget it'? His unit had been ordered to help extricate a French brigade which had become almost surrounded and in so doing nearly failed to extricate itself.

The Bulgars came on us like flies and though we mowed down line after line, they persisted with awful doggedness and finally gave us a bayonet charge which secured their victory. We only just had about 200 yards to escape by and we had to hold this until next evening and then dribble out as best we could.[11]

The Salonika campaign ended for Ledwidge when he was invalided out of the war zone to England via hospital in Egypt.

He was still in hospital, in Manchester, recovering from inflammation of the gall bladder, when the 1916 Rising forced him to reassess his loyalties. As a poet, Ledwidge had been an admirer of the work of the executed poet-leaders. He considered Pearse and McDonagh to be good friends. Some accounts of the events of Easter Week have Ledwidge, discharged from hospital, travelling to Dublin and attempting to join Pearse and McDonagh but being unable to do so. Such a version of events is inaccurate. Whatever Ledwidge might have wished to do he would have been unable to get to Dublin, as the boat service wasn't running. When he did manage to get back to Ireland, he brought with him the poem for which he is best known, honouring his friend and fellow poet Thomas McDonagh.

> He shall not hear the bittern cry
> In the wild sky where he is lain
> Nor voices of the sweeter birds
> Above the wailing of the rain
>   Nor shall he know when loud March blows
> Through slanting snows her fanfare shrill
> Blowing to flame the golden cup
> Of many an upset daffodil
>   But when the Dark Cow leaves the moor
> And pastures poor with greedy weeds
> Perhaps he'll hear her low at morn
> Lifting her horn in pleasant meads[12]

Like many other nationalists he now resented his obligation to fight for the British Empire, for that is how, from that point onwards, he saw the enterprise in which he was involved. In June 1917 he would write to an American academic,

I am sorry that party politics should ever divide our own tents but am not without hope that a new Ireland will arise from her ashes in the ruins of Dublin, like the Phoenix, with one purpose, one aim, and one ambition. I tell you this in order that you may know what it is to me to be called a British soldier while my own country has no place amongst the nations but the place of Cinderella.[13]

Ledwidge grew moody and sullen in the aftermath of the Rising, though much of his surliness may have been related to his war experiences. An altercation with an officer in Richmond Barracks arising out of a disagreement over the Rebellion was one of the events which, ultimately, led to his being court-martialled and to the loss of his lance corporal's stripe (though Dunsany, and others, have insisted that his heavy drinking was also to blame). His subsequent poem, 'After Court Martial', captures his sense of loss at the execution of the 'soldier-poets' of the Rising and his own disillusionment. It concludes:

And though men call me a vile name,
And all my dream companions gone,
'Tis I the soldier bears the shame
Not I the king of Babylon.[14]

When Ledwidge returned to active service it was not with the 5th Inniskillings but with the 1st Battalion, a Regular Army outfit, in the 29th Division, a unit much changed from its early involvement in the Gallipoli landings. And he was posted to an entirely different front. Ledwidge was one of the warm bodies required by Haig for his ambitious offensive plans of 1917 on the Western Front. He died during the disastrous Third Ypres (Passchendaele) offensive in July 1917. His unit was in reserve, building communications tracks composed of heavy wooden planks. On 31 July he was busy at this task near the infamous Hell Fire Corner, so-called because it seemed to draw enemy shell-fire like a magnet. Despite a continuous downpour, work on the wooden road continued, as did the sporadic German barrage. While he was drinking a welcome cup of tea, a shell exploded near Ledwidge, and he was, quite literally, blown to pieces.

Like millions of other young men who died in the Great War, Ledwidge deserved better. His talent as a poet and writer was developing rather than finely honed. He is rarely acknowledged in compilations of War poetry as a major voice. And perhaps that is as it should be. At the time of his death he was by no means the finished article. Neither could he be fairly and accurately described as a 'War Poet'. He did not write, as did Sassoon or Owen, either lyrically or savagely, about the Great War. His experiences in that conflict clearly informed, even enhanced, his work but the war was merely a backdrop to most of his romantic lyric verse. In one of his later letters he had written, to the poet Katherine Tynan, whose own son was a serviceman, of his dreams for the future:

If I survive the war, I have great hopes of writing something that will live. If not, I trust to be remembered in my own land for one or two things which its long sorrow inspired. ... You ask me what I am doing, I am a unit in the Great War, doing and suffering, admiring great endeavour and condemning great dishonour. I may be dead before this reaches you, but I will have done my part. Death is as interesting to me as life. I have seen so much of it from Suvla to Serbia and now in France. I am always homesick. I hear the roads calling, and the hills, and the rivers wondering where I am. It is terrible to be always homesick.[15]

Ledwidge lies in a graveyard three miles north of Ypres. A plaque erected in his memory in the picturesque village of Slane carries, as his epitaph, the first verse of his best known poem, 'Thomas McDonagh'. A more appropriate epitaph, however, one with a quality as elegiac as that of his most celebrated work, might be 'A Soldier's Grave' from *Last Songs* published posthumously in 1918:

> Then in the lull of midnight, gentle arms
> Lifted him slowly down the slopes of death
> Lest he should hear again the mad alarms
> Of battle, dying moans, and painful breath.
> And where the earth was soft for flowers we made
> A grave for him that he might better rest.
> So, spring shall come and leave it sweet arrayed
> And there the lark shall turn her dewy nest.[16]

TOM KETTLE

Tom Kettle's political pedigree was impeccable. Born in Artane, Dublin, in 1880, he was the son of Andrew Kettle, one of the founder members of the Land League. Kettle junior was an excellent student and a gifted orator who became auditor of the UCD Literary and Historical Society in 1898. In 1904 he suffered two major setbacks: his health gave way and he lost his brother. Physical and psychological recuperation brought him to the Tyrol and introduced him to the continent of Europe. He was called to the Bar in 1905 but quickly opted for a political career, joining the United Irish League and becoming the editor of a weekly journal *The Nationist* [*sic*], which lasted for six months. In 1906 he was elected to Westminster via a by-election in the East Tyrone constituency with a paper-thin majority of 16! He was re-elected in 1910 with a greatly increased majority of 118! In Parliament he was an excellent orator with a taste for the well-timed heckle and the apposite political barb. He once summed up the difference between the two main British parties: 'When in office, the Liberals forget their principles and the Tories remember their friends.'[17]

In 1909 he became Professor of Economics in the National University and decided to quit parliamentary politics. In that same year he also married Mary Sheehy. His involvement in political campaigning continued. He was active in seeking a solution to the great Lockout of 1913, retained his links with the Irish Parliamentary Party, and became a member of the Provisional Committee of the Irish Volunteers. In 1910 he published a volume of essays, *The Days Burden,* and was also responsible for a number of political pamphlets. On the debit side Kettle also began to drink heavily. His naturally melancholy temperament fell victim to the ravages of alcohol, and his health, mental and physical, began to suffer. In 1913 he was forced to seek treatment for 'dipso-mania' in a private hospital in Kent and, briefly, gave up his work in UCD.[18]

Kettle was in Belgium buying rifles for the Volunteers when war broke out, and during August and September 1914 he acted as war correspondent for the *Daily News.* What he saw taking place in Belgium filled him with a burning sense of indignation against Germany. He wrote a despatch to the *News* describing Germany as 'the outlaw of Europe' and adding that 'it is impossible not to be with Belgium in this struggle. Germany has thrown down a well considered challenge to all the forces of our civilisation. War is hell, but it is only a hell of suffering, not of dishonour, and through it, over its flaming coals, Justice must walk, were it on bare feet.'[19] He probably could have become a full-time war correspondent; instead he returned to Ireland and enlisted, according to his wife, Mary 'as an Irish soldier in the army of Europe and civilisation'.[20]

Kettle had volunteered for active service, but his poor health, his abilities as an orator, and his direct experience of conditions in Belgium (he had met with the Belgian king and prime minister) meant that he was far more valuable as a recruiter. He was given the rank of lieutenant and sent around the country to encourage others to enlist. His wife claims that he made over 200 speeches in the course of this work. It was in this role that Michael Fitzgerald, later of the Royal Irish Regiment, saw him in Bachelor's Walk in Dublin in 1914:

> I remember him climbing the steps up to the platform with his black top hat, his striped trousers and smoking a cigar. I have a vivid memory of him making a magnificent recruiting speech ... There was a very very big crowd, recruiting meetings were very well attended ... and there was no hostility to what was being said at all.[21]

The Home Rule Act, for which Kettle and the other members of the Irish Parliamentary party had struggled, received the royal assent in September

1918 but was accompanied by a Suspensory Act, leaving it in abeyance for the duration of the war. Kettle's participation in the Great War, was, in part, as one of many nationalist hostages to the ultimate delivery of Home Rule. He believed that 'used with the wisdom which is sown in tears and blood, this tragedy of Europe may be and must be the prologue to the two reconciliations of which all statesmen have dreamed, the reconciliation of Protestant Ulster with Ireland, and the reconciliation of Ireland with Great Britain'.[22]

Life as a non-combatant soldier was not without its drawbacks as far as Kettle was concerned. Long periods of boredom allowed him the leisure to drink heavily, and he was frequently carpeted for being inebriated while in uniform. On one occasion he was summoned to appear before General Sir Laurence Parsons, the CO of the 16th Division, because of some disciplinary infraction. Parsons, was undoubtedly conscious of Kettle's value but frustrated by his indiscipline. 'Lieutenant Kettle,' he upbraided him, 'this cannot go on. If you don't obey orders, the British Army cannot hold us both.' 'We'll be very sorry to lose you, General,' replied the insubordinate junior officer.[23] Ironically that was how it turned out, Parsons was replaced by Major General Hickie at the helm of the 16th and did not travel to France with the Division.

Kettle became increasingly restive through 1915 and made frequent appeals to be allowed go on active service. But he was still in barracks in Ireland (Newbridge) when the Easter Rising changed the entire dynamic of Irish history. Kettle was appalled by the actions of Pearse, Connolly and their supporters. As Lyons puts it, 'He shared the general feeling of outrage, in face of what most folk saw as dangerous folly, but he experienced too, a feeling of personal affront. He denounced the venture as madness. He saw it as destructive of what he had striven for throughout his adult life.'[24]

Two events were to change his attitude and affect his feelings towards the cause in which he had enlisted. The first was the murder of his brother-in-law, the pacifist Francis Sheehy-Skeffington. Skeffington had been arrested and taken to Portobello Barracks while trying to prevent the Dublin citizenry from looting. He had the misfortune to find himself under the control of a demented British officer, Captain Bowen-Colthurst of the Royal Irish Rifles. At about 10 a.m. on Easter Tuesday, Skeffington, along with two journalists Thomas Dickson and Patrick McIntyre, were murdered on the orders of Bowen-Colthurst. Mary Kettle was the sister of Hanna Sheehy-Skeffington, so Kettle shared the grief of the Sheehy family. His personal bitterness at the death of his friend and brother-in-law was accentuated by the fact that he wore the same uniform as the psychotic Bowen-Colthurst.

The second event which further soured his relationship with the British military was the execution of the leaders of the 1916 Rising. Thomas McDonagh had been a fellow professor; Pearse had been a friend of many years. His wish to go to France on active service was granted after Easter

Week (he sailed for France on 14 July 1916), but it was a much changed and chastened Kettle who joined the 16th Division as it prepared to play its part in the massive Somme offensive.

He endured the privations and miseries of trench warfare without complaint. One can speculate that a man as melancholy as he, who had seen whatever illusions remained to him shattered, was simply ready to die. In a letter to the Northern MP Joe Devlin, he talked, ambiguously, about death: 'I hope to come back. If not, I believe that to sleep here in the France I have loved is no harsh fate, and that so passing out into the silence, I shall help towards the Irish settlement. Give my love to my colleagues – the Irish people have no need of it.'[25]

Kettle quickly formed a bond with the ordinary soldiers under his command, and began to plan a book on the war and on the 16th Division. His collected observations of war were to appear in the posthumous volume *The Ways of War*. It includes this atmospheric description of an emblematic sentinel:

> A figure in khaki stands on the shelf of fire bag, his steel helmet forming a serious bulge over the parapet as he peers through the night towards the German lines. His comrade sits on the shelf beside him waiting to help, to report, to carry the gas alarm, the alarm of an attack. Over there in front across no man's land there are shell holes and unburied men. Strange things happen there. Patrols and counter patrols come and go. There are two sinister fences of barbed wire, on the barbs of which blood stained strips of uniform and fragments more sinister have been known to hang uncollected for a long time. The air is shaken with diabolical reverberations; it is stabbed with malign illumination as the Very lights shoot up, broaden to a blaze, and go out.
>
> This contrast of night and light and gloom is trying to the eyes. The rifle grenades and trench mortars, flung at short range, that scream through the air are trying to the ears. They may drop a traverse away, and other men not charged for the moment with his duty may seek shelter. But not he. Strange things issue from no man's land, and the eyes of the army never close or flinch. And so, strained, tense and immovable he leans and looks forward into the night of menace. But the trench has not fallen. As for him, he carried his pack for Ireland and Europe, and now pack carrying is over. He has held the line.[26]

He also expounds on the constant companion of the soldier, Death:

> In the trenches it is the day-to-dayness that tells and tries. It is always the same tone of duty: certain days in billets, certain days in reserve, certain days in the front line ... A few casualties every turn, another

grating of the saw teeth of death and disease, and before very long a strong unit is weak ... Everybody going up to the trenches from the CO down to the last arrival in the last draft knows it to be a moral certainty that there are two or three that will not march back. Everybody knows that it may be anybody. In the trenches death is random, illogical, devoid of principle. One is shot not on sight, but on blindness, out of sight ...[27]

Some time after his arrival at the front, Kettle had been offered the post of base censor. This would have meant his withdrawal from front line duties. He agreed to take up the position after the conclusion of the 16th's offensive against Guillemont and Ginchy. Many have seen as a sort of 'death wish' his refusal to accept a safe rear-echelon job. His wife alludes to this in her 'Memoir' in *The Ways of War*: 'Some critics have hinted that he died in France because he had not the heart to live in Ireland. Some even went so far as to suggest that he died in France because he knew he ought to have died in the GPO in Dublin.'[28] But, like Willie Redmond at Messines the following year, Kettle felt that he had something to prove. He did not want to leave himself open to the allegation that he was a mere 'platform soldier', a recruiter, in uniform but not in arms. He also, genuinely, wanted to lead his men into what was going to be their most rigorous test. He called them 'my Dublin Fusiliers'. 'What impresses and moves me above all,' he wrote, 'is the amazing faith, patience and courage of the men. I pray and pray and am afraid, but they go quietly and heroically on. God make me less inferior to them.'[29]

He survived the 16th Division's crippling assault on Guillemont, though he seems to have led a charmed life during the attack. He wrote his last letter to his wife before Guillemont. It is a letter full of self-recrimination:

> It is no longer indiscreet to say that we are to take part in one of the biggest attacks of the war. Many will not come back. Should that be God's design for me, you will not receive this letter until afterwards. I want to thank you for the love and kindness you spent and all but wasted on me. There was never in all the world a dearer woman or a more perfect wife and adorable mother. My heart cries for you and Betty whom I may never see again. I think even that it is perhaps better that I should not see you again. God bless and keep you! If the last sacrifice is ordained, think that in the end I wiped out all the old stains. Tell Betty her daddy was a soldier and died as one. My love, now at last clean, will find a way to you. Ever your husband, Tom.[30]

Between the successful assault on Guillemont and the subsequent attack on Ginchy Kettle spent a considerable amount of time in the company of Emmet

Dalton, then a second lieutenant in Kettle's battalion, the 9th Dublin Fusiliers. Speaking on RTE Radio many years later, Dalton recalled their encounters:

> he was in the advance trenches, the kick-off point, where I met him and talked with him. He was, of course, more an associate and friend of my father's than he was of mine, but he was very charming and delightful man and I spent some time with him, such little time as was available because within two days we were in the forefront and within three days he was dead ... I recall sitting with him prior to the movement up to the front line for the offensive. He recited to me a poem that he had written to his daughter, and he had it written down in a field notebook ... every officer carried one at that time, and it was a delightful little poem.[31]

The poem was, of course, the sonnet by which Kettle will always be best remembered, one which ranks alongside the best work produced by some outstanding poets who experienced the Great War. It was addressed to his three-year-old daughter Elizabeth (who was born on 31 January 1913 and who died in early 1997) and was entitled 'To my daughter, Betty, the gift of God'. It was Kettle's final testament, the valedictory of a man who had been broken in so many ways and who, in the face of death, could be ruthlessly honest and open about his failings, illusions and his legacy. The poem reads:

> In wiser days my darling rosebud, blown
> To beauty proud as was your mother's prime,
> In that desired, delayed, incredible time,
> You'll ask why I abandoned you, my own,
> And the dear heart that was your baby throne,
> To dice with death. And, oh! they'll give you rhyme
> And reason; some will call the thing sublime,
> And some decry it in a knowing tone.
> So here, while the mad guns curse overhead,
> And tired men sigh, with mud for couch and floor,
> Know that we fools, now with the foolish dead,
> Died not for flag, nor King, nor Emperor,
> But for a dream, born in a herdsman's shed,
> And for the secret Scripture of the poor.[32]

Dalton understood the import of the poem very clearly:

> I was very moved when I read it because Kettle quite obviously, by the tone of the poem as I now think of it, saw the difficulties that had arisen in 1916 in Ireland and questioned the validity of his own position

on the Somme and my position on the Somme, for that matter, whether we were right or wrong at this stage because he didn't realise initially that such a thing could happen and I suppose he felt sad about it, to think that he was fighting on the Somme and his own fellow country-men were suffering persecution, as it was, in his homeland.[33]

On 8 September 1916, the 9th Dublin Fusiliers were in trenches near Trones Wood opposite Guillemont. Heavy losses as a result of German shelling meant that Kettle had to take command of B Company while Emmet Dalton, then only 18 years old, became second-in-command of A Company. That morning both men were told to prepare their troops for the advance on Ginchy. Kettle wrote a letter to his brother with a grim sense of foreboding: 'Somewhere the Choosers of the slain are touching, as in our Norse story they used to touch, with invisible wands those who are to die.'[34] Even the journey to Ginchy was discomfiting. Emmet Dalton recalled that he was 'with Tom when he advanced to the position that night, and the stench of the dead that covered our road was so awful that we both used some foot powder on our faces ...'[35]

Ginchy was a readily defensible position guarded by a Bavarian division, on high ground which commanded the greatly denuded approaches to what was left of the village. But the 16th (Irish) Division, still recovering from its traumatic losses at Guillemont, swept through and beyond the village, unse-cured on either flank, and took the rubble of what had once been (and is today) a picturesque township.

But the 'invisible wand' was to touch the shoulder of Tom Kettle. The attack began at 5.00 p.m. Emmet Dalton was beside him when he was hit: 'I was just behind Tom when we went over the top. He was in a bent position, and a bullet got over a steel waistcoat that he wore and entered his heart. Well, he only lasted about one minute, and he had my crucifix in his hands.'[36] His pockets were emptied by another friend, M.H. Boyd, who intended that the contents be sent to Mary Kettle. However, a short time later Boyd him-self was blown to pieces by a German shell. Kettle was buried by members of a battalion of the Welsh Guards.

Kettle's fame and personal popularity ensured a fulsome reaction to his death. G.K. Chesterton wrote in the *Observer* that his 'fall in battle ought to crush the slanderers of Ireland as the fall of a tower could crush nettles'.[37] One person who was clearly crushed was Kettle's father, Andy. When told that his son was missing in action, the old man responded, 'If Tom is dead I don't wish to live any longer.' Within a fortnight of his son's burial he too was dead. The *Irish Times* wrote: 'As Irish Unionists we lay our wreath on the grave of a generous Nationalist, a brilliant Irishman, and a loyal soldier of the King.'[38] An unnamed friend wrote to Mary Kettle about his own personal sense of loss and grief, concluding that 'it is the loss of that rare, charming, wondrous personality summed up in those two simple words – Tom Kettle.'[39]

In her preface to *The Ways of War* Mary herself wrote, movingly about the hours before his death:

> His last thoughts were with Ireland, and in each letter of farewell written to friends from the battlefield, he protests that he died in her holy cause. His soldier servant, writing home to me says that on the eve of the battle the officers were served with pieces of green cloth to be stitched on the back of their uniforms indicating that they belonged to the Irish Brigade. Tom touched his lovingly, saying; "I am proud to die for it!" Ireland, Christianity, Europe – that was what he died for ... and with this mission of universal peace mingled his dream of a reconciled Ulster. He knew that there was no abiding cause of disunion between North and South, and he hoped that out of common dangers shared and suffering endured on a European battleground, there would issue a United Ireland.[40]

Kettle's final political testimony was published three weeks after his death. In it he says:

> I have mixed much with Englishmen and with Protestant Ulstermen, and I know that there is no real or abiding reason for the gulfs, salter than the sea, that now dismember the mutual alliance of both of them with us Irish Nationalists ... In the name, and by the seal, of the blood given in the last two years I ask for Colonial Home Rule for Ireland, a thing essential in itself, and essential as a prologue to the reconstruction of the Empire. Ulster will agree. And I ask for the immediate withdrawal of martial law in Ireland, and an amnesty for all Sinn Fein prisoners. If this war has taught us anything, it is that great things can be done only in a great way.[41]

It is one of the ironies of history that Emmet Dalton should have been present at the deaths of two of the greatest Irishmen of the early twentieth century, Michael Collins and Tom Kettle. The former is revered by most and reviled by a few but cannot be ignored; the latter is largely forgotten. Kettle has been overlooked by history because he chose his road 'not wisely but too well'. His cause was the same as that of Michael Collins, his methods and philosophy vastly different. As his biographer, J.B. Lyons, commented,

> He lived to see the Home Rule Act on the Statute Book but because of his unhesitating chivalry in the autumn of 1914, this knight in uniform, sans peur if not sans reproche, was destined to die in khaki in 1916, a year in which the retrospective distortions of historical perspective now decree it to have been de rigueur to have worn green.[42]

In his *Poems and Parodies* Kettle wrote: 'Memorial I would have ... a constant presence with those that love me.' For the best part of seventy years after his death Kettle's place was in the hearts of those who loved and admired him rather than in public memory. The poet and mystic George Russell (AE) recognised the great wrong which had been done to Kettle, in a poem published in the *Irish Times* in 1917 entitled 'To the Memory of Some I Knew who are Dead and who Loved Ireland'. It was written, partially, in response to Yeats' 'Easter 1916' which sponsored the myth of the Irish 'lost generation' of the 1916 Rising alone. In his poem, Russell recognised that other great loss of Irish intellects, to the Great War, by giving equal status in his poem to the memory of Thomas McDonagh and Thomas Kettle. He wrote of Kettle:

> You who have fought on fields afar,
> That other Ireland did you wrong
> Who said you shadowed Ireland's star,
> Nor gave you laurel wreath nor song.
> You proved by death as true as they,
> In mightier conflicts played your part,
> Equal your sacrifice may weigh
> Dear Kettle of the generous heart.[43]

Kettle's misfortune, like that of the Irish Parliamentary party, was to be overtaken by events and to be retrospectively castigated for flying in the face of a *zeitgeist* which had no validity when he made the choices which were to define his status and determine his future. Mary Kettle wrote: 'I think the chief reason his motives have been misunderstood is that few have gone to the trouble of understanding his wide outlook. He was a European. He was deeply steeped in European culture ... Mr Healy once said his idea of a nation ended with the Kish lightship. Tom Kettle's ideal was an Ireland identified with the life of Europe.'[44] Kettle himself wrote that 'while a strong nation has herself for centre, she has the universe for circumference ... My only counsel to Ireland is, that to become deeply Irish, she must become European.'[45] However, he was under no illusions about the flag under which he fought and the hypocrisy of British politicians who were prepared to defend the freedom of 'Little Belgium' and deny self-government to Ireland. 'England goes to fight for liberty in Europe but junkerdom in Ireland,' wrote Kettle sardonically.[46]

Kettle had no illusions about how he was likely to be judged by history. He put it succinctly in his poem 'Cancel the Past':

Cancel the past! Why yes!
We, too, have thought
Of conflict crowned and drowned in olives of peace;
But when Cuchulainn and Ferdia fought
There lacked no pride of warrior courtesies,
And so this fight must end.
Bond, from the toil of hate we may not cease;
Free, we are free to be your friend.
And when you make your banquet, and we come,
Soldier with equal soldier must we sit,
Closing a battle, not forgetting it.
With not a name to hide,
This mate and mother of valiant 'rebels' dead
Must come with all her history on her head.
We keep the past for pride;
No deepest peace shall strike our poets dumb;
No rawest squad of all Death's volunteers,
No rudest men who died
To tear your flag down in the bitter years,
But shall have praise, and three times thrice again,
When at the table men shall drink with men.

Perhaps the most appropriate epitaph for Kettle is contained in a verse which he wrote in honour of his earliest political icon, Charles Stewart Parnell. Although written in 1911, the terminology of the opening verse of 'Parnell' is military and oddly prescient and appropriate.

Tears will betray all pride, but when ye mourn him,
Be it in soldier wise;
As for a captain who hath gently borne him,
And in the midnight dies.

PATRICK MAC GILL

Born in 1890 Patrick MacGill was one of 13 surviving children of a poor farming family from Donegal. His illiterate father, on the advice of a local priest, sent MacGill to the village school, where he received a rudimentary education up the age of ten. He displayed no particular academic aptitude but did have an ability to learn and recite poetry. His departure from school was, in part, to do with the economic exigencies of his domestic situation and in part because he struck the schoolmaster with a pointer. The pre-teen MacGill was already exhibiting the rebellious tendencies which were to mark his adolescence.

At the age of twelve, after having worked on his father's small plot of land for two years he went to the hiring fair in Strabane and became a part of the white, Irish slave trade, suffering physical privation and abuse at the hands of Irish farmers who would have valued him more highly had he actually been a slave and of some financial benefit to them. For two years he endured this, sending home his wages every week in order to help sustain the increasing number of his brothers and sisters. In 1904 he went to Scotland to pick potatoes, 'a seasonal migration which still allowed mere boys and girls to be linked and lodged with semi-criminals, drunkards and gamblers in appalling working and living conditions'.[48]

While in Scotland, MacGill began to read and to write as he moved through a variety of different navvying jobs. He also discovered socialism and became a member of the Socialist Party in Glasgow. By 1909 his writing had led to a complete change of life for the self-educated Donegal man. He was offered a job as a journalist on the London-based periodical *Dawn*. The position paid £2 a week, a lot of money to someone used to hard manual labour and to labourer's wages. He supplemented his journalistic work with poetry and fiction, producing *Songs of a Navvy* in 1911 and his first novel, *Lanty Hanlon: A Comedy of Irish Life*, in 1912. His experience of child labour was crammed into his best known work, the autobiographical *Children of the Dead End* which was published in 1914.

From 1914 to 1919 the Great War provided the backdrop to MacGill's writings. He became Rifleman No. 3008 with the London Irish Regiment, and his engaged and committed writing articulated the anguish and disillusionment of his generation. The first work he produced which either utilised or recorded his wartime experiences was *The Amateur Army* (1915). He followed this with the *The Red Horizon* and *The Great Push* in 1916, the latter being an account of the major British offensive at Loos the previous year in which MacGill was wounded. *The Great Push* was written almost entirely as the battle itself raged. As he writes in his introduction, 'the chapter dealing with our night at Les Brebis, prior to the Big Push, was written in the trench between midnight and dawn of September the 25th; the concluding chapter in the hospital at Versailles two days after I had been wounded at Loos.'[49]

MacGill's approach to the subject of war was intensely personal and humane. His heroes were the ordinary soldiers whose heroism lay in their simple endurance. His attitude to war was that of the disputant and, towards the political 'mission' on which his 'betters' had embarked, the sceptic. As with his navvy stories he invokes a fraternity of suffering in his writings, making common cause with his fellow soldiers, implicitly excluding those who had not shared the experience of the trenches and explicitly condemning those who had provoked the conflict. He begins *The Great Push* by saying that

the justice of the cause which endeavours to achieve its object by the
murdering and maiming of mankind is apt to be doubted by a man who
has come through a bayonet charge. The dead lying on the fields seem
to ask, 'Why has this been done to us? Why have you done it, brothers?
What purpose has it served?' The battle-line is a secret world, a world
of curses. The guilty secrecy of war is shrouded in lies, and shielded by
bloodstained swords; to know it you must be one of those who wage it,
a party to dark and mysterious orgies of carnage.

The same sense of dislocation which comes across in his earlier writings is
very much in evidence in his war memoirs. Flanders is as alien to a Donegal
man as were the Scottish railroads. He wrote:

> Before I joined the Army
> I lived in Donegal,
> Where every night the fairies,
> Would hold their carnival.
>   But now I'm out in Flanders,
> Where men like wheat ears fall,
> And its death and not the fairies
> Who is holding carnival.[50]

In describing the reality of trench warfare MacGill's style is at times almost
lyrical, but it is a subversion of lyricism, a deliberately inappropriate use of a
comforting and congenial style, which is then contrasted with a downbeat
naturalism. The objects described are in stark contrast to the mode of
description:

> On the field of death, the shells, in colossal joy, chorused their terrible
> harmonies, making the heavens sonorous with their wanton and unbridled
> frenzy; star-shells, which seemed at times to be fixed on the ceiling of
> the sky, oscillated in a dazzling whirl of red and green – and men died
> ... We remained in the trenches the next day. They were very quiet,
> and we lay at ease in our dug-outs, read week-old papers, wrote letters
> and took turns on sentry-go. On our front lay a dull brown,
> monotonous level and two red brick villages, Loos and Hulluch. Our
> barbed-wire entanglement, twisted and shell scarred, showed countless
> rusty spikes which stuck out ominous and forbidding. A dead German
> hung on a wire prop, his feet caught in a *cheval de frise*, the skin of his
> face peeling away from his bones, and his hand clutching the wire as if
> for support. He had been out there for many months, a foolhardy foe
> who got a bullet through his head when examining our defences.[51]

Although never parochial or chauvinistic, MacGill, in his writings, memorialises the involvement of Irish troops in the Great War. As an emigrant who had joined a British based regiment (albeit an overwhelmingly Irish one) he was not surrounded by other Irish battalions, but his works are peppered with references to encounters with Irish troops in English and Scottish units. In *Red Horizon*, for example, the London Irish relieved a battalion of Scots Guards. 'In the traverse where I was planted, he recalled,

> I dropped into Ireland; heaps of it. There was the brogue that could be cut with a knife, and the humour that survived Mons and the Marne, and the kindliness that sprang from the cabins of Corymeela and the moors of Derrynane. 'Irish?' I asked.
>
> 'Sure,' was the answer. 'We're everywhere. Ye'll find us in a Gurkha regiment if you scratch the beggars' skins ...[52]

A story from *The Great Push* demonstrates his affection for even the most threatening of characters from his homeland. He devotes half a dozen pages to 'big, broad-shouldered, ungainly Gilhooley' (we are not favoured with a first name). Gilhooley was an accomplished bomber who enjoyed his work. He was square-jawed, potent and aggressive. 'It looked as if vast passions hidden in the man were thirsting to break free and rout everything. Gilhooley was a dangerous man to cross.' One story illustrates Gilholey's own unthinking physical courage and his healthy contempt for English officers.

> Once, when a German sniper potting at our trenches in Vermelles picked off a few of our men, an exasperated English subaltern gripped a Webley revolver and clambered over the parapet. 'I'm going to stop that damned sniper,' said the young officer. 'I'm going to earn the VC. Who's coming along with me?'
>
> 'I'm with you,' said Gilhooley, scrambling lazily out into the open with a couple of pet bombs in his hand. 'By Jasus! we'll get him out of it!'
>
> The two men went forward for about twenty yards, when the officer fell with a bullet through his head. Gilhooley turned round and called back, 'Any other officer wantin' to earn the VC.?'
>
> There was no reply: Gilhooley sauntered back, waited in the trench till dusk, when he went across to the sniper's abode with a bomb and 'got him out of it'.[53]

The main offensive operation referred to in *The Great Push* was the Loos offensive of September 1915. MacGill, a stretcher-bearer in the 1st London Irish Rifles, was a witness to the 'football' charge, subsequently romanticised and immortalised by Lady Butler in a famous painting. As MacGill prepared to go over the top, he wrote that 'I had a view of the men swarming up the ladders when I got there, their bayonets held in steady hands, and at a little distance off a football swinging by its whang from a bayonet standard.'[54] Later he notes that 'The boys on the right were dribbling the elusive football towards the German trench.'[55] According to myth 'each time the football was kicked into a German trench, there were loud shouts of "Goal"!'[56] But, according to MacGill's account, as the London Irish faced withering fire from the German lines, 'I saw, bullet-riddled, against one of the spider webs known as *chevaux de frise*, a limp lump of pliable leather, the football which the boys had kicked across the field.'[57]

MacGill's description of the carnage at Loos is all the more graphic because of his observational skills, his literary sensibility and the fact that, as a stretcher-bearer, he was left, quite literally, to pick up the pieces. As he dragged a wounded soldier into a shell hole,

> Men and pieces of men were lying all over the place. A leg, an arm, then again a leg, cut off at the hip. A finely formed leg, the latter, gracefully putteed. A dummy leg in a tailor's window could not be more graceful ... The harrowing sight was repellent, antagonistic to my mind. The tortured things lying at my feet were symbols of insecurity, ominous reminders of danger from which no discretion could save a man. My soul was barren of pity; fear went down into the innermost parts of me, fear for myself. The dead and dying lay all around me; I felt a vague obligation to the latter; they must be carried out. But why should I trouble! Where could I begin? Everything was so far apart. I was too puny to start my labours in such a derelict world.

Withering images abound like some of the grotesque scenes in a Breughel painting: 'A man, mother-naked, raced round in a circle, laughing boisterously. The rags that would class him as a friend or foe were gone, and I could not tell whether he was an Englishman or a German. As I watched him an impartial bullet went through his forehead and he fell headlong to the earth. The sight sobered me and I regained my normal self.' A few minutes later MacGill came across a colleague sitting in a shell hole, a bullet in his leg and an unlighted cigarette in his mouth: 'as I handed him my match box a big high explosive shell flew over our heads and dropped fifty yards away in a little hollow where seven or eight figures in khaki lay prostrate, faces to the ground. The shell burst and the wounded and dead rose slowly into the air to a height of six or seven yards and dropped slowly again, looking for all the world like puppets worked by wires.'

Robert Graves, at the time a 20-year-old subaltern, also captured the awfulness of the Battle of Loos in *Goodbye to All That*. He described how one officer, attacking an area nicknamed 'The Pope's Nose', had become exasperated with his troops:

> When his platoon had run about twenty yards he signalled them to lie down and open covering fire. The din was tremendous. He saw the platoon on the left flopping down too, so he whistled the advance again. Nobody seemed to hear. He jumped up from his shell-hole and waved and signalled 'Forward'. Nobody stirred. He shouted: 'You bloody cowards, are you leaving me to go alone?' His platoon-sergeant, groaning with a broken shoulder, gasped out: 'Not cowards, sir. Willing enough. But they're all f——g dead.' The Pope's Nose machine-gun traversing had caught them as they rose to the whistle.[58]

On the first day of the Loos offensive the London Irish lost nine officers and 235 men. The town itself was taken, but as the offensive dragged on into October it soon became clear that the gains being made did not justify the effort and expenditure of manpower. There was so much destruction that the Germans called the battlefield Der Leichenfield von Loos – the Field of Corpses of Loos; one Geman regimental diary actually claims that the Germans were so appalled at the carnage that they didn't even shoot at British wounded crawling back to their trenches. Among the dead that day was Rudyard Kipling's son John, who was serving with the Irish Guards. His father wrote of his loss:

> That flesh we had nursed from the first in all cleanness was given ...
> To be blanched or gay-painted by fumes – to be cindered by fires –
> To be senselessly tossed and retossed in stale mutilation
> From crater to crater. For this we shall take expiation.
> But who shall return us our children?[59]

One positive consequence of this new military débâcle was the dismissal of the first commander-in-chief of the British Expeditionary Force, Sir John French. This, however, was a mixed blessing, as he was replaced by Sir Douglas Haig!

In 1917 MacGill added *The Brown Brethern* to his wartime *oeuvre* and followed that in 1918 with *The Digger: The Australian in France*. A book of poems, *Soldier Songs*, published in 1919, was his final work inspired by his scarring military experience. Through the 1920s MacGill made a good income from writing, his novels selling thirty to fifty thousand copies each. He married a woman of independent means who also wrote fiction, as 'Mrs Patrick MacGill'. One of her works may have drawn upon her husband's experience; it was entitled *An Anzac's Bride*. MacGill moved, with his family, to the USA in 1930. It was a bad time to enter a United States in the grip of the Depression.

MacGill had hopes of benefitting from the needs of the burgeoning film industry for screen writers, but whatever plans he might have had did not materialise. With his novels going out of print and out of favour, his circumstances changed. His family was forced to sell off his large collection of books to make ends meet. The last years of his short life were probably as cheerless as his depressing childhood. He contracted multiple sclerosis sometime in the 1930s and died in Massachusetts in 1940.

MacGill's prolific output, his popular appeal and his journalistic origins resulted in an unwarranted contemporary condescension towards his work which was only properly rectified four decades after his death. The annual Patrick MacGill Summer School in his native Donegal brought him a new readership, and many of his works have been reprinted. In terms of Great War literature his poetry verges on the 'primitive', but his prose is sharp, committed, unsentimental and full of humanity. He tells it from the ordinary soldier's point of view, his themes being fear, boredom, death and the triumph of the human spirit in adversity. His humanity extends across the trenches to the supposed 'enemy', and he questions the validity of a conflict which sets the working classes of Europe at each other's throats. He celebrates the 'diurnal' heroism of the ordinary and does so with a humour and self-deprecation well illustrated by the poem which opens *The Red Horizon*; it is called 'The Passing of the Regiment':

> I wish the sea were not so wide
> That parts me from my love;
> I wish the things men do below
> Were known to God above
> I wish that I were back again
> In the glens of Donegal;
> They'll call me coward if I return,
> But a hero if I fall.
> 'Is it better to be a living coward,
> Or thrice a hero dead?'
> 'It's better to go to sleep, my lad,'
> The Colour Sergeant said.[60]

7 Prisons and Holding Camps

In a conflict in which the ordinary soldiers on both sides were victims, there was often a certain fellow feeling between men in opposing trenches. But there was also bigotry, hatred and rage, the sort of anger which was often turned against prisoners of war. Being taken captive was no guarantee of safe passage to a POW camp for the rest of the war. Most atrocities visited on disarmed troops occurred, as Robert Graves put it in *Goodbye to All That*, 'in the interval between the surrender of prisoners and their arrival (or non-arrival) at headquarters. Advantage was only too often taken of this opportunity ... The commonest motives were, it seems, revenge for the death of friends or relatives, jealousy of the prisoner's trip to a comfortable prison camp in England, military enthusiasm, fear of being suddenly overpowered by the prisoners, or, more simply, impatience with the escorting job. In any of these cases the conductors would report on arrival at headquarters that a German shell had killed the prisoners; and no questions would be asked. We had every reason to believe that the same thing happened on the German side, where prisoners, as useless mouths to feed in a country already short of rations, would be even less welcome.'[1]

On occasions both sides displayed a callous indifference to their own men who might have recently been taken prisoner by the enemy. The concept of the 'human shield' was alien to the philosophy of those who prosecuted the Great War. During the Battle of Loos, Patrick MacGill watched as German guns ploughed up prisoners from their own infantry:

> Across the level at this point came a large party of prisoners amidst a storm of shells. The German gunners had shortened their range and were now shelling the ground occupied by their troops an hour previous. Callous, indifferent destruction! The oncoming prisoners were Germans – as men they were of no use to us; it would cost our country money and men to keep and feed them. They were Germans, but of no further use to Germany; they were her pawns in a game of war and now useless in the play. As if to illustrate this, a shell from a German gun dropped in the midst of the batch and pieces of the abject party whirled in the air. The gun which had destroyed them had acted as their guardians for months. It was a frantic mother slaying her helpless brood.[2]

In the heat of battle, already desensitised troops could find ready justification for flagrant violations of the rules of war, but atrocities were far more likely to take place as an act of hot-blooded revenge or fury. In a letter written to his family after an attack by his battalion, the 7th Leinsters near Vermelles in June 1916, Lieutenant John Staniforth wrote about his troops: 'Oh, they were great. Of course, they were all quite mad. Three lads were sent back to our trench with six prisoners. On the way they stumbled across the body of one of our officers. Those prisoners will never reach any internment camp now, I'm afraid. As I said, we were all quite mad.'[3]

Private O'Neill of the 2nd Leinsters was mad enough after a German attack to get up from his stretcher and try and kill a German prisoner with his bare hands. This minor incident was recorded by Frank Hitchcock in his personal trench diary. It took place near Loos on 4 December 1916 when the Germans raided an outlying sap, killed a subaltern named Mouritz and wounded O'Neill. The private was rescued, but the party which brought him back to the British trenches picked up a German prisoner on their return. He was wounded in the foot, so his boot was cut off to facilitate treatment. Hitchcock wrote that 'The prisoner was a fine looking man of about twenty-two years of age. He couldn't speak any English, but seemed grateful to us for what we were doing. We had a lot of trouble with O'Neill who was also lying wounded in the dug-out, as when the stretcher bearers left the prisoner, O'Neill made a dive at him!'[4]

Soldiers like Jimmy O'Brien of the 10th Dublin Fusiliers could hardly be expected to be favourably disposed towards prisoners when they were getting contrary signals from chaplains. He recalled that 'there was a Fr Thornton, an Englishman and he said, "Well now boys, you're going into action tomorrow morning and if you take any prisoners your rations will be cut by half. So don't take prisoners. Kill them! If you take prisoners they've got to be fed by your rations. So you'll get half rations. The answer is – don't take prisoners."'[5] German prisoners were also vulnerable to non-combatants. In August 1918 Frank Hitchcock found himself in a base camp near Calais: 'On the southern fringe of the camp were two cages (a cage is a camp for prisoners, enclosed in barbed wire entanglements). In one of these were a hundred Boche prisoners, and in the other was encamped a Chinese Labour Corps unit, complete with their wives! In one of the Boche air raids a direct hit was obtained on the latter camp, and a number of "Chinks" were laid out. The following night the enraged "Chinks" retaliated on the Hun prisoners; having crawled under the barbed wire, they set on the sleeping prisoners and "did in" a number before the sentries were aroused.'[6]

Such atrocities were, of course, also visited on British and Irish troops by the Germans as well. Sometimes taking prisoners could be a risky business. In 1916, a Captain Louis Byrne of the Dublin Fusiliers wrote to the family of Lt. Louis Doran during the Battle of the Somme 'We attacked a certain position and we had just got to it when some Germans put up their hands to surrender. Your son went out to take their surrender and they shot him through the heart and he died at once.'[7]

However, most reactions to prisoners were surprisingly generous and empathetic. Anthony Brennan of the Royal Irish Regiment watched as German soldiers, captured during the first day of the Somme, were escorted through the British trenches:

> All through the day batches of prisoners were coming in. It was pathetic to watch them showing pictures of their wives and children to our 'tommies' who responded in the main by giving them tins of 'bully' and biscuits. I'm afraid many of the poor devils lost such valuables as wrist watches, cigarette cases, etc., at the hands of self-appointed searchers. I heard grim stories of prisoners who lost more than their possessions. I hope they were just 'stories'.[8]

Later Brennan testified to the essential decency of the average British soldier in his attitude towards captured enemy troops. He had been home in Kilkenny on leave and had missed the Battle of Messines. When he returned to his unit he was told 'a sorry tale of one of our Lance-Corporals who had, so I was told, deliberately fired at and killed a German who was coming in with his hands up. Our chaps took a very poor view of this and all kinds of maledictions were directed against the murderer.[9]

Even in the heat of battle it was possible for soldiers to show restraint. During the Irish attack on Ginchy in September 1916 the attacking elements of the 16th Division were taking heavy casualties from a German unit, roughly 200 strong, in a shallow trench. An unidentified second lieutenant wrote that 'To the everlasting good name of the Irish soldiery not one of these Huns, some of whom had been engaged in slaughtering our men up to the very last moment, was killed. I did not see a single instance of a prisoner being shot or bayoneted. When you remember that our men were worked up to a frenzy of excitement, this crowning act of mercy to their foes is surely to their eternal credit. They could feel pity even in their rage.'[10]

According to the less than reliable Michael McDonagh, another Dublin Fusilier was attacking a German trench in the centre of Ginchy which had inflicted more severe casualties. He spotted one particular German who had been especially effective and charged at him with his bayonet. The German simply laid down his rifle and raised his hands above his head. Despite the fact that this defenceless soldier had, only a moment before, been a potent killer, the 'Dub' slowed his charge and took him prisoner, commenting,

What could you do in that case but what I did? Sure, you wouldn't have the heart to strike him down, even if he were to kill you. I caught sight of his eyes, and there was such a frightened and pleading look in them that I at once lowered my rifle. I could no more prod him with my bayonet than I could a toddling child. I declare to the Lord the state of the poor devil almost made me cry. I took him by the hand saying, 'You're my prisoner.' I don't suppose he understood a word of what I said but he clung to me, crying, 'Kamerad, Kamerad!'[11]

The scene is a touching one but lacks credibility. It smacks of the sort of propaganda which was McDonagh's stock in trade, the elevation of the Irish soldier into a universally courageous, chivalrous and saintly being.

From the time of the 1916 Rising the loyalty of Irish troops, particularly those in the 16th Division, was constantly questioned by the military authorities. But that loyalty had been tested directly in the months prior to the Rising in the prison camps of Germany when the eminent Irish-born British civil servant Sir Roger Casement attempted to recruit his 'Irish Brigade' for use in the planned Easter insurrection. Casement's mission was woefully unsuccessful. It was an ill-fated and naive enterprise from the outset. In 1915, when his most determined efforts took place, he would have been trying to entice into his Brigade hardened veterans of Irish regular battalions. Few of the self-consciously nationalistic troops of the 16th Division would have made it to POW camps in Germany by 1915. As his biographer Brian Inglis has observed,

> If the great majority of the Irish Volunteers had preferred to stay with Redmond, even when he asked them to go to fight for the British in Flanders, it was inconceivable that Casement would find many recruits for his cause among the old sweats who had volunteered for service in the British Army even before the war broke out.[12]

Casement was following the precedent of the Boer War. There an Irish Brigade, led by Major John McBride, had fought for the Boers, and Irish prisoners had been persuaded by the Boers to switch sides. But, as Inglis points out,

> It had been relatively easy for the Boers to persuade a captured Irishman that he, like them, was a victim of Britain's imperialistic greed. But to the Irish involved on the retreat from Mons, it was the Germans who had appeared to be the imperialist aggressors – despoilers of little Belgium; and the conditions which they had met in captivity had done nothing to endear the Germans to them.[13]

The rebel leader's treatment at the hands of the Irish prisoners was hostile. He came to Limburg camp armed with a guarantee of Irish independence from the German administration. Corporal John Robinson recalled how 'On one occasion he was struck, and on another occasion I saw him get pushed. When he was struck, he swung his umbrella around to keep the prisoners off him, and when he was pushed, he walked out of the camp!'[14] Bryan Kelly, a student who had been transferred from a civilian internment camp in Ruhleben, recalled that Casement had been greeted 'by cheers for Redmond and shouts of "How much are the Germans paying you?"'[15] The recruiting forms he had handed round were torn up and thrown back at him. Some prisoners told their German captors, 'In addition to being Irish Catholics we have the honour to be British soldiers.'[16] He left the camp and on 9 January wrote to the Germans that, if enough money were made available, he might be able to bribe some men to join his Brigade but none would join for patriotic reasons. 'They are mercenaries pure and simple, and even had I the means to bribe them, I should not attempt to do so.'

The American-based Irish Republican leader John Devoy was highly critical of Casement's naive recruitment methods. 'Instead of approaching the men individually,' he wrote,

> he had them all assembled at a meeting at which he delivered an address which went over their heads. The good and the bad, the Orangeman and the Catholic, the half decent fellow and the blackguard, were all there to listen to his high patriotic sentiments, and, what was still worse, old Reserve men – whose wives were receiving subsistence money from the British Government and who naturally would think of the interests of their families before and above all else – were present. To step out of the ranks and volunteer for service against England under such circumstances required a degree of moral courage that is rare among Irishmen of that class.[17]

Casement managed to recruit about fifty men for his Brigade, most of them later claimed to have joined in the hope of better treatment. They were given special uniforms and removed to their own camp. None was ever landed in Ireland, it being deemed too risky for them as they would certainly have been tried for treason and shot had they been captured. By the time of the Rising, Casement was forced to admit that the whole affair had been 'a ghastly folly'. The very existence of the Brigade, however, allowed the British government and military to claim that the vast majority of Irish soldiers who had refused to join had been ill-treated by the Germans as a direct consequence. There is no evidence that this was the case, but the day after Casement's conroversial execution in August 1916 the British cabinet issued a statement giving its reasons for the refusal to grant a reprieve. It included a reference to the fact that

> Conclusive evidence has come into the hands of the Government since the trial that he entered into an agreement with the German Government which explicitly provided that the Brigade which he was trying to raise among the Irish soldier prisoners might be employed in Egypt against the British Crown. Those among the Irish soldier prisoners in Germany were subjected to treatment of exceptional severity by the Germans; some of them have since been exchanged, and have died in this country, regarding Casement as their murderer.[18]

Prison camp conditions could be emulated outside of prison camps. Life in front line trenches was as bleak and far more dangerous, but, in British training and transit posts such as the notorious Etaples camp in France, the regime was prison-like, right down to the virtual deprivation of liberty.

Lieutenant Charles Cecil Miller of the Inniskilling Fusiliers was doubly unfortunate in his World War I service. He became a prisoner of war after the German offensive of 21 March 1918, but he also spent a short period in Etaples, during which the camp was in ferment as a disorganised and spontaneous mutiny swept through the ranks. Miller had quickly become disenchanted with the administration of the camp, which was relentlessly and pedantically legalistic and harsh. No account was taken by the authorities at Etaples of the ultimate destination or the potential fate of the troops who were temporarily in their charge. Miller wrote: 'Discipline merely implies a measure of control and as such is very necessary, but when you make your control irrational, petty and irritating it is altogether wrong. This and much worse was what that little nincompoop of a commandant did at Etaples. Little or no attention appeared to be given to feeding or the entertainment of the men, but they were drilled without ceasing morning, evening, noon and night. Etaples is a dreary waste of sand dunes, and constant drilling in sand is a back-breaking performance. They were allowed practically no relaxation till they were drafted up to the front.'[19]

Despite the fact that there was a beach only a few miles away, few if any passes were issued to troops in transit, and the military police were constantly harrassing itinerant soldiers for their 'ticket of leave'. 'The military police were the worst feature of the whole affair,' observed Miller.

> They were a permanent feature there, and most of them were hefty blackguards who preferred staying at Etaples to taking the risk of the front line. The whole place represented a vast prison camp, with Thomas

Atkins, the man who was offering his life for his country, starring in the part of prisoner, with back breaking work, no relaxation, disgraceful food and miserable quarters. Under such conditions there is always the likelihood of a big burst up, and, but for the fact that the occupants of the prison house were constantly changing I think it would have happened long before.[20]

The 'big burst up' happened while he was there. It has been represented in fictional terms in the BBC drama 'The Monocled Mutineer'. Miller had vivid and unpleasant memories of the whole affair. It began when a Highland corporal attempted to engage a WAA corps woman in conversation. A military policeman warned him off in a manner which provoked the Highlander into retaliation. The MP shot him dead. Friends of the dead soldier who had seen the entire incident then chased the MP into the town of Etaples, pulled him out of a house in which he took refuge and killed him in the street with their bare hands. More fighting followed between troops and the much-despised MPs, and more deaths and injuries resulted. A measure of calm was restored, but discipline then began to fall apart. Soldiers, led according to Miller by 'some Colonials', refused to drill and escaped in their hundreds into the estaminets of Etaples. Miller was ordered to be second-in-command of a picket of fifty men and guard a bridge connecting the southern end of the camp with the town. The picket commander was, fortunately, a cheerful, relaxed individual unlikely to want to provoke an argument with the recalcitrant 'mutineers' on their return to the camp from Etaples. Which was just as well because none of the men on picket duty had ammunition in their guns. On the first night the 'mutineers' just good-naturedly charged the picket in numbers like a rugby scrum and brushed it aside. On the second night more violence was used, with 'a tendency to use fists and boots as well'. On the third night the gloves were to come off; the picket was to be issued with ammunition. But then this order was cancelled, instead outside help was called for in order to clear the town of troops. 'Concessions were made to men and the rigours of the training relaxed; calm was restored.'[21] (Ironically, some time later, when Miller was long gone, Chinese labourers struck for better conditions and their protest ended abruptly when it was suppressed by troops from the camp without compunction.)

His time in Etaples would have accustomed Miller to at least some of the rigours of prison camp life. He was to become a guest of the German nation after the first day of the massive 21 March offensive, an attack which netted so many prisoners that it put a huge strain on the resources of the Germans in dealing with them.[22] Miller was wounded when captured. His wound was slight enough, so that it was not life-threatening, but it clearly added to his total sense of dislocation and shock in the days after his surrender. As he wrote,

The time that follows is very blurred in my memory. It seemed to be constant railway travelling, sometimes in third-class compartments, sometimes in cattle trucks. In the former I had to stand up practically the whole time owing to the wound in my left thigh. Why we were being carted all round Germany I don't know, but I imagine that all the prison camps were full, there was a complete breakdown of arrangements, and they didn't know what to do with us.

He was placed, along with a number of others, in temporary accomodation in a place which he was unable to identify. 'After some days I and two or three other officers were hauled out of this place and put into a train again. This time we disembarked at Karlsruhe and I remember that some women on the platform had a spit at us, but very few women can spit straight'.[23]

Karlsruhe was a clearing camp for officers, a 'perfect oasis in the desert', as Miller put it. It was a well-known POW camp and well supplied with food parcels from Britain. Otherwise POWs existed on a diet similar to that of the German civilian population at large. Most of the nutrition was required for men at the front or for workers producing logistical aid. What was left was available to the ordinary population and prisoners. So, food parcels were a great boon. Miller was surprised that the Germans did not loot the contents of parcels more often. 'Here again the discipline of the Germans must be praised inasmuch as the vast majority of these parcels travelled through a semi-starving country and were delivered intact at destination. On the other hand it must be remembered that the parcel system enabled Germany to conserve a certain amount of her food resources, which would otherwise have been consumed by the prisoners, and at the same time she was able to avoid the responsibility of having caused the death of prisoners by starvation.'

Mainz became Miller's permanent camp in Germany. Designed to house 250, it held 600 men after the March offensive. The German officer in charge of the camp was an amiable individual nicknamed 'Johnny Walker' by the inmates because of his resemblance to the portly, jolly man on the whiskey bottle. 'He was an officer in a reserve cavalry regiment, was married to an Irish wife, whom of course we never saw, had spent a lot of his time racing in Ireland and spoke excellent English.' Unlike Karlsruhe, Miller's new accommodation was of recent vintage and food parcels didn't find their way there. 'To each officer there was an issue every five days of a medium-size loaf of German bread and a small quantity of beet sugar. That war bread was a pretty appalling compound, the foundation of which was maize, and its principal effect was to generate most remarkably unpleasant gases inside one. All the same, it was the most prized food, and it was frightfully difficult to make it last the five days, especially at night time when one was overpowered by hunger and could not sleep. Every morning, when the orderly summoned the room, he brought in a large metal jug filled with what looked like coffee, but was really a coffee substitute made from acorns and almost as bitter as quinine. That and your bit of bread had to carry you on till midday, when you assembled for what was called "mittag essen". This was generally a plate of gruel tasting simply of greasy water, followed by some sort of relish, which might be a small piece of dubious sausage, or raw fish, or sauerkraut made with slivers of swedes or mangles, but certainly not with cabbage. At 6 p.m. you had an almost similar meal. That was all the camp provided gratis, but one could buy a few things from the German canteen in the camp.'[24]

Their German captors used the few 'luxuries' available in the canteen as blandishments, to obtain hard currency. Prisoners would draw an order on their bankers for a specific sum of money. The order would be sent to a clearing bank in Holland. Once the signature was verified there, the Dutch bank would cash cheques and be refunded from Britain. The Germans, however, only allowed a rate of 20 marks to the pound. The going rate in 1918 was nearer 100 marks to the pound. The practice caused moral scruples for many patriotic but hungry prisoners: 'since it was money that helped the German to continue the war, it was not a very patriotic act on the part of the prisoner to draw more money than was necessary'.[25] Among the delights on offer to paying customers in the canteen were wine, cigars, and on some days beetroot or rhubarb. In order to cook, prisoners had to buy wood and a little coke for the stoves in their rooms. Miller writes:

> The wine which was sold was ghastly stuff, dregs and lees of wine, I imagine, and the cigars seemed to be composed chiefly of saltpetre. At the same time the awful monotony of existence made even this wine a temptation, and if you drank a bottle of the foul stuff, and at the same time smoked one of those vicious cigars, the pangs of hunger were for a time at any rate submerged by a nausea that made the thought of food intolerable. You see, the days were a nightmare of hunger and monotony. There was no English book in the camp, except most incongruously a copy of Mrs Beaton's cookery book in a very torn and battered condition, the opening page of which exhorted one to 'take two fat capons and baste them well.[26]

Boredom was a constant irritation for the POWs. There was nothing to do except roam the prison listlessly. There was no scope for organised games. 'Most of the officers in the camp were of the type that never bothered the mind except with concrete thought under the best circumstances, and had no mental reserves whatever to fall back on. When the canteen opened in the afternoon, most of the officers betook themselves there to get drunk with a minimum of delay. When the night came, you had to sleep in an overcrowded room with those drunks.'[27]

Miller's leg wound needed attention from the time of his arrival in Mainz, and eventually he had to be hospitalised. The prospect was less than inviting:

> I was in a blue funk because there was an acute shortage of anaesthetics in the Mainz hospital, and several prisoners who had been sent there had had gruesome experiences. The Mainz hospital was more like a front-line dressing station at the time of a big push than a hospital hundreds of miles from the front line, and I awaited my turn lying naked on a stretcher among other victims while the surgeon dealt with a body on the operating table. I nearly died of funk when they lifted me onto the said slab. My relief was enormous when someone from behind placed a wad of chemical stuff firmly over my nostrils because up to the last I had thought that I was going to get what was coming to me neat ... Wounds were so seldom dressed that the process when it happened was horribly painful. This was really I think not due so much to inhumanity as to the fact that the hospital staff was worked off its legs, and there was a dreadful shortage of dressings, even of the paper bandages in common use. I think at one time I was very near death in that hospital; more from sheer debility and tiredness than anything else I was losing hold of any desire to live and therefore of life.[28]

Miller was saved, according to his own account, by his sense of the love and anxiety of his own mother and by a diminutive German orderly named Hartmann: 'there was something of infinite tenderness and goodness about that little man ... which left the strongest impression on me, in that it hardly seemed to belong to this world.'[29]

There were few attempts to escape from Mainz, and none that Miller was aware of was successful. The prison had originally been built as a fortress and was surrounded by a dried-up moat. There were steps down into the moat, but there was a sheer concrete wall on the far side. This meant that there was only one way into this overwhelming obstacle and no way out:

> This was discovered by an officer who made a most daring solo effort at escape and succeeded in getting through all the wire and other obstacles, and got into the moat. He was there for several hours, trying desperately to find a way up the other side, only to be caught finally by the patrol. The only really feasible way of escape was to get out through the front gate, and the only method of effecting this was somehow to steal, make or procure a suit of workmen's clothes, to mingle unobserved with a group of the workmen, who sometimes came into the camp to do odd jobs, and to get out with them, avoiding both their detection and that of the sentry at the gates.[30]

Comhairle Contae County Council

Dun Laoghaire Rathdown Libraries
Deansgrange

Customer name: Hofmann, Marion
Customer ID: *********5430**

Items that you have borrowed

Title: They shall grow not old : Irish soldiers
and the Great War / Myles Dungan.
ID: 18518234769006
Due: **Monday 25 November 2019**

Total items: 1
1/11/2019 11:42
Borrow 2
Overdue: 0
Hold requests: 0
Ready for collection: 0

Items that you already have on loan

Title: Perfect Italian with the Michel Thomas
method : intermediate to advanced.
DLR20001010089
Due: Monday 4 November 2019

Thank you for using the SelfCheck System
2

Miller's wound, he claimed, left him in no position to contemplate an early escape, but by the time the Armistice was declared he and another prisoner had begun to devise a plan.

Prior to 11 November 1918 Miller had become well aware that the war was going against Germany. He could see that the population of Mainz was suffering increasing privations. The POWs feared that, if and when German discipline broke, things might go badly for the prisoners. There was talk of possible mass slaughter. But the end came in bizarre fashion. Prison camp officers, who normally wore dress uniform (not service uniform) one day arrived wearing lounge suits and soft hats. 'It appeared that the officer class had suddenly become unpopular throughout Germany, and down in the town the population were evincing a desire to rip the epaulets off them and, in the event of any resistance, to throw them in the Rhine.'[31]

When the war ended a short time later, the camp gates were simply thrown open. But this only made the first leg of the journey home easier for the prisoners. The local political and economic infrastructure had completely collapsed, in addition to which all movement of transport was back into Germany. As the Germans argued over the fate of the Kaiser and the future governance of their society, the prisoners of Mainz decided not to wait until someone arrived to liberate them and return them to their homes. They managed to persuade a Dutch steamboat captain to take them on board and he brought them from Mainz, down the Rhine to the Netherlands.

At around the time of the Easter Rising in Dublin the besieged British and Indian garrison at Kut al Amara in Mesopotamia (modern-day Iraq) was falling to the Turks, and 12,000 men were about to begin 'a veritable death march;'[32] among them was a 39-year-old Irishman, David Curran, an air mechanic with the Australian Flying Corps. Curran survived the march but did not last long in the Turkish prison camp which was the ultimate destination of the death column. Curran was a carpenter from Belfast and had left that city in 1902 bound for Capetown. Five years later he moved from South Africa to Australia and settled in Melbourne. Whether deliberately or through neglect and thoughtlessness, he completely lost touch with his family after he emigrated, and the first they knew about his move to Australia and enlistment in the Flying Corps was when they received notification that he had been taken prisoner.

The conflict in Mesopotamia was a Great War backwater (only one Irish unit, the 1st Connaught Rangers of the Indian Divison, was involved) and it was marked by initial British successes, in November 1915, against the Ottoman Empire, as General Townshend's force moved northwards towards Baghdad, taking Basra and Kut along the way. Defeat at Ctesiphon meant a rapid retreat and the development of a siege situation at Kut. Twenty-five thousand British and Indian troops were surrounded by 80,000 Turks. Attempts were made under General Aylmer to relieve the Turkish blockade (this force included the Connaughts), but the relief force made no progress, and the Kut contingent was, essentially, left to its own fate.

On 29 April the remaining defenders of Kut, now numbering about 12,000, surrendered. It was the biggest and most humiliating capitulation of a British force since the Battle of Yorktown in 1781. But the aftermath was far more traumatic. Some 2,500 sick and wounded troops were allowed to go free, in return for assurances of the release of an equal number of Turkish POWs, but the rest of Townshend's force was rounded up and led off to captivity in Anatolia, hundreds of miles distant. The death march began on 6 May 1916, and David Curran was among those forced to cover up to fifteen miles a day without water or shade and monitored by Arab guards who meted out summary and vicious punishment to all those who stumbled or looked like falling by the wayside.

One officer on the march, Captain E.O. Moulsey, watched the column from a boat; 'as they dragged one foot after another, some fell and those with the rearguard came in for blows from cudgels and sticks'. He reported seeing men 'dying with a green ooze issuing from their lips, their mouths fixed open, in and out of which flies walked'.[33] When the column reached Baghdad, the American consul there was so horrified at what he saw that he paid the Turkish authorities in the city to have 500 of the most seriously ill men sent back to Basra by boat. More than 160 of those men died on the journey back.

The remaining prisoners were kept in Baghdad for three days in a compound without shade or sanitation, and when they continued their march were stoned as they dragged themselves through the town of Tekrit, north of Baghdad. Flight Sgt. James McKenzie, an Australian comrade of David Curran, in a post-war statement described conditions:

> Whilst being *driven* to our place of internment, I suffered almost beyond human endurance (being beaten by rifle and whip). To fall out was (in most cases) to die. The food we were given consisted of *atta*, wheat (mostly whole), with no wood to cook it, and in the journey of about 600 miles we had meat on the track five times and very little at that. The Arabs in some parts were hostile ... but by far the posters of the column were the chief offenders.[34]

The treatment of General Townshend, who had ordered the surrender of Kut and whose too-rapid advance in November 1915, had led to the siege, was entirely different. He was taken by train to Constantinople and was given a house on the island of Prinkipo, off Constantinople, for the duration of the war. Of the 12,000 troops who began the march more than a third failed to complete it, and many who did were so weakened that they were unable to survive for long in the prison camps of Anatolia.

David Curran was deposited in a POW camp at Nesebin, but it was not long before he was admitted to the prison hospital. Conditions there were appalling. Flight Sgt. McKenzie also spent some time there and his statement relates that it

> was nothing less than a death trap. Six men of my unit entered with me, only two came out. When too weak to visit rear [*sic*] were placed in a separate room and left to die, laying in their filth for days. At this place I saw Turkish orderlies choke one of our men with water because he was not dead. They were wanting to bury him. The Armenian doctor came sometimes once a day. There was little or no medicines. Sanitation! I cannot describe it. The rooms were over-run with lice. Throughout Turkey sanitary arrangements are very crude and filthy. All clothing worn by me during my stay in Turkey was supplied by American or Dutch consuls or representatives.[35]

Curran was one of those who, weakened by the 600 mile march from Kut, succumbed to disease and died on 16 June 1916 in the Nesebin 'hospital'. His Red Cross Wounded and Missing Inquiry File includes a statement from a fellow air mechanic, K.L. Hudson, who told the Red Cross that Curran 'suffered badly from fever on the desert march and from exhaustion and exposure followed by malarial fever, for which he had practically no treatment. Formerly he was a strong, powerful man but became a walking skeleton.'[36]

Curran's parents were told in January 1917 that their son was a prisoner of the Turks. They, the Red Cross and the British authorities were unaware at the time that he had already died. A correspondence developed between his parents, Esther and Samuel Curran, and M.E. Chomley of the Australian Red Cross. Chomley attempted to reassure the Currans, who lived in Downpatrick, that everything possible was being done to improve the comforts of all POWs in Turkish hands:

> communications with our Prisoners of War in Turkish hands [he wrote] is very slow, but we are sending out parcels of food every fortnight. So far none have been acknowledged ... We have also sent some warm underclothing and boots, and quite lately a suit of clothes for each man. We also send cigarettes and tobacco once a fortnight. They are allowed to write occasionally, and you may write to them pretty often as long as you do not mention anything about the war.[37]

It is clear from the correspondence which follows that the Currans had completely lost touch with their son. Samuel Curran wrote to Chomley in July 1917 asking, 'Could you assist us in some way to get information about him. If we knew the name of the officer of his regiment or if we could trace the address he was at when he joined the Australian Flying Corps, we might be able to get some information about him from his landlady or some other friends; we don't know whether he was married or not.'[38] Chomley promised to do his best, responding, 'If we can find out anything about your son, we will let you know. I know how careless some people are, especially boys, about writing, and at a time like this it must be the cause of great anxiety to you.'[39]

Within three weeks of that exchange Chomley received a report that Curran had died the previous year; he wrote to a friend of the Currans, Maggie Malone of Killyleagh, Co. Down:

> I am extremely sorry to have to say that we have heard news, unofficially, of the death of David Curran. We were waiting for official information before writing to his parents. Perhaps it would be best if you were to tell them that we have received this information, and that we fear there is not much hope of it turning out to be untrue. We heard it from a letter of one of the other prisoners so he could hardly make a mistake.[40]

The reaction of Curran's mother was not unexpected, despite the fifteen-year separation from her son. She wrote to Chomley:

> We hope the sad news is not true and are anxiously awaiting for further news from you. If it is true we want you to get all information you can from the prisoner of war who communicated the news to you concerning his death. I wonder was he wounded or what was the cause of his death? I believe the Turks treated their prisoners very badly. Please try and find out all you can about him. I am heartbroken thinking about him.[41]

The Currans then got a cruel reprieve, thanks to an administrative error by one of Chomley's assistants. The young man mistook a returned Red Cross card for a communication from Curran and informed his parents of the good news. This was quickly followed by an apology for the misinformation from Chomley himself. In January 1918 Samuel Curran died, leaving his wife to continue alone the wait for confirmation of her son's death. That came after hostilities ended and those prisoners who had survived Nesebin were released.

A mother's last message to her son is included in the records of the Australian War Memorial. Esther Curran, who had not seen her son for fifteen years, wrote two stoic verses to commemorate his death:

Had He asked us well we know,
We should cry, Oh! spare this blow:
Yes, with streaming tears should pray,
Lord, we love him, let him stay.
But the Lord doth nought amiss,
And since He hath ordered this,
We have nought to do but still
Rest in silence on His will.

Frank Laird of the Dublin Fusiliers was a victim of the German offensive of 21 March 1918. He had been a safe twenty miles behind the lines, attached to a 16th Division entrenching battalion when the German bite swallowed him up. His unit had sat, like puzzled spectators, as most of the British army seemed to pass them moving westwards. By the time his 'navvies' got orders to withdraw, most of the bridges along their stretch of the Somme (near Peronne) had been blown up. Laird and his men managed to scramble their way across, but a few days later he was wounded in an ill-advised counter-attack outside the village of Morcourt. The bullet which should have killed him behaved in a fashion which would have been shunned by all but the most abysmal writers of fiction. Instead of penetrating his ribs, it shattered the whistle in his breast pocket. But he survived only to be taken prisoner.

As he lay, wounded, in a church, along with many injured Germans he was a witness to the efficiency of the Royal Flying Corps, which attacked the church and killed a number of the German wounded lying outside. 'Having been bombed by both German and British,' he wrote, 'I must say I much prefer the former. The German drones around and drops one here and one there, but these Britishers seemed to be dropping them one after another as quick as you could count. I heartily wished they would transfer their most commendable activities to another part of the front.'[42]

Despite the success (up to that point) of the German offensive, Laird's observations betray the evidence of a fighting machine which was grinding to a halt for lack of resources. He contrasted the plight of British and German wounded. Granted he was a prisoner of war whose own treatment would not have been on a par with that of a German officer, but

> the dressing stations were nothing like so well fitted up or organised. While the doctors I met seemed to be doing their best, they were without a great deal of the equipment which our men had. Perhaps the most conspicuous want to an ignorant layman like myself was linen bandages. They were using paper whenever they could possibly contrive to do so, and a very poor substitute it was.[43]

German transport was equally inadequate; chronic war shortages meant there were few rubber tyred vehicles,

> except a few staff cars used by the great ones. Some of the wounded went in handcarts, some succeeded in getting on to the iron-wheeled motor lorries, of which there was a scanty supply. The rest walked. There were cases where prisoners shot through the stomach had to walk considerable distances. When you had secured a coveted seat on one of the lorries, your troubles were not at an end. I cannot imagine a much more uncomfortable way of travelling than bumping over rough roads on those iron wheels, with a wound in your side or anything else.[44]

Laird marvelled at the pace and fury of the German advance, given the condition of *materiel* at their disposal.

Given the numbers of British prisoners who had succumbed to the German advance and the paucity of resources on the German side, it was hardly surprising that conditions in holding camps on French territory were abysmal. Laird's experience of a dressing-station at Le Cateau were of chronic overcrowding, wretched food and inadequate medical attention. What organisation there was had been imposed from within; a British officer-prisoner had taken charge and, using lightly wounded men as the orderlies which the Germans did not provide, made the best of a bad job.

After a couple of nights in Le Cateau, Laird was despatched, along with ten other officers and a hundred men, by train, to Germany. The journey lasted five days, its apparent aimlessness convincing the Dubliner that the Germans had no real notion of what to do with them. Periodically the train would stop, and the prisoners would be taken off and escorted to some large shed or reception area adjoining the station. There they would be fed soup or macaroni, the latter culinary delight indicating the success of the German offensive against the Italians. Their journey took them through Cologne and Berlin, through the flat plains beyond the German capital to reach the town of Hammerstein in West Prussia. There they detrained close to a hospital-prison and were counted three or four times by a fussy German commandant whose most notable feature was his facial hair.

The British prisoners felt hard done by after their tedious journey in overcrowded conditions and with insufficient food, but Laird acknowledges that their treatment was princely compared to that meted out to the unfortunate Russian prisoners who had been sent to Hammerstein before the Russian surrender. They had spent a week on a prison train with no food whatsover. Dozens had died of starvation shortly after their arrival, and hundreds more had succumbed to the neglect of their captors. There were 800 Russian graves in Hammerstein by the time Laird arrived.

British prisoners were, in relative terms, well treated by their captors in Hammerstein. Medical assistance was efficient in a Prussian sort of way, but it was still basic. The presence of a Russian doctor, himself a prisoner for three years, made conditions more tolerable. A local civilian doctor paid regular visits and, on being informed that Laird was from Dublin, assumed that he was a loyal Sinn Feiner and treated him with extreme cordiality. Time hung heavily and was passed in the playing of cards and in reading the few volumes in English which were supplied by a local German clergyman. This eclectic library included theological works, Dicken's *A Christmas Carol*, the essays of Washington Irving, *Little Lord Fauntelroy* and a tome entitled *Things Will Take a Turn*, about which Laird makes some condescending remarks.

Other inconveniences were the paltry diet and the dearth of cigarettes. Once their own supply had run out (which it did quickly because of the frequent necessity to bribe guards with tobacco to obtain extra food), they were forced to make do with the ersatz variety manufactured and sold by a man described by Laird in the casual anti-Semitism of the day as 'a rapacious old gentleman with a Jewish nose'.[45] He sold an extraordinary concoction which tasted to the hospital inmates like chopped-up timber. This vile mixture conformed to some mutation of the laws of supply and demand by rising in price every few days despite its patent unpopularity.

The circumstances of Laird's capture and the inadeqaucy of the mails meant that he experienced a phenomenon which is not unusual in time of war. On his repatriation he was able to read the glowing obituaries which had been written by friends and acquaintances about a man they assumed was dead. That assumption was based, in part, on the length of time it took for the first letter he wrote from Hammerstein to get to Dublin. It was written on 8 April and delivered exactly two months later. He received his first mail five months after he was taken prisoner. It would take three to four months for an exchange of letters. One of the many causes of delay was the fact that letters were retained by the suspicious and bureaucratic Germans for ten days before they were despatched. This was to ensure that prisoners had not used invisible ink when they were writing them.

Hammerstein was only a temporary staging-post for Laird. Along with eight other officers he was transferred to Schweidnitz in Silesia. The town boasted two illustrious natives – von Moltke, the great architect of Germany's military successes in the late 19th century, and von Richtofen, the air ace, who had a large house in a prosperous suburb of the town. The prison there was a large ugly building which had once been a workhouse or a reformatory. Divided into two separate camps (lagers), it was to be home to Laird and hundreds of other officers until 19 December 1918. One advantage of this more permanent if forbidding abode was the arrival of food parcels. When these arrived from home (often sent by families who were experiencing severe hard-

ships themselves), they would be opened by the Germans in the presence of
the fortunate recipients. Everything was examined thoroughly to ensure that
maps, compasses or any other aids to escape were not secreted in the parcels.

Apart from three daily roll calls prisoners at Schweidnitz were left pretty
much to their own devices. The least animate lolled about in bed all day, the
rest engaged in some activity. Inmates were allowed play football every second
day and go on regular country walks. A six-team soccer league interrupted
the relatively comfortable tedium. Cooking became a preoccupation for some
(the cleaning up was done by enlisted men); there were regular plays, concerts
and films. Laird's account of the entertainment provided has a surreal quality
to it, given the daily death and destruction being experienced by the peers
and colleagues of the men imprisoned:

> The cinemas generally turned up every second week, but the Boche films
> were inferior in intellectual depth and delicate humour to those which are
> to be seen at home. Lager one had set up a neat stage in their dining hall,
> and formed quite a good theatrical company, and we were allowed to go
> over and see most of their productions, which included a few really
> first-class plays and variety shows. Their 'ladies' were a particularly
> strong feature. Later on we had a stage rigged up in our own Lager and
> our local talent provided several excellent entertainments, and showed
> that we, too, could hold our own in the way of feminine beauty.[46]

In certain respects conditions at Schweidnitz were inferior. It was overcrowded and insanitary with insufficient space for daily exercise, but prisoners were
well treated by camp commandants, who 'were gentlemen, and really tried to
make things run smoothly'.[47] However, Laird's assessment must be put in
context. He was an officer and, on that score, was accorded better treatment.
(German officers in Britain were often accommodated in hotels.) In addition he
was an officer in the British Army. Britons and French tended to be meted out
far better treatment than, for example, Russians. His captivity came at the end
of the war when the Germans, facing defeat after the failure of their March
offensive, were far more accommodating with their prisoners.

Life was not nearly so comfortable for enlisted men. Many were forced to
work in mines on poor rations. Laird recalls

> the appearance of a batch of British Tommies who came to us to act as
> orderlies. They had been taken in March, and three months' work
> behind the line had reduced them to living skeletons. They were so
> weak that most of them could scarcely walk, and they looked at death's
> door. They were a striking contrast to the fat and contented Fritzes
> whom I had seen at work so often in France. It took some months of
> decent food to get them back to the [sic] normal again.[48]

The location of their prison, about as far away from the Western Front as it was possible to be within the borders of Germany itself, made escape a doubtful proposition. In addition, conditions in the camp, compared to the misery and insecurity of the trenches, would hardly seem to justify the effort by anyone other than the fanatically committed. During Laird's sojourn no one managed to escape, though there were a few attempts. Most escapees remained at liberty for a few hours, or days at most. One Royal Flying Corps officer managed to get as far as the Franco-German border but was recaptured at Aachen. He had been sent a map, a German passport (complete with name, photo and profession) and a travel permit by a previous escapee. The documents had been concealed in the binding of a book which had managed to escape examination by the German guards.

His escape was engineered with the co-operation of a group of orderlies who went to church on Sunday night in the dark. The RFC man took the place of one of the group and simply walked into the night at an appropriate moment. When the orderlies returned, before they were counted, someone took the vacant place. For the next two days during roll call an officer who had already been counted would simply steal along the back of the group and fill the spot left vacant by the RFC flyer. This charade was continued for six roll calls, giving the escapee a forty-eight hour start before the Germans were even aware of his absence. After hiding outside Schweidnitz for a week, he boarded a succession of trains before being recaptured almost within sight of his objective.

The Germany of which Laird and his comrades (including Charles Cecil Miller, see above) were temporary guests was in no position to be hospitable. It had been rationed to the brink of starvation. Substitutes were on sale for most goods. People wore wooden shoes and paper clothes, smoked tree bark and washed with brick dust instead of soap. But there were no substitutes for good nourishing food. As a consequence, 'a fat one was hardly ever seen, and the children all looked pinched, thin, and weakly ... Everything in the country, too, had a used-up appearance. The army and its equipment, the railway trains, the agriculture, conducted with cows for the most part as substitutes for horses, all went to show that the Empire was on its last legs.'[49] It was a Germany where Socialism crept and finally sprang towards the sun, but without ever taking root.

On 9 November 1918, the Revolution which swept Germany reached Schweidnitz, and a Soldier's and Workmen's Council took command of the situation. Hohenzollern eagles were ripped from helmets and shoulder straps and acquired by POWs as mementos, in exchange for the contents of food parcels. Uncertainty attended the post-Revolution period, as a counter-revolt was expected. Paranoia replaced *ennui* as the dominant condition. Some prisoners feared that either element in any civil strife would kill their captives

in order to prevent them from taking sides. Most POWs were more concerned that the socialists would not be as efficient in delivering their food parcels

Both fears were unfounded. Natural German efficiency is an ingrained
instinct which cannot be supplanted by a mere revolution. The officers at
Schweidnitz continued to be far better fed than their erstwhile captors. After
the armistice they had almost unlimited access to the town and were,
ironically, able to purchase supplies of food which were beyond the means of
the ordinary Silesian. Upon their departure, the prisoners got a much more
lively send off than the reception accorded returned German army units
(however, this rapture may have been the enthusiasm of Germans familiar
with the laws of supply and demand who hoped for a reduction in the price
of basic foodstuffs in the wake of the departure of the free-spending Allied
soldiers). The inmates of the Schweidnitz prison camp left the town on 19
December, bound for Danzig and home. The final anecdote in Laird's book
might serve as an illustration of how Britain was in scarcely better a state
than was Germany. On the other hand his own interpretation might be
adequate. The boat on which they sailed landed in the Scottish port of Leith
on Christmas Day. 'As we stepped ashore, a native called out, "Is anyone
short of matches?" One of us said "Yes", whereupon the gentleman produced
a box from which he picked out two and handed them over. Then we knew
there could be no mistake and we had really landed in Scotland.' Laird
himself, though he had come through injury and imprisonment and survived,
was not to be granted a long life after his demobilisation. In an enigmatic
preface to his unfinished but published work *Personal Experiences of the Great
War* his wife observes that 'as a result of his war service he developed a fatal
illness. He died on January 6, 1925.'

The Great War was an anthology of tragedy. Entire families, like the Stackpoles
from Kilkenny (a father and two sons), were wiped out.[51] The composition of
the Ulster Division meant that on the first day of the Somme whole streets
of Belfast and entire rural villages lost most of their men. Against this sort of
background, the poignant story of Lance Sergeant William O'Reilly of the 1st
Battalion, Royal Irish Fusiliers would probably be a mere footnote – except
that we can follow that story through a hoard of forty letters preserved by his
family. It's a moving narrative, all the more so when one considers that the
experiences of William O'Reilly were shared by thousands of others. The loss
felt by his family was shared by millions.

He was born in 1882 to a farming family in Cortubber, near Kingscourt in
Co. Cavan.[52] The town of Kingscourt (which also happens to be the author's
birthplace) was then a small market town close to a railway junction and
adjacent to the Co. Meath border. He was an Army reservist when the war

broke out, having served with the Royal Highland Regiment during its tenure in India, which began in 1902. As a consequence he was called up immediately, returned to Edinburgh to re-enlist and was despatched to join the 1st Battalion, Royal Irish Fusiliers with the rank of lance sergeant.

In 1914 O'Reilly was a thin, rather ascetic-looking man in his thirties with dark greying hair, a high forehead and a brush moustache. During the brief period between his pre-war and wartime service he had returned to Ireland where he married Kate Smith, of Shancor, Kilmainhamwood, Co. Meath. One or both sets of parents didn't entirely approve of the match, because the couple eloped in order to get married. O'Reilly also became involved with the National Volunteers, and his military background ensured that he was involved in the training of the local force before his call-up.

His battalion, a Regular Army unit, was mobilised in England in early August 1914 and rushed to France shortly after fighting broke out. Assigned to the 10th Brigade, 4th Division of the British Expeditionary Force, they disembarked at Boulogne on 23 August 1914 and their first action was at Le Cateau three days later. Here, according to Henry Harris in *The Royal Irish Fusiliers*, 'they were thrown piecemeal into the line ... to cover the retirement of the BEF from Mons. This introduction was more movement than fire, for the men it meant long retreats, some at night, stumbling along broken roads, and subject to shelling.'[53]

The 'Faughs' (as the Royal Irish Fusiliers were nicknamed) were next involved in the pivotal Battle of the Marne, as part of the advance guard of the 4th Division. It was here that trench warfare began, and it was at around this time that William O'Reilly became a prisoner of war. References in his letters to trench warfare suggest that he lasted in action until after the Marne at least. He may well have been one of the Faugh's casualties at the first Battle of Ypres where, for example, one company (A Coy) lost half of its operational strength when the Germans carved a slice out of the Ypres salient.[54] O'Reilly spent his first period in captivity in the German prison camp of Limburg, a typical POW camp consisting of lines of raised wooden accommodation 'huts' as well as some more permanent brick and concrete structures. As discussed above, Limburg is best known in Irish history for the visits of Sir Roger Casement as he attempted to recruit disaffected Irish soldiers to join his putative 'Irish Brigade' which was to have been armed and equipped by Gemany for use in the 1916 Insurrection.

In his book *Roger Casement* Brian Inglis notes that 'When Casement arrived at Limburg on December 4th, and addressed an assembly of NCOs, most of whom had been in the British army for years, he found them uncompromisingly hostile. After two days when he retired to bed with a throat infection, he had secured only a couple of volunteers, Sergeant MacMurrough and Corporal Timothy Quinlisk; and both of them, he thought, looked rogues.'[55] (Quinlisk later threw in his lot with Sinn Fein but was discovered to be in the pay of the British authorities and was assassinated on the orders of Michael Collins.)[56]

One of the unimpressed NCOs was William O'Reilly, though shortly after Casement's first visit to the prison camp he received news which might have made him slightly more amenable to Casement's blandishments. His new wife Kate, now settled in his family's home in Cortubber, had given birth to their first child, a daughter named Anna. Casement, however, returned to Limburg in early January to a hostile reception from most of the prisoners. O'Reilly opted to stay put.

On 17 April 1915, tragedy struck. Kate Smith died of peritonitis at the age of 24. O'Reilly didn't hear the news of his wife's death until 8 May, after which he began a series of letters to his sister-in-law Annie, now entrusted with the care of her tiny infant niece. Annie Smith had, by then, given up a good job as a cook in England to return to Kilmainhamwood and look after the child.

In his first letter to his sister-in-law a clearly numbed William O'Reilly wrote:

> I have received a letter from Father Lennon today telling me of Katey's death. I have not quite grasped it yet and can hardly believe it's true. It's too awful and all the plans I had made to make the old place nice for her. It drives me mad when I think that I will never see her again or hold her hand in mine. You at least Annie know what it means to me. Will you ask mother to keep the Baby. She will have five shillings a week from the Government. I also received your parcel; many thanks for it Annie, it was kind of you to send it. I shall be very glad to hear from you. I'll conclude now, Annie. Yours, Wm O'Reilly.[57]

The 'mother' to whom O'Reilly referred was, in fact, his mother-in-law Jane Smith. His next letter to his sister-in-law, in reply to one of hers, is not for another month. In it he tries to persuade her to move from her own family home in Shancor, to Cortubber, where his ageing father was living at the time. It is also clear that he still clings to the belief held by the earliest POWs and members of the British Expeditionary Force that the war would be of a short duration:

> My poor darling's death [he wrote] must have been a terrible shock to you Annie. I shall never forget it. She wrote me a very cheery letter just about a week before and told me Baby had red hair. I'm awful anxious to see it, it's a great responsibility and I shall never marry again. You say you are going home to remain, Annie dear. I'm going to

apply for a postman's place in Kingscourt and think I shall get it when I return, so, Annie, what do you think of coming to live in Cortubber; it would make me very happy and we could devote ourselves to the Baby. I don't know, Annie, how you will look at this, and I cannot put all I would wish in this, but I think, Annie, you will understand and I hope, Annie, you will consent and you would be secure in case anything happened to me ... My only consolation in this terrible time is that she is surely in heaven and that I may meet her again. Annie dear, by whose wish or order was she buried in K'wood. They should have buried her in Inniskeen. I hope, dear Annie, you will see your way to what I suggest. I should like to see you there when I return. [In a postscript he adds:] I wouldn't make altogether a bad brother.

Ten days later, in a letter dated 18 June, he reiterates his offer:

You may be sure, Annie, my Baby will be alright should anything happen to me. She is a dear legacy from my wife and will always be doubly dear to me. I shall have to be father and mother to her, so that when my time comes I can go with joy in my heart. Annie, if you agree to go to Cortubber, would you go as soon as you can. The Estate Agent – Mr Ceely Maude – is looking after my interests, so you would not have much trouble, and, Annie, my poor father wants some one. You must remember my Katey was very dear to him, and he has not had much comfort in his life.

Annie Smith, perhaps unwilling to take on two dependents, declined his offer and continued to bring up her niece in her own family home at Kilmainhamwood.

As time went on, O'Reilly's letters become less stiff and formal. He begins to build up a relationship with his daughter and sister-in-law through the pages of his prison-issue notepaper. He starts to refer to his growing child as 'Her Majesty the Baby', and he also stoically accepts that the war will continue indefinitely ('I suppose the sun is shining there now and everyone busy. It's much the same here from day to day. Still, I suppose it will end sometime. It will be a sensation to be free again.')

The arrival of the first photographs he had seen of his young daughter, in September 1915, brought O'Reilly even closer to her. Her dutiful aunt was also coaching her diligently to ensure that the first word she would utter would be 'Dadda', a fact appreciated by him in his letters. In other correspondence that month he displays that sense of guilt which is often associated with Roman Catholic Ireland the philosophy that if life happens to be good at any time one will pay for that happiness with misery further down the road. He writes of his marriage, 'I suppose we just had to fulfill our destiny. We were just too happy and that is bad for poor mortals.'

Prison life in Limburg, even in the early years of the war, when food shortages in Germany were not so severe as they would become later, was an austere existence, brightened for the prisoners by the arrival of Red Cross parcels and other support from home. O'Reilly had some responsibility in Limburg for the distribution of these. In one letter he mentions that 'I have a lot of parcels to distribute amongst my men' and itemises the names of people who have sent them, asking Annie to drop them a card of thanks, as he is not in a position to so do.

Annie Smith's letters, which do not survive, obviously outlined the part being played in the upbringing of little Anna by Andy Smith, her brother. Their 'father-daughter' relationship clearly evokes pangs of jealousy in her real father, which he regularly acknowledges. On 15 May 1916, for example, he admits, 'I'm getting quite jealous of Andy. I'm afraid we will fight over her.' And again, on 4 April 1917, 'I'm thinking that with so many relations fond of Baby she won't have a place for Dadda. Tell my dear Baby I have a big knife and I'll cut Uncle Andrew's head off when I come home if he annoys my Baby, and put him into the well with the trout.'

Finally, in December, 1916, William O'Reilly left the Limburg prison camp but only to make his way, still a prisoner of war, to a sanatorium in Leysin in Switzerland. Leysin was, essentially, a resort for those suffering from tuberculosis, but its altitude, clear, dry air and high average daily sunshine, were helpful in clearing up other complaints, such as bronchitis or asthma. O'Reilly affords us very little information as to the reason for this transfer. He doesn't seem to have been suffering from TB (14 per cent of the prisoners coming to Switzerland from Germany were). He may have been suffering, as we shall see, because of a deterioration in his kidneys. Whether his studied avoidance of the subject of his malady is because he was kept in ignorance of it, or because he didn't wish to worry his relatives about the state of his health, is unclear.

In January 1917 he wrote that he'd been examined by a doctor who had professed himself satisifed with the condition of his heart and lungs. But in that same letter, written from the Pension Beau Site, one of about half a dozen which housed ailing soldiers, he mentions that 'I got cold in the kidneys and am in bed at present.' He also speculates as to why he had been transferred in the first place, seeming to suggest that he had been malingering. This was clearly not the case. 'I think I got here,' he wrote,

> because I was suffering from a severe cold and the Doctors thought my lungs were affected. I stuck tight to that cold until after the final

inspection. [There was nothing much the matter with his lungs, as can be inferred from his remark:] plenty of snow here and its very cold. Those whose lungs are bad have to lie on an open verandah from 9–12, 1–3 and 6–7 and they don't like it.

His move to Switzerland also gave him some hope of seeing his daughter. Unlike German prison camps, neutral Switzerland allowed visits to POWs. He had written to Annie Smith at the end of December 1916 saying that he would 'make a special application and I have not the slightest doubt it would be agreed to as I have some regimental friends who would back it up'. Naturally, she was to make the trip with young Anna, now two years old. He insisted that well publicised fears 'that all who come here are dying of consumption' were unfounded; 'there's no danger for any one who comes here and takes care of themselves.' By January, however, he had been disabused of his earlier optimism, being forced to acknowledge that 'with regard to bringing Anna out I was too previous. The order has been cancelled and only wives are allowed out.'

In the main the letters are characterised by a remarkable degree of stoicism. Only occasionally does the near despair he must have felt show through. On 23 January 1917, writing from Leysin, he tells his sister-in-law, 'No, there is no chance of getting away from here. At least not yet. Even if I escaped my own government would send me back.' The following month there are intimations of mortality in the line 'A Sergeant here, a fine young chap, died today.' Despite constant references to his well being and to the fact that he is gaining weight, he does write at the beginning of March 1917, 'It's bitter cold here now. Hard frost and coal is scarce. Food is getting tight also.'

Then comes the first hint, in a letter sent later in March, that a prisoner exchange might result in his early release, 'to make room for more invalids. A week later, encouraging such speculation, the first batch of prisoners' wives reach Leysin: 'I went up to see them arrive and the hugging and kissing was awful. One of them nearly came through the carriage window, wouldn't hardly wait till the door was open.' Given his own situation, it can only have been a bittersweet moment for him.

As time dragged on and the rumoured release failed to materialise, disillusionment with officialdom begins to assert itself in his correspondence. Censorship of letters, to which he has not previously referred, becomes an issue.

You mentioned [he writes on 1 May 1917] about a scarcity of something in your letter and the censor scratched it out in the usual intelligent official fashion. Such things may be published and broadcast in the papers but must not be mentioned in a letter ... We are still hoping for the transfer home and so are the boys in Germany as it would leave more room here and a better chance for them. The French expect to go this month. Of course, our officials at home have plenty to eat and good salary. Maybe the censor might rub out this, so I'll say no more on that subject. [After the visit of the French General Pau and the departure of the French prisoners he wrote (30 June 1917):] We are sick waiting for the transfer home and it does not give us a high opinion of our authorities God save the mark. It's much better to be a conscientious objector.

The absence of any confirmation of the release of prisoners makes him, quite understandably, maudlin and sentimental. Every single letter from Leysin contains references to his daughter and many to the countryside around his home: (24 May, 1917) 'The scenery [in Leysin] is beautiful but a whitethorn hedge or a whin bush would be more to my taste. I get homesick when I see daisies and buttercups in the fields;' (19 June 1917) 'I'm tired of looking at Swiss mountains. I just go out and lie in the grass and think of dear old Ireland.'

Highlighting the contrast between the treatment experienced by the occupants of the various sanatoria around Leysin and the inmates of German POW camps was the fact that a couple of the prisoners actually married while still, officially, incarcerated. Not even the sombre nature of their residency in the Hotel Beau Site exempted the newly wed soldiers from post-nuptial pranks. 'The last one was a Sergeant' (13 May, 1917). 'He got married in Lausanne and someone hung a bell under the bed and secured it well into the springs. They suspected tricks and made a good search but didn't find it – all in the hotel knew it was there – and it made an awful noise, so now we are all ting a ling when we meet.'

On 20 August William O'Reilly sent his last letter from Leysin, type-written for the first time and interrupted so that he could convey the information that 'You can tell Anna that her dear Daddy will soon be home. Isn't it great news. I suppose, Anna will be watching for me every day.' He had been examined and passed as fit enough to go home.

But the correspondence doesn't end there. His next (undated) letter is from No.1 General Hospital, London, and mentions, ominously that 'that old pain in my side has hampered me lately so they are keeping me here to fix it up and I hope it won't be long. I'm in hopes of being transferred to an hospital in Dublin, but they won't let me go so far. Although I worry the doctors on every chance they only laugh.'

His handwriting, which had already deteriorated noticeably since his first letters in 1915, now begins to worsen even more. His psychological state is just as brittle. On 26 September he writes to Annie,

I was just despairing of hearing from you at all and its pretty miserable being among strangers with no letter. [He attempts to reassure her, or perhaps he's reassuring himself:] Now, my dear, there is nothing to worry about, except that the cure takes time. It's just a question of rest and diet and medicine; only its jolly hard to be thrown into bed after 3 yrs imprisonment. Still I'm getting home by stages. First Switz. then England next Dublin and then Shancor ... I'm sending you a box full of kisses for Baby, nice big ones, and I'll expect that big hug when I get to Dublin. Love to you all. Yours Affectionately, Willie.

It was to be his last letter. There is, however, one more in the collection, from a nurse at the Hospital, Sister F.S. Oldfield. She gives us the first indication that either the severity of O'Reilly's condition had been kept from him, or that he had been keeping it from his sister-in-law. The former appears more likely to have been the case. In the letter, dated 3 October, she says,

I am writing to tell you that your brother-in-law, L/Sgt O'Reilly has not been so well the last two days, & the doctors think his condition serious. If you wish to come over here to see him please write to me at once & I will send you a railway pass which will enable you to obtain a return ticket for a single fare. Please, if you write to O'Reilly do not let him know I have written to you, as there is no need to alarm him about his condition.

Given the relatively upbeat nature of her communication with her brother-in-law, the letter must have come as a severe shock to Annie Smith. She needed no second bidding. The pass was issued and she prepared to take Anna, now almost three years old, to see her father for the first time. But it was already too late. William O'Reilly was not fated to live to see his daughter. He died on 6 October 1917, aged thirty-five. Just one of the nine million soldiers who died in the War to End All Wars. Annie Smith was to leave for London with his child the following day. His death certificate gives as the cause of death 'Chronic Nephritis Uraemia', an inflammation of the kidneys.

His story, and that of his orphaned daughter who was reared to adulthood by Annie and Andy Smith, is no more or less tragic than that of thousands or even millions of fathers, sons or brothers who died between 1914 and 1918. His death was a relatively benign, physically painless and dignified one when compared with the horrific deaths of many of his splintered, pummelled and torn peers. But one poignant question remains in the minds of those familiar with his story. It is a question which too obviously presupposes the existence of a larger determining force in human lives but can be posed even by those who do not presume that such a force exists. It is this: Would it have been too much to have allowed William O'Reilly to have seen his daughter before he died, or for little Anna O'Reilly to have seen her father and carried some living memory of him through her life?

William O'Reilly is buried beside his wife Kate in the Old Cemetery, Kilmainhamwood, Co. Meath.

8   'It's Draughty in the Trenches-oh'

'It may be hot in Flanders
But it's draughty in the trenches-oh'

(Contemporary folk song)

Imagine an advertisement in a daily newspaper along the following lines:
'Wanted: Able-bodied men to share crowded accommodation with thousands
of lice-ridden compatriots. Narrow, roofless, rat-infested, subterannean premises
with excellent views of incoming ordnance. No central heating. Frequently in
need of repair. Food basic. Bring CV and sense of humour. Rent free.' The
trenches of Flanders, Picardy and Gallipoli offered variants of that prospectus
for four years. Holes in the ground became home for hundreds of thousands
of men. Privation and boredom became so oppressive that men yearned to go
into action, until the time came to actually do so.

The imagery of the Great War is dominated by the trench. It is as if no
other army had ever 'dug in' before the winter of 1914. And, when measured
against the trench warfare of the 1914–18 war none really had![1] The lengthy
series of parallel scars which were scored into the French and Belgian landscape were wounds which bled continuously for four years, haemorrhaging
thousands of lives. And yet they also represented a sort of security. Below
ground there was some measure of sanctuary. Above the parapet there was
only death and destruction. Towns, villages and forests disappeared: there
was no safety there.

Into this Hell, which not even Dante or Breughel would have had the
imagination to envisage, came hundreds of thousands of ordinary souls, men
without any experience of these extremes. Their senses were assaulted, their
spirits were violated. They were called upon to discover inner resources and
heroism just to get through an average day.

Lieutenant John Staniforth of the 7th Leinsters offered his parents an
oddly beguiling and colourful view of his working environment in May 1916:
'I wish you could come out here just for a flying visit and see what things are
like' It could have been the prelude to a diatribe or a campaigning Phillipic.
As it happens it was not. He asked his family to envisage approaching the
front at night by train and resuming the journey by bus:

163

Then the bus would come to a few blackened shells that was once a village, and you would be told it was unsafe to drive any further, and you'd have to get down and walk. Before long you'd top a little rise, and then stand and catch your breath with the whole Front spread out before your feet. Imagine a vast semi-circle of lights: a cross between the lights of the Embankment and the lights of the Fleet far out to sea; only, instead of fixed yellow lamps they are powerful white flares, sailing up every minute and burning for twenty or thirty seconds, and then fizzling out like a rocket – each one visible at ten miles distant, and each lighting up every man, tree and bush within half a mile. Besides these you will see a slim shaft swinging round and round among the stars, hunting an invisible aeroplane; and every instant flashes in the sky like the opening of a furnace-door and there is a clap of thunder from the unseen 'heavies'. The whole makes a magnificent panorama on a clear night.'[2]

Staniforth had changed his tune by August when he informed his family, 'It's all just heat, flies and monotony. I'd give worlds for green fields and blue water, instead of stony white chalk, blinding in the sun-dazzle and scorching to touch.'[3]

Second Lt. Tom Allen of 1st Irish Guards had little enough time to experience trench life. He was in France when the fighting stagnated to such an extent that both sides dug in along a front from Picardy to the Belgian coast, but he was dead by late February 1915. If Staniforth offered his family a safe panoramic view of the trenches, Allen offered his a close-up. It was of the system in the Loos–Lens area:

Getting along a trench is not as easy as you think. For one thing it is not straight for more than four yards (it is 'traversed' to prevent enfilade and shell fire having much effect). Then there are all sorts of odd off-turns, to officers dug-outs, or other lines of trenches: at other places there are steps down and other unknown steps up where a piece of parapet has been blown in, or some walls of a traverse have collapsed. In these mazes where we have fought each other so often and each side has held the ground in turn, you can never be quite sure whether a trench won't lead you straight to the German lines. In more than one place in our present line we actually do have communication trenches connecting our and their lines.[4]

Charles Cecil Miller, an officer with the 2nd Inniskillings, tried to convey to his family a sense of what it was like to live in the open and underground, exposed to the elements for days and weeks on end:

It must be very difficult for anyone who hasn't seen a trench to visu-
alise trench life, and it is not very easy to describe. You live in a broad
deep cutting below the level of the earth and the enemy opposite you
does the same. Above you is the sky and all around you is naked earth.
Your objective is to prevent the enemy from doing damage to you so
far as you can, and at the same time to do him as much damage as you
can. His designs on you are precisely similar. You are each protected by
barbed wire, and, always provided you are sufficently vigilant you
should be able to stop the enemy infantry in the opposite trenches from
doing you much harm, as the advantage under the conditions lies with
the defence. If however his artillery chooses to blow you up from a
distance, you can do nothing except ask your own artillery to intervene
with counter battery work on the enemy's artillery ... [5]

This became an option later in the conflict, but in the early days of the war
the British Expeditionary Force was so chronically short of ammunition that
it could only respond to German strikes on a piecemeal basis.

Except in the case of a rare large-scale offensive, most aggressive activity
along the frontlines took place after dark:

The night was of course the wakeful time in trenches, patrols were out
then, and anything in the nature of an attack or raid was far more likely
at night than during the day. At the same time you generally got previous warning of an attack in force, as the enemy would put down a heavy
preliminary bombardment with the object of smashing up your wire so
that they could get through easily. To attack against unbroken wire was
suicide – you were just shot down at a few yards range while you struggled to cut or force your way through the wire.[6]

The Meath poet, Francis Ledwidge, served initially with the 10th Division
in Gallipoli but by 1917 his battalion, the 5th Inniskillings, had been posted
to France. Writing to his friend, the poet Katherine Tynan, he offered this
lyrical description of the trenches at night:

Entering and leaving the line is most exciting, as we are usually but
about thirty yards from the enemy, and you can scarcely understand
how bright the nights are made by his rockets. These are in continual
ascent and descent from dusk to dawn, making a beautiful crescent from
Switzerland to the sea. There are white lights, green, and red, and
whiter, bursting into red and changing again, and blue bursting into
purple drops and reds fading into green. It is all like the end of a beautiful world. It is only horrible when you remember that every colour is

a signal to waiting reinforcements of artillery and God help us if we are caught in the open, for then up to a thousand reds, and hundreds of rifles and machine-guns are emptied against us, and all amongst us shells of every calibre are thrown, shouting destruction and death.[7]

Those of a less poetic bent were more oppressed by the daily reality of coping with the elements which seemed to conspire to make an unenviable situation altogether worse. J.F.B. O'Sullivan of the 6th Connaughts wrote to his mother about his frantic efforts to shore up his battalion's HQ dugout as incessant rainful threatened to make it uninhabitable:

> Helped by Bulger, Smith's batman, and by my own batman McConnell, I got the stairway cleared out and then tried to lessen the sticky slime clogging the floor: I would hold open a sandbag, whilst Bulger pushed in handfuls of mud, and then pass the half filled bag up to McConnell who crouched waiting on the upper steps. The over-all slush was lowered by a few inches, though ever more kept oozing in almost as fast as it was scooped out; and by late morning we gave up in despair – 5 inches of mud still carpeting the place.[8]

'Comfort' levels often depended on the distance between the two front lines. If they were separated by more than a few hundred yards, then it was relatively safe to work on the deepening and draining of trenches and the enlarging of dugouts. But if the enemy trenches were only some forty to fifty yards distant (which was often the case), then home improvement was a pointless and dangerous exercise. The very act of moving about, let alone full-scale construction, invited a response from enemy snipers. Both sides' trenches were well within range of mortars and grenades (Mills bombs and hand bombs) and so subject to random demolition. And, with the enemy just a few paces away, constant vigilance was required in the event of an attack or a raid. Practical architecture is not viable under such stressful conditions.

There is one story, probably apocryphal, of an Irish battalion in the Ypres area doing a deal with a nearby German unit following days of heavy rain. The trenches were awash and the German troops, miserable to the point of being suicidal, climbed over their parapets to escape the water and mud. As they did so, they appealed to the British troops opposite (which in one version was an Irish unit) not to open fire. Defying any possible disciplinary action, the Irishmen put down their guns and clambered out of their own waterlogged trenches.[9]

As luck would have it, the winter of 1915 was one of the worst on record. It also marked the introduction of the 16th (Irish) Division to the trenches of the Western Front. Anthony Brennan served with the Royal Irish Regiment and, while he acknowledged that 'Casualties in the winter months were few', he did not appreciate the debit side –

> when we had to live in four foot of slimy mud and sleep in dug-outs which were dry on the rare occasions when we were lucky, and were unfailingly rat infested, and lousy. As the winter advanced and the rainy season descended upon us, conditions in the trenches became worse and worse. Our beautiful brick-fashioned structure of sand bags, so nice to look upon during the dry summer days, collapsed ignominiously after a few days' heavy rain. All along the front traverses fell in, usually at about 2.00 a.m., and tired men, just settling down to a couple of hours' sleep after a wearisome ration party, or a spell of sentry duty, were hauled out to dig a way clear from fire-bay to fire-bay before daylight made the task impossible.[10]

Though the members of the 10th (Irish) Division in Gallipoli might have had other hazards to contend with there were, as Major Bryan Cooper describes them, certain advantages attached to a drier climate:

> While in many respects fighting in Gallipoli was more unpleasant than in France or Flanders, yet its trench warfare had certain advantages over that engaged in there. Though the heat by day and the cold by night were trying, yet there was but little rain, and it was easy to keep the trenches dry. Except on the Kiretch Tepe Sirt and close to the sea, the soil was firm, so that the sides of trenches did not require much revetment, and repairs were not constantly called for. Above all, the character of the enemy gave the defender an easier time.[11]

The stalemate at Gallipoli and the absence of any great need for emergency fatigue duties spent repairing trenches devastated by rain in the small hours of the morning led to a more predictable routine there. 'Stand To', the period just before dawn (and dusk) when every available man would take up his position as it was considered the most likely time for an enemy attack, would be followed by the rum issue and breakfast. In Henry Hanna's account of the fate of D Company, 7th Royal Dublin Fusiliers (*The Pals at Suvla*), there is an account by an unnamed member of the company of a typical morning:

> 4.45 a.m. – 'Stand to Arms! Stand to arms!' I am half asleep and hear it echoed through the trenches, but I still lie on, so up comes the Sergeant: 'Come out of it my lad. Stand to arms, stand to arms.' So out I get, grasp my rifle, with bayonet fixed, work the bolt, see that it is loaded, close it up again, and get into a firing position. At daybreak the

order comes down: 'Unfix your bayonets and carry on as usual.' Then we all unfix, and all but the sentry sit down or carry on as they like, and the sentry remains on watch. The sentry is one man in every four at night and one in every eight during the day.

7.00 a.m. 'Come on there, here's this rum (strong language). Would you hurry up? Do you want this rum or not?' So shouts the sergeant-major, and we all gather round for a quarter-pint of neat rum, and it warms one, I can tell you.

7.30 a.m. Breakfast. 'You cooked that bacon fairly well this morning, and these biscuits are all right.' 'Yes, they're not bad, and the tea's all right, not too bad for Gallipoli.' And so on. 'The meals are discussed, though not always with the same satisfaction.'

8.30 a.m. Rifle inspection. Usually means the sergeant making numerous rude remarks about the state of one's rifle, bayonet, etc.

9 to 11.30 a.m. Improvement of trenches, digging deeper, repairing parapets, making dug-outs more comfortable, etc. etc. and of course all this time the sentries go on and come off as usual. Dong, Dong, Dong, Dong – four beats on the iron crowbar. A warning sound. Everyone hears it, and in about two minutes we're all safe in our dug outs. What's up now, you wonder. Well it's an enemy aeroplane in sight, or else the enemy's artillery are going to shell our trenches. The Dongs are a signal from headquarters, and then a few more casualties, some wounded, some killed – all part of the day's work. Then people at home talk about 'Fight to a finish' etc. while if they had a day of this they'd be peacemongers for the rest of their lives. Dong, Dong, two beats on the crowbar, and everyone is alive again. The danger, whatever it was, has passed.[12]

Gallipoli could be cold at nights, but Allied troops were withdrawn from the area before having to undergo the rigours of a full Turkish winter. Troops on the Western Front suffered some of the coldest winters on record between 1914 and 1918. Peter McBride was relatively fortunate, he joined up in Omagh in May 1916 and served initially with the cavalry regiment, the King's Own Irish Hussars. From there he went to the Inniskillings but didn't enter the trenches until January 1917. There his good fortune ended:

That was the coldest winter for fifty years. The first night we went up we had no overcoats because they were afraid there might be a thaw; there was very very severe frost. We only had leather jerkins and wading boots, and those were very necessary because when we went up there was no front line at all, there was only a series of shell holes and we sat on the edge of a shell hole on a bit of a board; there were about six of us in our section, with our feet in the water. The water was freezing around our legs all night and we sat there for about 36 hours.

The twenty-mile withdrawal of the German army to the well fortified Hindenberg Line in March 1917 resulted in a move for McBride to positions near St Quentin. From St Patrick's Day 1917 to 19 April 'we were in the open all the time, in snow and sleet and very cutting sleety rain and we were under fire of course but we didn't have many casualties. In those six weeks we didn't have our clothes off, I don't think we ever had a roof over our heads, and I don't think we ever had a hot meal. And when we were eventually relieved on the 19th of April I remember our platoon officer (there were only four of us survived) said, '16 Platoon, what's left of you, fall in.'¹³ Most of the casualties had come from frostbite.

John King from Waterford had joined the 1st Battalion, Royal Irish Regiment in 1907. He came from India to the Western Front in late 1914 and reckoned that winter was one of the coldest for years:

> You'd put your clothes on and leave them on until they fell off. It was very severe coming from a warm country to the frozen swamps of France and Belgium. You didn't see only your knees with mud. As you know, Belgium is a low country, and once the sod is lifted from it you're into a quagmire and that's what you were in. Maybe you went in for forty-eight hours. Maybe everything went quiet for that forty-eight hours and then you were relieved. Of course, you didn't come out with the same strength as you went in with. You'd casualties in every way ... from shelling and trench mortars and different things. There was no peace of mind, you were always on the go. You were on the go and they were on the go.¹⁴

The moist, cold, subterranean and altogether alien environment of the Western Front trenches gave rise to a whole new set of ailments. 'In addition to battle casualties,' Colonel Wallace Lyon recalled, 'the troops suffered from a disease called Trench Fever, generally thought to come from the bites of lice who in turn had been infected by rats'.¹⁵ First cousin to Trench Fever was Trench Foot, an affliction not unlike frostbite. War correspondent Phillip Gibbs was more sympathetic towards its victims than were Staff officers who managed to keep their feet dry and thus avoid it. In his book *The Realities of War* he described its causes and effects:

> Men standing in slime for days and nights in field boots or puttees lost all sense of feeling in their feet. These feet of theirs, so cold and wet, began to swell, and then go 'dead' and then suddenly to burn as though

touched by red hot pokers. When the 'reliefs' went up, scores of men could not walk back from the trenches, but had to crawl, or to be carried pick-a-back by their comrades. So I saw hundreds of them, and as the winter dragged on, thousands ... Brigadiers and Divisional Generals were gloomy, and cursed the new affliction of their men. Some of them said it was due to damned carelessness, others were inclined to think it due to deliberate malingering at a time when there were many cases of self-inflicted wounds ... There was no look of malingering on the faces of those boys who were being carried pick-a-back to the ambulance trains at Remy siding near Poperinghe with both feet crippled and tied up in bundles of cotton wool.'[16]

Ultimately, contracting frostbite or Trench Foot became a military misdemeanour which carried sanctions other than acute discomfort. Soldiers were instructed that it could and should be avoided by changing their socks frequently and by rubbing whale-oil onto their feet: 'if the individual carried out orders regarding sock-changing and massage, the chances were 80 to 1 against his getting frost bitten. Frost bite, under these circumstancs, was regarded from a disciplinary point of view, and became a crime.'[17] Captain Frank Hitchcock wrote.[18]

The peripatetic nature of the British army soldier often meant that uncommon diseases turned up in unlikely places. In November 1916, for example, Captain Frank Hitchcock, found himself confronted in Belgium by an ailment which was more appropriate to the Tropics: 'I remember when we were there 8645 Pte. Corbally had a bad attack of malaria one night. I gave him several glasses of whisky, and lent him my great-coat. The treatment cured him all right, but next night several men complained of having malaria!'[19] One can make the supposition that Corbally had seen service in Gallipoli and that either the disease had incubated or this was a recurrence.

The unwitting agents in the spread of much of the disease which infected the infantry were the ubiquitous lice and rats that infested the trenches. The rat posed a very obvious threat; that of the louse was more insidious. Three-quarters of a century after his introduction to the trenches of Picardy, Dubliner Jack Campbell still had vivid memories of the healthy and well-fed rodents with whom he shared his accommodation:

I often wonder how many unfortunate lads died of rat bites. I remember one time my company was visiting an old loft. It had been used for a long time by troops coming out for rest and that kind of thing. There was a young lad alongside me and in the nighttime he shouted, 'Oh, I've been bitten.' Well we got a bit of candle, and right enough a rat had taken a piece out of his cheek. We put a first aid dressing on, and he saw the medical officer in the morning, but it was too late and two or three days afterwards he died. His face and his neck were black and swollen from the poison of the rat ... If you had a bit of food, the only place you could save that was in your stomach, because it doesn't matter where you hid it: those bloody rats would get it.'[20]

Body lice hosted on troops in impressive numbers. Only a convincing delousing when in reserve could get rid of them. When in the front lines it was futile to attempt to deal with them individually. They simply had to be tolerated and often became the subject of elaborate games or mordant army wit. According to Jack Campbell, a standard army joke was to 'take one out, look at it, put it back and say, 'Remanded for a week.' James Maultsaid of the 14th Royal Irish Rifles and his comrades used to while away many nights sitting around a candle with their shirts off. On a given signal a general hunt would begin for lice. 'A time limit of ten minutes was laid down and and the winner was the man that caught the most.'[21]

The detritus of the Great War (which included a distressing number of unburied corpses) offered the rodent population of northern France an unparalleled food source. Rat numbers were the only ones which rose during the conflict, and many of the better fed rodents grew to prodigious sizes.

As the French had not buried all their dead after their great offensive, they were left to decompose in the sun, and the majority of them provided a feast for the rats. I saw many rats on the ridge and in the valley. They were a colossal size, almost as big as dogs. Rat chasing was a great recreation when in the line on Vimy Ridge.[22]

In a place which he calls 'Sandbag Villa' near Wytschaete, Frank Laird claims to have seen two dead rats in the farmyard which were the size of a small terrier:

Sometimes the men amused themselves by baiting the ends of their rifles with pieces of bacon in order to have a shot at them at close quarters. They skipped about like kittens over the feet of anyone who left the dug-out after dark, and even made free with the dug-out itself. Our Captain, energetic and hopeful as always, determined to make it rat-proof, and spent the whole of one morning having wire netting nailed over every loophole by which they could enter. It was an arduous job, and one corporal nearly lost his stripes over it, but eventually all was satisfactorily finished, and the Captain sat down to a game of bridge in the afternoon with an air of 'something accomplished something done.' The game was underway a short time when Poulter found a rat sitting beside him on the bench! Captain Thompson averred he had brought it in his pocket, an allegation to which Poulter's love for practical jokes gave some colour, but I think on the whole the rat came in on his own to show up the preventitive measures.'[23]

For the fastidious and the naturally hygienic the paucity of opportunities to wash properly and to change one's clothes regularly was offensive. John Breen of the 3rd Royal Irish Regiment was upset that 'you were filthy dirty the whole time ... We'd often be fifteen and sixteen days, maybe three or four weeks without a change of clothes. It'd all depend on what time you'd be relieved. We were lousy ... we were in a terrible state.' Adverse conditions often did not make commanding officers any less demanding as regards standards of personal appearance. Prior to one of its most active periods at the front, in September, 1916 (Guillemont and Ginchy), the CO of the 6th Connaughts, Lt.-Col. J.S.M. Lenox-Conyngham[24] insisted to his officers (among them Lt. J.F.B. O'Sullivan) on the preservation of rigorous sartorial standards. 'The Saturday morning (2nd) started off cheerfully enough. After some tea and bread for breakfast we cleared the table for the day's office work, but were halted in this by the CO's pointed remarks about the number of unshaven faces around him. Taking the unsubtle hint, I climbed upstairs and managed to shave with a cup of water McConnell found for me.'[25]

The extended period in action around Guillemont had a damaging effect on O'Sullivan's feet, which had been continuously soaked in a drenched dugout for more than 48 hours:

> So I scraped away the outer layers of mud, slowly unpeeled the puttees and took off boots and socks. The feet were raw, cracked and pulpy, and required great quantities of Murphy's boracic powder before the socks and boots could be comfortably replaced. Rewinding the muddy puttees was a slimey job. After this my loud-voiced smugness was too much for Sandy [Campbell] and he immediately followed suit; and very soon everyone in the dug-out was drying and powdering his feet.[26]

In Gallipoli the sea offered an inviting but potentially risky answer to all hygiene problems. The Gunning brothers needed little urging to clean up during their rest periods at the beach:

> ... we stripped and got in and Sergt. A gave us a tip how to wash in a prehistoric fashion. That was by grabbing a handful of sand from the bottom and rubbing it on our hands, neck, arms, etc. to scrape the dirt off us. Even while in the water, there were some shells bursting in the sea about half a mile away ... Later on, after I left, C. wrote saying that

they were bathing one day, and a shell fell right in amongst them, and four or five of the poor chaps were killed in the water.[27]

The diet of the troops varied tremendously. It often depended on the resourcefulness of the battalion quartermaster and what he could beg, borrow, cadge or simply steal. When troops were on front line duties they were often dependent on the competence and courage of the Army Supply Corps, whose job it was to bring rations to the infantrymen. In some sectors both sides took particular pleasure in targetting the supplies of the enemy; in others there was a tacit arrangement exempting ration parties from attack. In the former case British troops often went hungry if ASC supply vehicles were hit by shells or mortars when their approach was detected by the Germans. As Charles Miller put it in his memoir, 'rations were sent up nightly from the quartermaster's stores generally a few miles away. This was not always possible however and in particularly hot corners you might have to exist for your allotted spell (generally four days) on what you and your men could carry in.'[28]

Jack Campbell was doomed in the early days of the war to serve in a sector where the 'brass' on both sides were not the malleable types and where they took the interdiction of supplies seriously. Ultimately, however, common sense prevailed.

We went hungry on a lot of occasions when trench warfare started. At night time if the shelling wasn't too heavy we could hear the transport bringing up the rations to the German lines and of course they could hear the transport behind our lines coming up with it. That was the signal for the artillery to open up and blow the transport off the roads and too often they were successful. With the result that at about nine or ten o'clock at night the word would be passed along, 'Sorry, lads, no rations tonight. Transport couldn't get through.' Now you'd been there all day and that meant you'd to go all through the night and all through the next day until the next evening to see if the transport would be able to get through then. I think it was by mutual agreement that that ended because if we couldn't get our rations up and the Germans couldn't get theirs up, what was going to happen to the men in the trenches? After a short while, things began to level out and the rations and supplies would come up regularly.[29]

At Gallipoli there appears to have been no inclination on the part of the Turks to call the supply of rations a 'draw' and leave well enough alone. According to Major Bryan Cooper,

Drawing rations was one of the most dangerous occupations on the Peninsula, especially at Anzac, and was usually performed at the double. The beaches, where the supply depots were situated, were among the enemy's favourite targets, as they knew that there were always people moving there, and they shelled them persistently. In France, the ASC are said to have safe and 'cushy' jobs; but this was certainly not the case in Gallipoli. Their work, in addition to being dangerous, was not exciting, which made things worse; for though Death is the same wherever he comes, it is easier to encounter him in a charge than when cutting up bacon.[30]

Even when supplies did make it through, the food available to front-line troops was usually unappetising. It generally consisted of 'bully beef' and 'biscuit'. The beef usually came in tins and was plentiful, so much so that 'in some sections the trench was revetted with unopened bully beef tins!', according to Col. Wallace Lyon. Army 'biscuit' was an all-purpose food which had the practical advantages of being virtually imperishable and 'bulking up' when eaten. It could be taken dry or mixed with water to create a sort of cereal or porridge. Despite its nutritional qualities it was no balm for the taste buds. As one Australian sodier observed, 'The man who invented the army biscuit was an unmitigated rascal. As an eatable there is little to choose between it and a seasoned jarrah board.'[31]

When in reserve troops could often manage to supplement their diets by making purchases from the local population or by trading with other soldiers. For those in a position to do so, a little pilfering from Army supplies was often indulged in. For at least one Irish battalion this looting took on a political aspect in May 1916. Anthony Brennan, Royal Irish Regiment, writes:

> At length we arrived at a large village near the Fricourt sector. Here we spent a week or two; going up several nights to the trenches with rations for the Ulster division. It was rather ironical, in a way, for an old National Volunteer to be thus helping to feed his late enemies of the Ulster Volunteers. Any qualms I might have had on the matter were adequately eased by occasional pilferings of the Ulsterman's 'plum duff'.[32]

When the Army Service Corps brought up supplies, they were left in the reserve trenches. From there they had to be transported by hand by troops assigned to fatigue duties. It was an uncomfortable and often hazardous occupation. In the winter of 1915 Brennan was often assigned to those duties. The geography of the front line usually involved two sets of parallel front line trenches and reserve trenches a few hundred yards further back with communications trenches linking them. In Brennan's sector the communications trench was so full of mud that winter that soldiers preferred to traverse open ground and run the risk of exposing themselves to snipers rather than wade through the mire:

> Later when the weather broke that much-traversed path became muddy and slippery, it was a way of tribulation for many an overburdened ration-carrier, and many a heartfelt curse went up to Heaven from the lips of an exasperated 'Tommy' as he measured his length on the slushy earth, or slid headlong towards the ubiquitous shell-hole. Given a large four-cornered box of biscuits; a couple of sand bags loaded with any-thing from the tins of 'Bully' to bricks for the Captain's dug-out, and slung around one's neck a rifle and two bandoliers of ammunition, and the things that could happen to one's person and one's temper on that three hundred yards of slippery, uneven footpath on dark night were enough to try the patience of the meekest of 'Tommies'.

Bill McMahon, a Dubliner, spent the war in a Horse Transport section in constant danger from shelling.

> You had to bring in rations, ammunition, barbed wire – the water car had to go in, the field kitchens had to be brought up. Up around Ypres was the worst of the whole lot. On the roads up around Ypres at night it was really horrific. They were knocking hell out of the roads to keep the reinforcements from going up and materials from going in. Those roads were always getting hell.

McMahon had at least one narrow escape:

> I was with the 18th Hussars at this particular time and a horse cast a shoe. It was the last month of the war, we were coming back from having spent all day trying to get in, but there was no getting through at all. This was up at Le Cateau. The horse cast a shoe and two of us dropped out with the blacksmith and drove a nail into the shoe. During that time the unit moved on quite a distance. Coming off the fields onto the road the horse struck up a spark. It was getting dark then in the evening, five o'clock in the evening in the month of November. There was a Jerry overhead looking for our guns. When he got the spark, he dropped a bomb. It fell straight down into the middle of a lorry loaded with ammunition. Up she goes. Well, there was upwards of sixty horses and men of the Royal Horse Artillery between where our connecting file was and our main unit and they were absolutely blown to pieces. There was men taken out of those horses' bellies.[33]

The hierarchy of the trenches was clear as far as shoulder insignia went. Officers enjoyed whatever privileges were available (the biggest and most 'comfortable' dug-outs, the allotment of fatigue duties to others etc.). NCOs came next in the pecking order, and the private soldier made his own arrangements. Among privates there was often a sort of inverse snobbery. Middle-class privates stepped out of their world when they took their place among the 'other ranks'. When Anthony Brennan was posted to the 2nd Royal Irish Regiment along with some friends who had had cadet training, he

> found a certain amount of hostility towards us prevailing amongst other members of the platoon [No.14 platoon] This was due to the fact that we had come from the 'Cadet' Company, about which they had all sorts of funny ideas. To them we were 'swells' of a kind, and for a good many months we had to put up with various forms of 'pin-pricks' and many unjust and unmerited 'fatigues', because of this erroneous idea.

Brennan and his friends, Dick Breen and Frank Waldron, didn't help by establishing themselves on one occasion in a separate dug-out: 'Our other fellows did not like it and thought it was just a bit of Cadet Corps "stand-offishness" … we had been missing some of our belongings, including the contents of parcels sent out from home, and one night while we were at work Dick Breen slipped quietly away from our party and went back to our dug-out just in time to surprise two of our dear comrades from the platoon.' The thieves heard him coming and got away, but thereafter the thefts stopped. 'Most of the Waterford chaps in the platoon were old soldiers in the sense that it was not safe to leave anything lying about.'[34]

In a class-ridden era, even in the squalor of the trenches it was still possible to preserve the differences between the social classes. Captain Charles Cecil Miller, Inniskilling Fusiliers writes:

> If you were an officer, you brought into trenches an air cushion to put your head on and something to wash and shave with. Of course, while in trenches you never got out of your clothes, and very seldom out of your boots, and then only in the day. When not on duty in the trench, you lived in the dug-out, generally with the other company officers, and most dug-outs contained one or two rough wooden frames with rabbit wire fitted to them, on which you reposed in all your clothes during such time as you could snatch an hour or two's sleep.[35]

The most obvious status symbols of the officer in the front line were the absence of any need for hard physical labour and the occupation of the bigger dug-outs. Lieutenant John Staniforth described:

A world of moles, burrowing always deeper and deeper to get away from the high explosives: an underground city with avenues, lanes, streets, crescents, alleys and cross-roads, all named and labelled and connected by telegraph and telephone. 'No.3 Posen alley' was my last address, and you reach it via 'Piccadilly', 'Victoria Station', and 'Sackville Street'. After you've wandered for perhaps two hours you'll see a hole at your feet with a mass of wires of all sizes and colours running along the ground and disappearing into it. Go down twenty or thirty steps, down mud steps, and you come into a low, long cave, lit by candles stuck in bottles and a swinging hurricane lamp.[36]

There, according to Frank Laird, between rifle inspection in the morning and dusk 'Stand To' officers had 'little to do but smoke. The others had leisure on their hands, except the Captain, whose pen was generally busy. The quantity of manuscript of all kinds which he had to pass through his hands in the line fairly astonished me. Indents, strength reports, wind reports, etc., etc., seemed to be cropping up all day long.'[37] Officers also bore responsibility for the censorship of letters and for writing to bereaved relatives to console them on the deaths of their loved ones.

In Gallipoli the composition of the soil made it more difficult to scrape out a dugout 'worthy' of an officer. This was especially true at Anzac Cove, where the Irish 29th Brigade landed and where officers occupied dug-outs which had been hacked out of the cliffs by Australian and New Zealand soldiers. In his account of the 10th Irish Division at Gallipoli Major Bryan Cooper advised that.

The dug-out that is dug for another is not so elaborate. You burrow into the vertical face of the hill until a cavity large enough to contain a man is created, and leave it for the occupant to make the best of. Before he has learnt to do this, he has probably bumped his head several times and filled his hair with earth. At the same time, however small it may be, it is unwise to forsake the burrow constructed for you by the experienced inhabitant and strike out a line for yourself. Two officers who attempted to do this were quickly disillusioned. Their first effort installed them in a cemetery, where a corpse was awaiting burial. Their second reopened a recently filled-in latrine, 'while the third found them in the midst of buried Turks. Then they gave it up.'[38]

The bane of the life of the Great War soldier was fatigue duty. 'Fatigues' were aptly named as they tended to be onerous and tiring and were often undertaken at a time when troops were most exhausted. When troops were

officially 'resting' (that is, not on front line duty), they were often called upon
to work hardest. Lt. J.F.B O'Sullivan, 6th Connaught Rangers:

> This term 'rest' became a standard joke. Everyone made it, each with
> an air of great originality – and always got a laugh, or at least a sym-
> pathetic snigger ... The periods when a battalion was holding the front
> trenches were so filled with fatigues, raids, and back-breaking work
> parties that many a tired man welcomed the return to the death-dealing
> 'line'.[39]

The cover provided by darkness was usually the cue for 'fatigues' to begin.
Frank Hitchcock's diary contains many dispirited entries, such as the one for
9 June 1915:

> Returned from fatigue at 3 a.m. We were all pretty jaded and disgrun-
> tled with this task. Every night on the same work, hacking through
> corpses and filling sand-bags! The ground was a swamp, and churned
> up by shell fire which prevented drainage. Nothing broke the monotony
> of this working party; the same smell of gas, and sickening smell of
> decomposing human flesh hung round the locality. Every now and then
> shrapnel would burst over us to break the stillness of the night. Otherwise
> the only sounds were the sighing poplars and the everlasting croaking
> of the frogs.'[40]

Sgt. F. de Margry was one of a number of Channel Islanders drafted into
the 2nd Royal Irish Regiment from a cavalry regiment soon after the war
became bogged down and the cavalry became, for the time being at least,
supernumerary. De Margry was unusually tall for that time (six foot) and, as
the trenches were constructed for the protection of men of smaller stature, he
was forced to spend most of his time in the front line with a permanent
stoop. As a man used to dealing with horses he just might have had some
ideas above his station. These would quickly have been dispelled by his first
chore with his new battalion:

> I was given some wooden stakes and a couple of reels of barbed wire to
> carry to the front line, so, after joining the others similarly loaded up,
> we moved off in the dark, taking a 'B' line to our destination across
> some very rough ground pitted with shell holes half full of stinking
> water and intermittently lighted up by bright aerial flares fired from the
> trenches. We hadn't gone very far in this slow and laborious fashion
> when we tripped more and more over dead bodies (most of them
> belonging to Princess Pat's Canadian Infantry who'd been gassed) and

their long rifles scattered around them. Job to repair barbed wire defences in no man's land ... I can't say I felt any too happy about this, my first experience of such an exposed position, specially while subjected to enemy fire from most directions and handicapped as we were in our work, due mostly to lack of stout protective gloves, sufficient light to see what we were doing, and previous experience under such strange conditions. About an hour before dawn we trudged wearily back the way we had come to find on arrival at our assembly point that we had lost 15 men (roughly 10 per cent) during those few hours on night fatigue ... Our first experience of front line night fatigues was repeated daily, varied only by the different tasks we had to perform and the nature of the loads we had to carry and dispose of, with casualties pretty much the same most nights. In fact, according to my reckoning based on that average, all or most of us couldn't hope to escape the same fate beyond another fortnight or so ... [41]

Such were the constant hazards of fatigue duty. Every night casualties were taken among units doing nothing more adventurous, significant and aggressive than digging holes in the ground. De Margry, however, was lucky; the Royal Irish were transferred to a safer sector of the line shortly afterwards.

The Irish soldier was often accused of lacking the discipline of the Englishman and the Scotsman to endure adverse conditions. He was said to lack the stoicism of those neighbouring races and to be at his best only in attack. The stereotypical Irish soldier is the mythical one who appeals to his commanding officer after three days of torrential rain, 'Please sir, can we attack the Germans?' So, in concluding this section on the physical conditions which Irish (and other troops) had to tolerate, let us hear a most comprehensive whinge, not from an Irish soldier but from a Channel Islander (Sgt. de Margry) serving with an Irish unit, the Royal Irish Regiment:

After being relieved in our turn a week later, we moved back to our 'rest camp', where for another week we were sent up and down the line, daily or nightly, engaged on various arduous fatigues ranging from ration parties to trench maintenance, or latrine digging to hauling heavy ammunition boxes to the front line, or laying barbed wire entanglements in no man's land to building timber tracks for heavy vehicles – in fact, quite a variety of back-breaking jobs, specially on bully and biscuits which was more or less our staple daily ration. Water was so scarce that one had to save half one's morning mug of tea for shaving purposes and wait for rain to get a wash of sorts. Once in a blue moon one had a quick shower at Divisional Baths (generally miles away) and a clean change of underwear, so it's no wonder we were almost permanently lousy. Our drinking water (rationed) was so heavily chlorinated as to be almost undrinkable, and more often than not our tea was greasy and onion-flavoured due to the dixies being used for soup or stews serving as receptacles afterwards for tea-making – without any sort of cleaning for want of facilities.[42]

The tedium of the trenches, whether they were in France, Belgium, Turkey or Bulgaria, was relieved with spontaneous irregularity and unpredictability by the appearance of mail from home. This often had a somewhat peculiar effect on morale. The arrival of mail would boost the troops, but many would then become morose and melancholy once they read their correspondence and were forcibly reminded of home. The Gunning brothers, Frank and George, landed at Suvla Bay with the 7th Dublin Fusiliers in August 1915. The arrival of the first mail (and in Frank's case the last – he was invalided out on 19 August) was, initially, a cause of much excitement. The Gunnings received six letters in all from various family members and friends.

> We read them over two or three times, and they made us feel terribly homesick and miserable. Lots of chaps got newspapers, cigarettes, etc. and I had the pleasure to see the *Punch* Summer Annual. Some of the jokes were good enough; but, at the time, I thought it seemed awfully tragic for people at home to be laughing over such silly things, while we were in such a game of life and death. But now, at home, I say, why shouldn't they? Especially our womenfolk, for they need something amusing to drive away trouble and anxiety from their minds for at least a little while.[43]

Bryan Cooper revealed how officers could be ambiguous about the correspondence they received:

> Nor did one's own mail consist entirely of personal letters, for the officers who survived found themselves in September receiving many letters from the relatives of their comrades who had fallen begging for details of how they died. These letters were not easy to answer, since details were often lacking, and the writer was always afraid of inadvertently opening the wound again; but it was a labour of love to reply to them. More amusing semi-official letters were also received, such as the demands of railway companies for sums of three-and-sixpence due by men who had travelled without tickets four months earlier. As even sup-posing the men in question had not been killed or wounded, they had certainly received no pay for more than a month, and were unlikely to

receive any for an indefinite period, so the prospect that the Company Officer would be able to recover the debts before being killed or wounded himself did not seem large.[44]

Parcels, however, were always welcome. These usually contained food (often including some impractibably perishable goods) and were used to supplement meagre or tedious army rations. 'The most welcome gift of all was tinned fruit, since these and the syrup that came with them quenched thirst. Lemonade tablets, too, were welcome, and sauces and curry-powders to disguise the taste of the eternal bully-beef, were much appreciated. Some things failed to stand the climate; chocolate usually arrived in a liquid condition, while a parcel of butter became a greasy rag.'[45]

The regular renewal of his love affair with alcohol was a constant objective of the soldier 'at rest'. In the front lines the rum ration filled that need, the more so if one could trade with a teetotaller and get his supply as well. Peter McBride of the Inniskilling Fusiliers was a non-drinker ('there was great competition to get my ration of rum'). One day in 1917, near Nieuport, someone found a fully laden winecellar and looted it: 'Everybody on that front was drunk that night, except myself and the adjutant.' The ranks of the intoxicated included two men on sentry duty who were subsequently court-martialled and each sentenced to 11 years. 'The Germans could have walked through that evening.'[46]

Failure to get the rum ration to the front lines risked mutiny. Edgar Poulter with the 7th Dublins in Suvla watched a soldier bringing up rations. Poulter noticed that he was carrying something on his head. From somewhere a sniper let loose at this lone figure and a bullet went under the jar and creased his scalp. Naturally he dropped whatever it was he was bearing on his head. As he did so, it smashed and Poulter realised to his chagrin that it was the battalion rum jar. 'There was more desolation about that ... than about his wounds.'

A more varied selection of alcoholic beverages was available to soldiers 'at rest' behind the lines. These could usually be got in what were known as 'estaminets'. In this country they would be classed as 'shebeens', that is, private drinking establishments of dubious legality. Corporal Davy Starret, batman to Col. Percy Crozier of the 9th Royal Irish Rifles, was stationed near Neuve Eglise in early 1916.

The estaminets here were rough shows, filled with French girls. One at the corner of the cross roads was always full, for there the girls could swear in English, or what they called English. Strange how soon foreigners pick up all our worst words. 'Here's you blazing beer and I hope you'll stick it up your a—e!', they would say. The name of that house consequently amongst the men cannot be printed. Over a year after, when I was with the 40th Division, I met an Ulster boy, who told me that after we left the place was blown to bits. I was not sorry to hear it.[47]

'Estaminet' proprietors were often unscrupulous when it came to the quality and the price of the drinks they served. They tended to operate on the basis that they were 'the only game in town' and act according to the extent of their monopoly. Soldiers were often provoked into a response by the iniquity of the tariff structure or by the amount of alcohol they had consumed. Wallace Adelbert Lyon's first meeting with his new platoon in the 7th Leinsters came just in time to save one offending proprietor. Intending to introduce himself to the men under his command, he walked into a local 'estaminet':

> There I beheld a bunch of soldiers milling around an upturned beer barrel, the head of which had been stove in and out of which protruded the kicking legs and part of the body of the French proprietor. As they pushed him in, the level of the beer rose and they dipped their mugs in it. When they pulled him up, the unfortunate Frenchman renewed his protests. Quickly I thought of the duke of Clarence drowned in a butt of Malmsey wine; then I thought, 'My God, he'll be another,' so I intervened. The Frenchman was furious. I thought he might have been grateful to me, but he was all for going to the Colonel, the General, or anyone else he could think of, and it took quite a time to pacify him and to point out that he would be better off if he accepted my offer to pay for the damage, plus insult. Finally he agreed. I thanked God I knew enough French to make him understand and that I had escaped the trouble of a court martial which would have been the worst possible introduction to the men I was to lead in battle. I then fell in the platoon, gave them the hottest troopers' telling off I could think of, and ordered a kit inspection in half an hour. It cost me the best part of a fiver in French francs, but the men were not unmindful of it and I had no more trouble.[48]

The impression often created of the Great War is of constant turmoil and almost daily offensive actions of one kind or another. This was not the case. Major battles such as the Somme or Messines were rare events in the life of the average soldier, and smaller-scale raids or other types of skirmishes hardly more frequent. One of the main enemies of the soldier of the 1914–18 war was sheer boredom. In his war memoir Wallace Lyon observes that

If a soldier is well fed, kept clear of lice and with constant attention to feet and clothing, he can stand a remarkable degree of cold and still remain healthy. It was the dreariness of being among the rats, the stench of death, the dirt and the unceasing drain of casualties that told most on the troops morale. It was seldom we had the satisfaction of seeing the results of our efforts. Sometimes at dawn the mist would suddenly rise to reveal a Boche behind his own front line in a crouching position with his trousers down – a chance seldom missed, but for the most part we had to endure our own casualties without being able to see what we had inflicted on the enemy.[49]

Lyon's image of the compromised German soldier was part of the macabre humour with which Allied troops staved off boredom and rationalised and objectified their experience. The British graffiti, spotted on a German grave marked by a wooden cross, which read 'He died to strafe us all,' was typical. Many examples of the humour of the British and Irish troops are similarly black and macabre. Frank Hitchcock wrote about an attack by the 2nd Leinsters at Vimy Ridge in October 1916: 'A skull was lying on the top of Uhlan Alley communication trench. Some wag had stuck a derelict *kepi* on it in grim humour. A very macabre sight for those ascending the ridge for the front line!'[50] Even as lofty a personage as General Alexander Godley allowed some tasteless and morbid humour to come through in a joke at the expense of Sir Ian Hamilton's Gallipoli staff. Writing to his cousin Lord Kilbracken in July 1915, he recalls gleefully that

Before the Maoris arrived they asked us what was their strength and did they require any special diet? I replied that there were 500 of them but that the question of their diet should offer no difficulty as I trusted that, during their stay with the Division, enough Turks would be killed or taken prisoner to go round.[51]

Terence Poulter who began with the Dublin Fusiliers, served out the war with the Royal Fusiliers, a London-based regiment. Poulter was fond of the wit and puckish wisdom of the cockneys under his command. One of those was a Sergeant Major Woodward, who accompanied Poulter on a patrol into no man's land on one particularly appalling night when both were soaked completely through. 'We were going from shell hole to shell hole. He stopped, put his hat back on his head and said, "D'ye know sir, there's one poor bastard I always pity on a night like this." I said, "And who the hell is that?" "The poor policeman on London Bridge".'[52]

Sometimes that peculiarly humorous illogical 'logic' for which the Irish are renowned asserted itself. In late December in Loos a decision was taken to fill in a hideously waterlogged communications trench known as 'Russian sap'. The day before it was filled in, the GOC of the area, Major General Capper, decided to have a look for himself. Capper was a tall aristocratic individual who was forced to stoop as he wallowed through the mud of the sap – 'to find a perfectly collected sentry, head and shoulders above the parapet, looking out towards the enemy, oblivious of any danger. The GOC told him not to expose himself and asked, 'Have you not got a periscope?' The sentry eyed the general, and replied: 'Sure, what good would it be, sir? Aren't they just after breaking two on me?'[53] One Irish soldier invalided home was asked what had struck him most about the war. 'What struck me most?' he replied. 'Sure, it was the crowd of bullets flying about that didn't hit me!'[54]

The more knowing wit of the cynical Northern soldier comes across in the tale of an officer of the 36th Ulster Division who was sent out on an administrative fool's errand:

> Early in the spring of 1917 a return was required from GHQ of all officers, NCOs and men who spoke Chinese as they were required for the Chinese Labour Corps. We were told that nil returns were not to be sent in except after personal enquiry of the men in the companies. One morning we stood to; as I went round with the rum I asked, 'Do any of you men talk Chinese?' As my men came from the factories and shipyards of Belfast where linguistic attainments are rare, my enquiry was received with a silence which I knew was highly charged with contempt. I would fain have hidden my diminished head in a rat-hole. As I passed from one fire-bay to the next, I heard a voice behind me say, 'Holy Jesus, what more will they want for a bob a day.'[55]

Sometimes the humour took a more practical turn. Wallace Lyon once exacted some measure of revenge from a fellow officer of the 2nd Leinsters who had survived a German attack, by simply failing to acknowledge that it was happening:

> Seeing in what a weak state we were, the Boche decided to make a strong raid on our lines, and as usual started the proceedings with a hearty barrage. It was customary to have an officer on duty in the front trench or breastwork, and the rule was for the relieving officer of the watch to come up and take over, so that there would be an officer there all the time. We had an officer called Kelly, who was a very pleasant chap but inclined to be sleepy and slack in this respect. On this particular night he must have been very tired, for he slept in his shelter through a bombardment that would have wakened the dead, followed by an infantry attack which normally provoked a stand to arms for all

hands. We beat them off and took a few prisoners, while Kelly still slept, so when firing died down we chose one good-sized German wearing thick glasses and sat him on Kelly's chest! That woke him alright! He thought he had been taken prisoner and nearly died of fright, but the lesson was learned, and after that his response to the call of duty was always smart.[56]

In a war situation a soldier has a relationship with his comrades, his allies and his enemies. There may be little interaction with the latter, but a relationship still exists. In the case of the Great War contact between Irish and French troops was rare: 'We never really mixed. We had our own sectors, they had theirs, except when a battalion was next to a French one where you probably put an officer across and they put one across to you.'[57] Communication (often bitter recrimination) took place at staff level.

Whenever other ranks came into contact with the French Army, there was bound to be a certain element of culture shock. In November 1915, for example, at St Eloi, a Corporal Leavy received a Medaille Militaire from the French nation. Afterwards he gave an account of the ceremony to Capt. Frank Hitchcock: 'Begad, sorr. 'Twas grand entirely, Froggie General and all. He shook me by the hand, and to me utter astonishment, kissed me on both sides of me face, and me with the two days' growth.'[58]

Occasionally a British Army officer would be asked to liaise with his French equivalent whenever they found themselves holding the same stretch of the front line. Charles Cecil Miller was given that task when the 2nd Inniskillings were transferred to the St Quentin area and were due to take over the line from a French battalion.

> I remember very little about the French [wrote Frank Hitchcock] except that they had a most amusing and sprightly old Colonel who appeared to have been hit in every part of his extremely fleshy person and who took great delight in showing his wounds – stripping himself almost naked to do so – at the slightest provocation; also that their ideas of cleanliness and sanitation in trenches were not ours, but nevertheless they appeared to thrive on them.[59]

This is a constant refrain in the memoirs of officers, and others were not as tolerant or restrained as Miller. Eric Dorman-Smith, in a letter home on 29 May 1915, observed huffily that 'We took over a new bit of the line last night. Poor trenches made by the French dug out like a pigsty.'[60] The temperamentally crochety Lt. Noel Drury was stationed with the 6th Dublins in Serbia in November 1915. He confided to his diary (and probably to anyone who would listen): 'The 10th Division is now holding its own portion of the line, and is not responsible to the French for support or reserves. It's a good job we are clear of them for such filthy troops I never saw. They have not the rudiments of sanitation or cleanliness in camps nor billets. They are typical of the French nation for selfishness, thinking their convenience alone is to be considered.'[61]

There are also frequent scathing references to the fighting qualities of the French soldier. This is very much in keeping with the tendency for soldiers from any unit at any level (from army down to platoon) to see troops in other units as, somehow, lesser beings. Only in the case of Charles Miller does perceptiveness overcome prejudice. He cast a cold eye over the different approaches of the two armies:

> The British Army, incidentally has certain shibboleths, one of which, and it has cost the lives of scores of thousands of soldiers, is that when you are attacked in overwhelming force you mustn't run away. The French, who are much more logical than we, and who consider results and not prestige, invariably run away under such circumstances, and when the right moment comes run back again and deliver a counter attack. The British shibboleth of course extends only to the actual men in the line; the brigadiers and divisional generals run away all right, only they call it moving their quarters. This does not apply to quite all the generals but to the very great majority of them.[62]

In the many contemporary memoirs and accounts which exist of the Great War there are remarkably few references to the native French or Belgian populations. Estaminet proprietors and prostitutes make regular appearances but, with the exception of accounts of the first and last months of the fighting, there is virtually no mention of the farmers or townspeople who would have owned the land over which the war was being fought. There is, of course, a perfectly simple explanation for this, that the native population had long since removed itself, or been removed from the war zone. Where it hadn't and where the fighting suddenly caught up with French inertia the consequences could be tragic. Corporal David Starret of the 9th Royal Irish Rifles was in Armentieres in 1916 when German forces broke through Portuguese defences and began a heavy shelling of the area.

> It was painful to see the French folk looking dazed-like at their houses and possessions going up into the air, and women and children catching wounds and death from flying fragments of red-hot iron. Some in the roads, some on their own doorsteps, and some in the rooms they refused to leave ... it took all my powers of persuasion ... to lead some

of the refugee natives to safety. A bunch of some score wouldn't heed me and tramped on into a couple of bursts, that left nothing but scraps to show the sort of people they'd been ... Bethune, when we reached it again, had changed from a town of laughter and song to a shambles. Women killed in heir nightgowns, men lying stark naked by bursts, children disembowelled, babes smashed to pulp. War is certainly a beast from hell. Staggering through these streets, just a wounded remnant of a once proud Brigade, we saw sights that even now return to memory like the worst of nightmares.[63]

What was true of the French was equally true of the native Belgian population and the remnants of the Belgian army. In the writings of Frank Hitchcock there are a couple of unflattering references to the Belgian population around the devastated city of Ypres. 'We had a poor regard for the Flemish peasantry,' he wrote in *Stand To*:

> they robbed us right and left. It was a well-known fact that the people around the back areas of Ypres lived on British rations, bully beef and tins of Maconochie especially. The men used to say: 'Faith, they are so bloody mean they work their dogs!' In the weeks after the Armistice, while the Belgian population was friendly towards British troops it had started to turn on its own. It was time for revenge and those who had fraternised with the Hun had their houses smashed up. I saw all kinds of furniture being thrown out of the windows of two houses going through the town. In the majority of cases, the objects of hate were the women of easy virtue who were known to have 'liased' with the enemy. All these had their hair closely cropped in order to brand them before the world. I saw one of the unfortunate victims being chased by some inhabitants across a field in the pouring rain.[64]

As for relations with the enemy (German or Turkish in most cases) this varied between outright antagonism, grudging respect and occasional fraternisation. It was not possible to ignore the Germans, especially if your trenches were only a few yards away from theirs. That was what Terence Poulter of the 10th RDF found in Ophy Wood in 1917.

> The lines were near enough that you could hear the Germans talking at night. The trenches were three or four hundred yards apart but they had saps out and they were manning these saps. On one accasion we had the Germans over to have a chat with us we were that friendly. They came out of a sap and nobody fired at them. Captain Noel Dwyer, who was a divil from Mullingar, he got out with his walking stick and had a chat with them.[65]

Fraternisation of any kind was disgouraged by the High Command. Soldiers were encouraged to think of the enemy as 'the Hun' or 'the beastly Boche'. Antipathy was nurtured on stories of the rape of nuns and was further cultivated by propaganda tales like that of the Crucified Canadian. This myth had virtually complete currency for the duration of the war and it changed and developed as the conflict progressed. Sometimes the unfortunate Canadian soldier had been taken prisoner and crucified in the trench with nails being hammered into the palms of his hands while his comrades were forced to listen to his screams. On other occasions he was attached to a barn door with German bayonets. Gradually the number grew from one Canadian prisoner to six. However clumsy a piece of propaganda it might have been, it was augmented by the more subtle myth that, as a consequence, Canadian troops never took German prisoners, preferring instead to bayonet them.

In *Goodbye to All That* Robert Graves avers that 'The troops with the worst reputation for acts of violence against prisoners were the Canadians (and later the Australians).[66] The Canadians' motive was said to be revenge for a Canadian found crucified with bayonets through his hands and feet in a German trench. This atrocity had never been substantiated; nor did we believe the story, freely circulated, that the Canadians crucified a German officer in revenge shortly afterwards.'[67]

Stories like this obviously had some impact on front-line troops few of whom needed any persuasion to despise the Army which shelled them and blasted their comrades into oblivion on a daily basis. But most soldiers were able to process the propaganda for themselves and form their own judgements. They were especially sceptical of what they read in English papers.[68] Frank Hitchcock was well able to judge the merits of Press propaganda from his own daily observation of the truth. 'The Huns strafed the tower of Ypres Cathedral all morning ... Our Press used to amuse us immensely with its accounts of the Hun's "frightfulness" in bombarding churches. Both sides invariably used church towers as artillery observation posts.'[69]

On Christmas Day 1914 ordinary soldiers from both sides made a gesture to each other which was in keeping with their humanity and which defied their conditioning. All along the front line (mainly at the instigation of the Germans) troops dumped their rifles and climbed out of their trenches to greet each other. Chocolate, cigars and cigarettes changed hands. Burial parties got to work unimpeded. Impromptu games of soccer began in no man's land. The General Staff had apoplexy. It was not in the interests of the High Command that German soldiers, who had been depicted as unfeeling monsters, should be revealed to their Irish, English, Scottish and Welsh counterparts as ordinary human beings. Sir John French, Commander in Chief of the BEF 'issued immediate orders to prevent any reoccurence of such conduct and called the local commanders to account'.[70]

Colonel (then Captain) E.H. de Stacpoole of the 2nd Leinsters was in the front line when this spontaneous Christmas truce began with

> the Germans lighting up their trenches with lanterns and shouting, 'If you don't shoot we won't shoot' and we agreed to have a quiet night for a change. Next day they marched out, a crowd with shovels, to bury their own dead, who were lying in front of our trenches and we went out and had a chat with them. Through all this our Brigadier lost his Brigade, but I think it was a good thing ... They had perfect English and the Colonel had been married in London that Spring and somebody produced a programme from the Music Hall in Cork, where he'd been a week before and a voice was heard saying, 'Let's have a look at the artists. I was in that line.' So we said goodbye and shook hands and went back to our trenches. Hostilities didn't begin again until the New Year. Then we had to give orders to men to fire their rifles because the Germans wanted to keep up the truce. We actually had to shoot some Germans before they realised that we actually meant business.

The Christmas 'Truce' was an example of fraternisation on a vast scale but on a daily basis there were instances of 'petty-fraternisation'. Tommy Irvine of the 36th Ulster Division used to have shouted conversations every day with a German who had heard him sing and play. The German would begin by calling him 'Paddy' ... 'I never met the man at all but I could hear him from the other side shouting, "Paddy". I said, "Hello". He shouted, "Play music." He used to call me "Paddy" all the time. He knew we were all Paddies.'[71] On some occasions both sides sensibly ignored each other. This was especially true during conditions of torrential rain which made both sets of trenches uninhabitable. Frank Hitchcock wrote in his diary of just such an incident in St Eloi in November 1915:

> All morning spent in trying to drain out the water. Sump pits were dug, as the only trench pump available would not function. Fatigue parties worked away with old biscuit tins, and baled the water out over the parados. We all walked about in the open as the Saxons were also walking out on their parapets. Their trenches, although on the high ground, were waterlogged, and we watched them bailing and pumping water into the large mine crater.[72]

On other occasions it went beyond casual toleration and strayed into good neighbourliness. A story has been recorded of a group of Munster Fusiliers in the Somme sector who began fixing barbed wire defences in broad daylight in an area where the enemy trenches were only twenty yards away and where

German soldiers could legitimately expect to fall foul of that barbed wire on a regular basis. However, out of indifference, curiosity or respect for the courage and foolhardiness of others this bizarre fatigue detail drew no fire from the German lines. As the work proceeded the Germans looked on, clearly relaxing, as one does, at the sight of others working. One of the Munsters, however, found himself in need of a mallet and approached the German trenches to see if he could borrow one. By means of an elaborate mime he communicated his needs to his enemy and was lent a mallet without a murmur. Furthermore he later returned it intact. His remark on leaving it back, which would have been completely incomprehensible to the Germans was, apparently, 'High hanging to the man that caused this war – ye now who I mean – and may we be all soon busily at work hammering nails into his coffin.'[73]

Units serving in sectors of the line where neither side was overly enthusiastic about raiding, shelling or otherwise disturbing the even tenor of life often developed quite a rapport and became quite 'tame' and trusting. Having been drawn closer together by their mutual misery in the rain of St Eloi in November 1915, the 2nd Leinsters and the Saxon battalion across from them became almost friendly. When Frank Hitchcock did his rounds in the morning 'The enemy shouted out "Good Morning" to me. When I was in front of the largest crater, I watched six Germans coming up in the open, and getting into one of their advanced posts. Six more got out with their rifles slung, and with braziers in their hands, yelled "Good-bye" to me and went back to their main trench. The relief started to try and fraternise with us immediately.'[74]

The following year near Vimy Ridge Hitchcock found the atmosphere entirely different. Attempts at fraternisation by the Germans were actively discouraged but at least one German nonetheless managed to make a tour of the British trenches:

> Espionage was practised successfully by the enemy in our divisional sectors at Vimy Ridge and at Loos, towards the end of this year. One day a daring Hun got as far as the Lorette heights dressed as a sapper officer. He made a thorough reconnaissance of our machine-gun emplacements and departed. That night practically every machine-gun position got a direct hit from shell-fire.

To guard against a repetition GHQ ordered a series of passwords to be used by soldiers with business in different parts of the line. Words like rabbit and apple were used and, not unreasonably, some men found it difficult to remember from day to day what the password was:

On one of the dark nights of this tour, seeing a man approaching me, I called out, 'Halt, who goes there?' only to get the following unusual reply, 'Begad, I was a rabbit last night, a spud the night before, and I'm damned if I know what I'm meant to be at all to-night.' It was 8645 Pte. Corbally.[75] He apologised profusely when he recognised me. I told him the pass word and went on my tour laughing. Corbally was a treasure.[76]

Even in the heat of battle there could be an unexpected amount of mutual compassion. The German defenders of Guillemont in September 1916 took very heavy casualties from the attacking 16th Division battalions. These included the 6th Connaughts and after the fighting had died down Lt. J.F.B. O'Sullivan did his best to help some badly wounded Germans:

Near the edge of the village a groaning and agonised German, with half his thigh blown off, feebly beckoned to me; and before going on I made some futile efforts to staunch his bleeding. Then, heading for the main east-west street still vaguely indicated through the pulverised rubble I stumbled over a weeping and terribly mauled little man whose head cringed away from an expected bullet, and instead of the bullet put my water bottle to his lips. He grabbed it with both hands and tried to drain it. As the bottle was firmly attached to my equipment I finally had to drag it away from the poor creature in order to free myself.[77]

At the Third Battle of Ypres in November 1917 Captain Devoy of the 1st Dublin Fusiliers witnessed an extraordinary act of compassion on the part of a young German soldier towards a Fusilier, Second Lieutenant Seale: 'When I went back to have a wound dressed I found Seale lying in a shell hole badly hit through an artery high up in the leg. Lying beside him was a young Boche, scarcely more than a boy, holding the severed ends of the artery tightly with his half frozen fingers, which were blue with cold ... He undoubtedly saved Seale's life.'[78]

The writings of those Irish Great War veterans who have left their memoirs behind or of the men who have spoken about their experiences reveal a grudging admiration for the German soldier. As far as Terence Poulter was concerned

Starvation beat them in the end. The lack of stamina from completely bad food. They had bread that we found that was completely black and as hard as iron. You'd need a sledgehammer to break it. They'd give you anything for a bit of chocolate. Bully beef they'd go mad for. The British soldier bore no animosity to the German. When we got up amongst the Germans in the occupied territory in Cologne for instance you'd see the British Tommy go up and say 'Hello Bochy come and have a drink'![79]

Denis Kelly of the Irish Guards concluded that 'They must have been good because it took nearly the whole world to beat them. We had the best of sympathy for them, and they for us.' This regard for the ability of the German soldier was undiminished when it was occasionally tempered by human frailty. The Germans had an opportunity of a breakthrough in the Armentieres sector in 1916 but, according to Corporal David Starret of the 9th Royal Irish Rifles, they were forced back by a British counter-attack because they 'had got at drink on their advance. But what could one expect. Probably they'd not had a square meal for weeks and booze is not friendly to empty stomachs.'[80]

Not all veterans, however, were so tolerant of their enemy. Jack Campbell died at the age of 96 and for seventy years nurtured a hatred of Germans which derived from his experience of the Great War. His animosity would undoubtedly have been accentuated by the undimmed effects of a German mustard gas attack in 1918. But to his dying day Campbell firmly believed that:

> There's no such thing as a good German, even now. I wouldn't trust the Germans because I saw what they did during the war. I saw, and others besides me saw. When we went up from the Ypres front the next battlefront we went on was Givenchy in France. We were there on the 28th January 1915. We happened to be successful in an attack we made on the German line and a bunch of us happened to go down a dugout to see if there was any rations lying around. You were always scrounging rations and we knew that they used to get tins of sausage and things like that. When we got down there was seven lads down there. They had no equipment, no rifles, no ammunition. all they had was their jacket and pants. They were all dead, and we found the remains of nine German stick bombs down there as well … them lads had been bloody murdered. They were prisoners of war, they were sent down there and they threw the bloody bombs after them. After that I know what I call Germans. And after that you can guess what we did.[81]

Stories of Turkish atrocities were just as common as were those of German outrages and just as much a product of the semi–official war time propaganda machine. Fr John Fahey was a Tipperary-born chaplain to 11th Battalion of the Australian Imperial Force force in Gallipoli. In a letter to Archbishop Clune of Perth on 5 August 1915, which was reprinted in the *Catholic Press,* he wrote, clear in the knowledge that what he had to say would be published:

> No doubt people in Australia are expecting to hear of Turkish atrocities. Well, I have not seen a single case of mutilation, nor has any such case been reported. I am inclined to think the Turk is more of a gentleman than the German. According to newspapers it would seem that the

Turks are hopeless cowards and their army a disorganised rabble. It is a mistake. They are fighting bravely and are not wanting in courage, although they are not up to the standard of our men.[82]

Stories of Turkish atrocities were obviously running in tandem with Turkish tales of Allied outrages, as Colonel Joseph Livesley Beeston discovered at Gallipoli. Beeston was an Irish-born doctor serving with the 4th Field Ambulance of the AIF. One day he was dressing the wounds of a badly injured Turkish prisoner:

he had been hit some days previously, in the abdomen, and smelt horribly. When I began to remove his clothing, he cried piteously, and held up his hands imploringly. I am sure he thought I was going to mutilate him. The same silly stories were current regarding Turk treatment of our wounded. I never saw anything that would give the least color [sic] to that story.[83]

As an opponent the Turkish soldier was feared and admired by most Irish soldiers. The 10th Division, along with the other elements of the force sent to Gallipoli, was comprehensively defeated by the Turks and by the incompetence of their own operation. However, after defending the peninsula against the initial Allied surge, according to Major Bryan Cooper, the Turks were quite prepared to limit the damage and sit out the campaign leaving the initiative with the attacking forces:

The Turk is inflexibly stubborn in defence, and when stirred up to make a mass attack, he appears fearless of death: but he is not an enterprising foe. Except at one or two points ... where the opposing trench lines were close together, and trench mortars and bomb-throwers raged perpetually, he was content to leave the enemy to the attention of his snipers. These, of course, were persistent and ingenious, and any point in a trench which could be overlooked, either from a tree or from high ground in the enemy's lines, required to be specially defended. Otherwise, however, the Turk was not much disposed to institute aggressive enterprises, and his bombardments, though intensely annoying, and causing a good many casualties, were not to be compared in intensity with those employed by the Germans in Flanders.[84]

Today the towns and villages which were devastated by the concentrated fighting along the long narrow Western front have been restored. There is little physical evidence remaining of what went on there eighty years ago.

The trenches have long since been filled in and ploughed back into the land, although it is still possible to see evidence of their existence from the air. As one travels through the tiny villages of rural Picardy the one persistent reminder of the carnage which was visited upon this quiet, sleepy region is the presence of thousands of small white crosses in unexpected cemeteries often concealed by staves of corn or fully grown sunflowers. On 29 December 1915 the French National Assembly passed a law giving the land on which temporary British war cemeteries were located as 'the free gift of the French people for a perpetual resting place of those who are laid there'.[85] Today there are more than 2,000 such cemeteries tended by 500 gardeners and cared for by the Commonwealth War Graves Commission. Some cemeteries are dedicated to Irish regiments, others are dotted with crosses which bear the name of Irishmen who fell while serving with English, Scottish or Welsh units.[86] Few Irish names are scribbled into the visitors' books which are left at each of these tiny graveyards.

Some of the Irish who over the years have visited these places of peace and contemplation have themselves been veterans of the Great War. In the 1930s Anthony Brennan returned to France before its second descent into war within a generation and visited the cemetery at Bazentin le Petit where he had lost his best friend Frank Waldron during the Somme offensive of 1916:

> Although the village had been rebuilt and the cemetry was once more a respectable cemetry the topography of the ground had not changed. It was a peaceful scene nevertheless. An old man in a straw sombrero and two of his womenfolk were busy binding sheaves of corn just above and adjacent to the Cemetery, and not fifty yards from the site of the windmill which had played such a fateful part in our little battle. The windmill itself had disappeared. In a neighbouring field a man with a couple of horses was busy cutting the ripe corn. The contrast of this peaceful August afternoon to the July day of 1916 was as striking as the memories it revived were sad and poignant. It was so long ago and so unreal in the light of one's present existence. Only the recollection of dying men and suffering souls and the unchanging landscape remained to prove that the 'I' of then and the 'I' of now were identical ... [87]

Common sense would hold that Anthony Brennan had been fortunate to survive the Great War and that his friend, Frank Waldron, had not been so fortunate, but at least one survivor Jack Campbell, is not so sure:

> I happened to be one of the lucky ones. Or was I lucky because ... I think it would be a humane thing for any of us that got gassed to let us die. Because any that I know that's been gassed we've suffered on down through the years. I'm still suffering from the effects of the gas, the

doctors here could tell you that. I've gone through the pain and the misery and the hardship on down through the years and the longer I live the longer I'll suffer. I'm 96 years of age now.[88]

For the young men who fought in the trenches of the Great War the world could never be the same. They had experienced death, danger, misery, hunger and disease at first hand. They had witnessed and endured events which left indelible marks. Not all cared to recall what they had seen and experienced; those who did so in old age, like Jack Campbell, often found the memories more vivid and real than the commonplace images of their daily lives. As Campbell told me when we met in 1990,

> If I'm speaking to you now and talking about the Battle of Mons or this, that or the other thing I'm not here with you at all. I'm there, where it occured. I'm looking at everything as I saw it when it did occur. I can see the stone on the side of the road, the broken branch of a tree, an old broken gate and all those things. I'm not seeing you.[89]

The generation of men which carried those pictures in their heads has now passed but such is their power that it will be a long while before the words and the images of the Great War have been erased from modern memory. For 20th-century man it was the event which first put some shape on his century. It marked the end of a sort of innocence and the acquisition of unsought wisdom, for those who returned. Of the men who did not survive Lawrence Binyon wrote:

> They shall grow not old, as we that are left grow old,
> Age shall not weary them, nor the years condemn.
> At the going down of the sun and in the morning
> We will remember them.[90]

Notes

Preface

1 It should be also recognised that the Somme Association has done a lot for research into southern Irish regiments as well.

1 Taking the Shilling

1 By which I mean that the Irish military tradition lay in the supply of Irish soldiers to foreign armies, a subject I have dealt with in *Distant Drums* (Belfast, 1993).
2 Denis Kelly (Irish Guards) from Dysart in Co. Roscommon was typical. He joined up in England. He had the option of returning to Ireland to avoid enlisting. When asked by Jim Fahy of RTE why he joined he replied, 'I had nothing at home here, there was nothing in it, no work or money or nothing.' The only thing vaguely exceptional about Kelly was his rural background. As was often the case with large rural Irishmen of farming stock, Kelly was recruited into the Irish Guards.
3 *Leitrim Observer*, centenary issue.
4 McDonagh, Michael *The Irish at the Front* (London, 1916), p. 2.
5 Ibid., p. 4.
6 Ibid., p. 5.
7 Ibid., p. 13.
8 Flanagan, Frank, 'Reminiscences', p. 8 (copy in the possession of the author).
9 Dalton, Emmet, interview with Kieran Sheedy; in the RTE Archive.
10 The War Office also displayed an anti-nationalist bias by refusing an application from NUI colleges to establish an OTC (a cadet training establishment) similar to the one in Trinity College. This meant that NUI students were often unable to qualify for commissions without enlisting as privates and rising through the ranks.
11 Cooper, Major Bryan, *The Tenth (Irish) Division in Gallipoli* (London, 1918; reprinted Dublin, 1993) p. 137.
12 Drury Papers, National Army Museum, London, vol. 3, pp. 128–9.
13 Coogan, Tim Pat, *Michael Collins* (Dublin, 1990), p. 31.
14 Phillips, James, interview with Kieran Sheedy; in the RTE Archive.
15 Laird, Frank, *Personal Experiences of the Great War* (Dublin, 1925), p. 3.
16 Gibbon, Monk, *Inglorious Soldier* (London, 1968), p. 4.
17 Ibid., p. 5.
18 So called because Kaiser Wilhelm was reputed to have instructed his commanders to brush aside King George's 'contemptible little army' on their way to Paris.
19 Campbell, Jack, in conversation with the author, 1990.
20 Two of the Campbell brothers died. Frank, who was in the Dublin Fusiliers was killed on the Somme, and Jack buried him; that night he himself was gassed. At Vimy Ridge, Pat, serving with the Royal Engineers, was killed by a shell. Joe, who was with Irish Guards, survived, as did the oldest brother, also with the Guards (a sergeant major).
21 Poulter, Terence, interview with Kieran Sheedy; in the RTE Archive.
22 De Stacpoole, E.H.M., interview with Kieran Sheedy; in RTE Archive.
23 Then a captain he was wounded at Ypres in 1915. Frank Hitchcock records in his book on the 2nd Leinsters *Stand To* (p. 33): 7 June, 1915. 'Very hot weather. D Company on our right was shelled in the evening. Capt. de Stacpoole was severely wounded, and some men killed. I saw de Stacpoole lying in his dug-out with his back peppered with shrapnel.' De Stacpoole subsequently became a lieu-tenant-colonel commanding the 1st Batt. the Royal Scots.

24 This was only the case, obviously, in Ulster and in Connaught where Protestants composed 8 per cent of the numbers recruited but only 4 per cent of the population. (Figures from Patrick Callan, 'Voluntary Recruiting for the British Army in Ireland during the First World War', PhD thesis, University College, Dublin, 1984)

25 Browning was later killed during the 1916 Rising.

26 Hanna, Henry, *The Pals at Suvla Bay* (Dublin, 1916), p. 14.

27 There was, for example, a 'commercial' element associated with the 10th RDF. The 7th RDF 'Pals' was by no means the only unit with a sporting connection. In September 1914, 50 professional golfers enlisted in the Kings Royal Rifle Corps and at least one Irishman, the Curragh pro. R.C. Lewis, was a member of this unit. It became known as the 'Niblick Brigade' (cf. William Gibson, *Early Irish Golf*, Kildare, 1988, p. 87).

28 Ibid., p. 17.

29 This indeed happened to many of them after the evacuation from Gallipoli. Downing had said, according to Edgar Poulte, 'I would advise you all to go out as a sporting body, a Pals Battalion, and when the casualties start, we'll commission you in the field. We'll pick our officers from this company.' 'So we all went out as good solid privates,' Poulter recalled. 'Right enough, after the casualties started on the peninsula some had pips painted on their shoulders and were told they were commissioned from that date to fill up vacancies.'

30 Poulter, Edgar, interview with Kieran Sheedy in the RTE Archive.

31 Barry, Tom, *Guerilla Days in Ireland* (Dublin), p. 8.

32 Dalton, Emmet, interview with Padraigh O'Raghallaigh; in the RTE Archive.

33 Patrick Callan, 'Voluntary Recruiting for the British Army in Ireland during the First World War,' PhD thesis, UCD (1984), p. 2.

34 It was equally difficult to obtain recruits in Britain between 1915 and 1916 when compulsory military service was introduced.

35 Again the pattern in Britain and Northern Ireland was similar.

36 Staunton, Martin, 'The Royal Munster Fusiliers in the Great War' MA thesis UCD p. 12.

37 Codd, Pauline, *Recruiting in Wexford*, Trinity History Workshop, 1986, p. 16.

38 Staunton, op. cit., Evidence of James McDonnell before Kilrush Petty Sessions, 12 July 1915, p. 7.

39 *Leitrim Observer*, centenary issue.

40 O'Brien, Dennis, interview with Kieran Sheedy; in the RTE Archive.

41 Ryan, Mary, Browne, Sean and Gilmour, Kevin, *No Shoes in Summer* (Dublin, 1995), p. 128.

42 Laird, op. cit. pp. 71–72.

43 Lyon, Wallace Adelbert, memoir, Imperial War Museum, p. 56.

44 O'Malley, Ernie, *On Another Man's Wound* (Dublin, 1979), p. 26.

45 McDonagh, *The Irish at the Front*, op. cit., p. 129.

46 *Drogheda Independent*, 2 May 1916.

47 Gibbon, op. cit., pp. 31–32.

48 Laird, op. cit., pp. 80–81.

49 Coogan, op. cit. Prologue.

50 Drury Papers – vol. 2, p. 130 – week ending 29 April.

51 McDonagh, Michael, *The Irish on the Somme* (London, 1917), pp. 128–9.

52 Gibbon, op. cit., p. 35.

53 Barry, op. cit., pp. 7–8.

54 Brennan, Anthony, memoirs, Imperial War Museum.

55 O'Malley, op. cit., p. 50.

56 Drury papers, vol. 3, p. 31 – 15 Sept. 1917.

57 Gibbon, op. cit., p. 115.

58 Ibid., p. 116.

59 Fitzgerald, Michael, interview with Kieran Sheedy; in the RTE Archive.

60 Kelly, Dennis, interview with Jim Fahy; in the RTE Archive.

61 Dalton, Emmet, interview with Padraigh O'Raghallaigh; in the RTE Archive.

62 Figures from Patrick Callan, Voluntary Recruiting, op. cit.

63 Lt.-Col. F.E.Whitton, *The Prince of Wales Leinster Regiment*, vol. 2, pp. 261–2.

64 Hitchcock, Capt. F.C., *Stand To: A Diary of the Trenches 1915–1918*, (Norwich, 1988), p. 130.

65 Ibid., p. 218.

66 Ibid., p. 331.

67 Whitton, p. 366.

68   Ironically some of its unpopularity was connected to British policy in Ireland. In his history of the Leinster regiment F.E. Whitton wrote that 'On the 5th February there took place a visit of the Canadian Irish Rangers to Limerick it appears that the propaganda arising from the suppression of the rebellion was having a bad effect on recruiting in Canada and so this regiment was sent over to see that Ireland was not given over to massacre and rapine as had been reported' (p. 379).

69   Martin Gilbert, *The First World War* (London, 1994) p. 377.

70   Callan, op. cit., p. 358.

71   Over the four years of the war something of the order of 40,000 Dublin men offered themselves for enlistment in the Royal Dublin Fusiliers and were rejected due to poor health. This was not unusual in a city with such acute levels of poverty.

72   Ibid., Appendix E.

73   'Casey' Imperial War Museum, p. 9.

74   Ibid., p. 12.

75   The provenance of this memoir is dubious, but the above facts, as outlined, were not uncommon and, even if fictionalised, have a ring of truth.

76   O'Malley, op. cit., pp. 49–50.

77   Dalton, Emmet, interview with Padraigh O'Raghallaigh; in the RTE Archive.

78   O'Malley, op. cit., p. 93.

79   Gilbert, Martin, *First World War*, op. cit., p. 413.

80   The Irish in Australia, who formed a sizeable portion of the volunteer Australian army, also played a significant part in the successful campaign against conscription there.

81   Lt.-Col. F.E.Whitton, *The Prince of Wales Leinster Regiment*, vol. 2, p. 269.

82   Poulter, Edgar, interview cited.

83   Lt.-Col. F.E.Whitton, op. cit, vol. 2, p. 377.

84   Poulter, interview cited.

85   O'Malley, op. cit., p. 309.

86   Barry, op. cit., p. 12.

87   Ibid., p. 99.

88   Ibid., p. 104.

89   Denman, Terence, *Ireland's Unknown Soldiers* (Dublin, 1992), p. 181.

90   Gregory, Adrian, *The Silence of Memory: Armistice Day 1919–46* (Oxford, 1994), p. 198.

91   Callan, op. cit., p. 361.

92   I have dealt with this subject before in two previous works, *Distant Drums* (Appletree Press, Belfast, 1993) and *Irish Voices from the Great War* (Irish Academic Press, Dublin, 1995) and hope to do so in much more detail at some future time.

93   Kiberd, Declan, *Inventing Ireland*, (London, 1995), p. 240.

94   The mentality which would deny the fact that there is any Irish contribution to commemorate reasserted itself when the then Labour/Fine Gael coalition government decided to send an Army representative to the Remembrance Day event in St Patrick's cathedral in 1985. The move aroused much virulent opposition.

95   Among whom I myself must be numbered.

96   Letter from the Taoiseach, John Bruton, to Deputy Paddy Harte, 19 December 1996; copy in possession of the author.

2   The Killing Machine

1   Hitchcock, Frank, *Stand To: A Diary of the Trenches, 1915–1918* (Norwich, 1988) p. 34.

2   J.F.B. O'Sullivan memoir, Imperial War Museum, p. 5.

3   Ibid., pp. 6–7.

4   McBride, Peter, interview with Kieren Sheedy; in the RTE Archive.

5   Byrne, Ned, interview with Kieran Sheedy; in the RTE Archive.

6   Brown, Malcolm, *The Imperial War Museum Book of the Western Front* (London, 1993), p. 59.

7   Lt.-Col. F.E. Whitton, *The Prince of Wales Leinster Regiment*, vol. 2, p. 234.

8   Ibid., p. 236.

9   Hitchcock, op. cit., p. 150.

10   Laird, Frank, *Personal Experiences of the Great War*, (Dublin, 1925), p. 118.

11   Gilbert, Martin, *The First World War*, (London, 1993), p. 383.

12   Nightingale papers, British Public Record Office PRO 30/71/3.

13   Greacen, Lavinia, *Chink: A Biography*, (London, 1989), p. 40.

14   Fahy, Jim, interview with Denis Kelly; in the RTE Archive.

15 Starret, David, memoir, Imperial War Museum, pp. 109–110.
16 Hitchcock, op. cit. p., 102.
17 McMahon, Bill, interview with Kieran Sheedy; in the RTE Archive.
18 Johnstone, Tom, *Orange, Green and Khaki* (Dublin, 1992), p. 213.
19 Col. Wallace Lyon, Imperial War Museum, p. 60.
20 Charles Cecil Miller, memoir, Imperial War Museum, p. 20.
21 King, John, interview with Kieran Sheedy, 1973; in the RTE Archive.
22 De Margry, memoir, Imperial War Museum, pp. 8–9.
23 Wallace Adelbert Lyon, memoir, Imperial War Museum, p. 62.
24 Anthony Brennan, Diary, Imperial War Museum, 11 August.
25 Hitchcock, *Stand To*, op. cit., pp. 230–31.
26 Ibid., pp. 237–45.
27 Ibid., p. 239.
28 Nightingale papers, British Public Record Office PRO 30/71/3.
29 Ibid.
30 Breen, John, interview with Kieran Sheedy; in the RTE Archive.
31 Brown, op.cit., p. 135.
32 O'Sullivan, J.F.B., Imperial War Museum, pp. 24 & 29.
33 Greacen, Lavinia, op. cit., p. 41.
34 Kirkpatrick, Ivone Imperial War Museum, pp. 29–30.
35 De Margry, memoirs, Imperial War Museum, p. 12.
36 Ibid., p. 16.
37 Hitchcock, op. cit., p. 106.
38 Brennan, op. cit., p. 10.

3 Irish Chaplains at the Front

1 Leonard, Jane, *Catholic Chaplaincy*, Trinity History Workshop publication, (Dublin, 1986), p. 10.
2 Ibid., p. 13.
3 Ibid., pp. 1–2.
4 Ibid., p. 4.
5 McDonagh, Michael, *The Irish at the Front* (London, 1916), p. 11.
6 Cooper, Bryan, *The Tenth (Irish) Division in Gallipoli* (Dublin 1993), p. 48.
7 Lt.-Col. F.E. Whitton, *The Prince of Wales Leinster Regiment*, vol. 2, p. 311.
8 McDonagh, Michael, op. cit., pp. 104–5.
9 Which is more than can be said for McDonagh himself, who glorified war at almost every opportunity while purporting to decry it.
10 Hanna, Henry, *The Pals at Suvla Bay* (Dublin, 1916), p. 134.
11 Op. cit., McDonagh, pp. 109–10.
12 Ibid., p. 112.
13 Ibid., p. 113.
14 Hitchcock, Frank, *Stand To*, op. cit., p. 44.
15 McDonagh, op. cit., p. 105.
16 Leonard, op. cit., p. 11.
17 McDonagh, op. cit., p. 108.
18 Ibid., p. 94.
19 *Merry in God. A Life of Fr William Doyle S.J.* (No author named; London, 1939), p. 253.
20 O'Rahilly, Alfred, *Fr William Doyle S.J.* (London, 1932) p. 410.
21 Laird, op. cit., pp. 109–10.
22 Ibid., p. 153.
23 *Merry in God*, op. cit., pp. 256–7.
24 O'Rahilly, op. cit., p. 548.
25 Dungan, Myles, *Irish Voices from the Great War* (Dublin, 1995), pp. 171ff.
26 *Merry in God*, op. cit., p. 323.
27 Hanna, op.cit., p. 133.
28 Drury Papers, volume 1, p. 116.
29 Ibid., p. 141.
30 Cooper, op. cit., p. 122.
31 Leonard, op. cit., p. 7.
32 Ibid., p. 7.
33 Ibid., p. 7.
34 Ibid., p. 11.
35 Drury diaries, vol, 3, p. 27.
36 Ibid., vol. 3, p. 102.
37 Gilbert, Martin, *The First World War* (London, 1994), p. 189.
38 Laird, Frank, *Personal Experiences of the Great War* (Dublin, 1925).
39 Leonard, op cit., p. 10.
40 McDonagh, Michael, *The Irish at the Front* (London, 1916), p. 50.
41 McKernan, Michael, 'Padre: Australian Chaplains in Gallipoli and France' (Sydney, 1986), p. 2.
42 Ibid., p. 1.
43 He is discussed in more detail below
44 Ibid., p. 36.
45 Ibid., p. 128.
46 McDonagh, op. cit., p. 116.
47 McKernan, op. cit., p. 48.
48 McDonagh, op. cit., p. 116.
49 Ibid., p. 115.

50 Lt. G.G. Allardyce, letters, Australian War Memorial, to his father, 27 Feb. 1917.
51 McKernan, op.cit., p. 143.
52 From an anonymous memoir in the Australian War Memorial, 3 DRL 7359.

4 *'Shell Shocked – The psychological effects of the Great War'*

1 'We had shellshocked men who talked to phantoms.'
2 Kelly, Denis, interview with Jim Fahy; RTE Archive.
3 Tobin, Paddy, letter obtained from Kevin Myers, p. 8.
4 Brennan, Anthony, memoir, Imperial War Museum, p. 14.
5 Greacen, Lavinia, *Chink: A Biography* (London, 1989), p. 43.
6 De Margry, memoir, Imperial War Museum, p. 15.
7 Hitchcock, Capt. F.C., *Stand To*, op. cit., p. 77.
8 Laird, Frank, *Personal Experiences of the Great War* (Dublin, 1925), p. 52.
9 O'Sullivan, J.F.B., letter to his mother, Imperial War Museum, p. 1.
10 Op. cit., p. 34.
11 Nightingale papers, British Public Record Office, PRO 30/71/3.
12 Ryan, Mary, Browne, Sean and Gilmour, Kevin, *No Shoes in Summer* (Dublin, 1995), p. 128.
13 Graves, Robert, *Goodbye to All That* (London, 1929), p. 94.
14 Brown, Malcolm, *The Imperial War Museum Book of the Western Front* (London, 1993), p. 34.
15 Graves, op. cit., pp. 88–9.
16 Research has shown that many winners of the Victoria Cross became chronic alcoholics or were otherwise psychologically scarred.
17 Whitton, F.E., *The Prince of Wales Leinster Regiment*, vol. 2, p. 476.
18 O'Sullivan, op. cit., pp. 25–6.
19 Lake, W.V.C., extract from memoirs, Imperial War Museum, p. 4.
20 Crozier, Percy, *A Brass Hat in No Man's Land* (London, 1930), p. 110.
21 Crozier, Percy, *The Men I Killed* (London, 1937), p. 49.
22 David Starret, memoir, Imperial War Museum, p. 100.

23 Jack Campbell – 1 Batt Royal Highlanders, interview with author.
24 Drury Papers, National Army Museum, vol. 1, p. 107.
25 Martin Gilbert, *The First World War* (London, 1994), p. 61.
26 Greacen, Lavinia, *Chink*, op. cit., p. 46.
27 C. Hitchcock, op. cit., p. 277.
28 Putkowski, Julian and Sykes, Julian, *Shot at Dawn* (London, 1993), p. 11.
29 Ibid., p. 16.
30 Crozier, *The Men I Killed*, op. cit., p. 52.
31 Putkowski and Sykes, op. cit., p. 18.
32 Drury Papers, vol. 1, p. 140.
33 Graves, op. cit., p. 94.
34 Brown, op. cit., p. 98.
35 Kipling, Rudyard, *The Irish Guards in the Great War* (London, 1923), p. 47.
36 Putkowski and Sykes, op. cit., p. 30.
37 Kipling's interest in the Irish Guards came through his son who was killed while serving with the regiment.
38 Kipling, op. cit., vol. II, p. 263.
39 Putkowski and Sykes, op. cit., p. 36.
40 Nightingale papers, British Public Record Office PRO 30/71/5 22/6.
41 Ibid., 1/5.
42 Ibid., 3/5.
43 Putkowski and Sykes, op. cit., p. 59.
44 Crozier, Percy, *The Men I Killed*, op. cit., p. 43.
45 Putkowski and Sykes, op. cit., pp. 67–8.
46 Crozier, op. cit., p. 47.
47 Ibid., p. 50.
48 Ibid., p. 52.

5 *Irishmen in the Anzac Forces*

1 Connor, John, 'Irish-Australian studies', Paper delivered at the Seventh Irish Australian Conference, July 1993, p. 320.
2 McDonagh, Michael, *The Irish on the Somme* (London, 1917), p. 180.
3 Gilbert, Martin, *First World War* (London, 1994), p. 267.
4 I will be dealing primarily with Australian soldiers in this chapter.
5 Cooper, Major Bryan, *The Tenth (Irish) Division in Gallipoli* (reprinted Dublin, 1993), p. 52.
6 Drury Papers, vol. 1, p. 101.
7 Ibid., vol. 3, p. 96.
8 Cecil Malthus, *Anzac: A Retrospect* (Auckland, 1965), p. 67.

9 *Letters of Lord Kilbracken and General Godley*, 1898–1932, p. 135.
10 Ibid., p. 49 – 23, Aug 1915.
11 Ibid., p. 135.
12 Ibid., p. 104, 29, Dec. 1917.
13 Ibid., p. 37 – 20, April 1915.
14 Ibid., p. 38 – 9, May 1915.
15 Connor, John, Paper, op. cit., p. 320.
16 Ibid., p. 321.
17 Freeman, R.R., *Hurcombe's Hungry Half Hundred: A memorial history of the 50th Battalion AIF, 1916–1919* (Sth Australia, 1991), p. 169.
18 O'Donnell, Jack, *Songs of an Anzac*, (Dublin, 1918), p. 23.
19 Connor, op. cit., p. 323.
20 O'Donnell, op. cit., p. 18.
21 Australian War Memorial 131, John Joseph O'Connor.
22 Connor, John, 'Everard Digges La Touche' p. 5.
23 Ibid., p. 5.
24 Ibid., p. 5.
25 Bean, C.E.W., *The Story of Anzac*, vol. I of the Official History of Australia in the War of 1914–1918 (Sydney, 1921), p. 44.
26 Connor, op. cit., p. 6.
27 Bean C.E.W., op. cit., vol. II, p. 517.
28 Connor, op. cit., p. 7.
29 Letters of Lt. G.G. Allardyce, 4th Battalion, AIF, Australian War Memorial, 30 Sept.
30 Ibid., Sept. 1915 (no date supplied).
31 Ibid., 27/7/16.
32 Ibid., 13/1/17.
33 Ibid., 19/4/18.
34 Fallon, David, *The Big Fight* (London, New York, etc. 1918) p. 2.
35 Ibid., p. 22.
36 Ibid., p. 17.
37 Ibid., p. 16.
38 'And the Band Played Waltzing Matilda' (Bogle).
39 The above information was ferreted out by the invaluable John Connor of the Dept of History, the University of New South Wales, Australian Defence Force Academy
40 Fallon, op. cit., pp. 107–8.
41 Papers of Joseph Livesley Beeston, Australian War Memorial pp. 59–60.
42 And, of course, the USA.

6 'The Foolish Dead' – Three Irish Writers of the Great War

1 Brooke, contrary to popular belief had virtually no direct experience of warfare. He was peripherally involved in the Royal Naval Division's attempt to relieve Antwerp in 1914. He died in the Aegean on 23 April 1915 having been taken ill with acute blood poisoning some weeks before the Gallipoli campaign got underway.
2 Curtayne, Alice, *Francis Ledwidge. A Life of the Poet* (London, 1992), p. 82.
3 Heaney, in – Bulger, Dermot ed., *The Selected Poems of Francis Ledwidge* (Dublin, 1994), p. 11.
4 Curtayne, op. cit., p. 83.
5 Bulger, op. cit., p. 12.
6 RTE Radio documentary, 'Blackbird of the Boyne'.
7 Johnstone, Thomas *Orange Green and Khaki* (Dublin, 1992) pp. 135/136
8 Dunsany himself, according the Charles Cecil Miller, who took up a commission in the 2nd Inniskillings was 'the most extraordinary member of the officers mess ... a poet and playwright of some renown, though I believe more appreciated in the United States than in England. He also was a reservist and not a regular soldier, and I should imagine that even this connection with the Army was purely a matter of family tradition, because anything more unsoldierly than Lord Dunsany never existed. I must say that Dunsany was perfectly honest about his intention to avoid any active participation in the war if he could do so, and I remember him once explaining the situation, as he viewed it, to a few of us subalterns in the mess. According to Dunsany the deaths of any of us meant nothing but a small matter of personal sorrow to those who were connected with us; but his own death would entail the loss of something which could never be replaced, and which moreover, had it not been lost, would have been of eternal joy and benefit to countless generations then unborn.'
9 Gilbert, Martin, *First World War*, (London, 1993), p. 189.
10 Curtayne, op. cit., p. 151.
11 Ibid., p. 159.

12 *Selected Poems of Francis Ledwidge*, p. 157.
13 Curtayne, p. 180.
14 *Selected Poems of Francis Ledwidge*, p. 66.
15 Curtayne, op. cit., p. 170.
16 *Selected Poems of Francis Ledwidge*, p. 76.
17 Kettle, Thomas, *The Ways of War* (Dublin and London, 1917), p. 24.
18 Lyons, J.B., *The Enigma of Tom Kettle* (Dublin, 1983), p. 240–1.
19 Ibid., p. 3.
20 Ibid., p. 3.
21 Fitzgerald, Michael interview with Kieran Sheedy, 1973, RTE Sound Archive.
22 Lyons, op. cit., p. 268.
23 Ibid., p. 279.
24 Ibid., p. 284.
25 *Ways of War*, op. cit., p. 34.
26 Ibid., p. 172–3.
27 Ibid., p. 171.
28 Ibid., p. 35.
29 *Ways of War*, op. cit., p. 12.
30 Lyons, op. cit., p. 299.
31 Dalton, Emmet, interview with Padraigh O'Raghallaigh, RTE Sound Archive.
32 Kettle, Thomas, *Poems and Parodies* (Dublin, 1916), pp. 15–16.
33 Dalton, op. cit.
34 Lyons, op. cit., p. 300.
35 McDonagh, Michael, *The Irish on the Somme* (London, 1917) p. 162.
36 Ibid., p. 162.
37 Lyons, op. cit., p. 302.
38 *Ways of War*, op. cit., p. 39.
39 Ibid., p. 39.
40 Ibid., pp. 7–9.
41 Ibid., p. 163.
42 Lyons, op. cit., p. 14.
43 Kiberd, Declan, *Inventing Ireland* (Dublin, 1996), p. 240.
44 *Ways of War*, p. 4.
45 Ibid., p. 4.
46 Ibid., p. 5.
47 Kettle, *Poems and Parodies*, p. 55.
48 Burnett, John, *Children of the Dead End*, introduction, v.
49 MacGill, Patrick, *The Great Push* (London, 1984), introduction.
50 Ibid., p. 50.
51 Ibid., p. 34.
52 MacGill, Patrick, *The Red Horizon* (London, 1984), p. 83.
53 *The Great Push*, p. 24.
54 Ibid., p. 70.
55 Ibid., p. 73.

56 Bredin, Brigadier, A.E.C., *A History of the Irish Soldier*, p. 426.
57 *The Great Push*, p. 81.
58 Graves, Robert, *Goodbye to All That* (London, 1929), p. 131.
59 Gilbert, Martin, *The First World War* (London, 1994), p. 200.
60 *The Red Horizon*, p. 13.

7 *Prisons and Holding Camps*

1 Graves, Robert, from *The Penguin Book of First World War Prose* (London, 1990), p. 315.
2 MacGill, Patrick, *The Great Push* (London, 1984), p. 94.
3 Brown, op. cit.
4 Hitchcock, Frank, *Stand To. A Diary of the Trenches*, 1915–18 (Norwich, 1988), p. 215.
5 Sheedy, Kieran, RTE Archive interview.
6 Hitchcock, Frank, op. cit., p. 263.
7 McDonagh, Michael, *The Irish on the Somme* (London, 1917), p. 188.
8 Brennan Papers, Imperial War Museum, p. 10.
9 Ibid., p. 21.
10 McDonagh, op. cit., p. 150.
11 Ibid., p. 191.
12 Brian Inglis, *Roger Casement* (London, 1973), p. 286.
13 Ibid., p. 286.
14 Ibid., p. 301.
15 Ibid., pp. 301–2.
16 Denman, Terence, *Ireland's Unknown Soldiers* (Dublin, 1992), p. 142.
17 Inglis, op. cit., p. 309.
18 Ibid., p. 389.
19 Charles Cecil Miller papers, Imperial War Museum, p. 25.
20 Ibid., p. 25.
21 Gilbert, Martin, *The First World War* (London, 1994), p. 360.
22 One of the prisoners taken by the Germans who did not survive was Michael Moran, winner of Irish Professional Golf Championship from 1910–1913. He had gone to France in 1915 with the South Irish Horse. He died of his wounds in the War Hospital at Le Cateau in April 1918. In 1913 he had tied for 3rd place in the British Open won by J.H.Taylor. One of the great unanswered questions is, would he

have won the Open after the war had he
survived? William Gibson *Early Irish
Golf* (Kildare, 1988).

23 Miller, op. cit., pp. 35–6.
24 Ibid., p. 39.
25 Ibid., p. 39.
26 Ibid., p. 39.
27 Ibid., p. 39.
28 Ibid., p. 40.
29 Ibid., p. 40.
30 Ibid., p. 41.
31 Ibid., p. 42.
32 Gilbert, Martin, *First World War*
    (London, 1994), p. 247.
33 Ibid., p. 247.
34 Australian War Memorial, AWM 30
    B3.1A POW Statement of No. 11 Act.
    Flight Sgt. James McKenzie.
35 Ibid.
36 Australian War Memorial, Red Cross
    Wounded and Missing Inquiry File for
    David Curran, statement by 1st Air
    Mechanic K.L.Hudson.
37 Ibid., Letter 12/3/17 ME Chomley to
    Samuel Curran.
38 Ibid., Curran to Chomley, 9/7/17.
39 Ibid., Chomley to Curran 11/7/17.
40 Ibid., Chomley to Malone, 31/7/17.
41 Ibid., Mrs E. Curran to Australian Red
    Cross Society 3/8/17.
42 Frank Laird, *Personal Experiences of the
    Great War*, p. 166.
43 Ibid., p. 167.
44 Ibid., p. 167.
45 Ibid., p. 177–8.
46 Ibid., p. 187.
47 Ibid., p. 193.
48 Ibid., p. 195.
49 Ibid., p. 197.
50 Ibid., p. 200.
51 Memoirs of Anthony Brennan, 2 Royal
    Irish Regiment, p. 16 – Imperial War
    Museum.
52 Information supplied by Ms Eilis Lambe,
    grandaughter of William O'Reilly (do.
    with most other personal details not
    contained in the correspondence)
53 Henry Harris, *The Royal Irish Fusiliers*
    (London, 1972), p. 87.
54 Ibid., p. 88.
55 Brian Inglis, *Roger Casement* (London,
    1973), p. 300.
56 Ibid., p. 412.
57 Letters of William O'Reilly, private
    collection, 8 May 1915 (all subsequent
    letters are dated where dates are available).

8 *It's Draughty in the Trenches-oh*

1 They were even given names, most were
   called after familar street and place names
   in Britain but some in the Somme sector
   bore the slightly surreal titles of Fluff,
   Hazy, Foggy and Muggy. In the Tyneside
   Irish sector of the Somme the German
   trenches were named Tara and Usna and
   were separated from the Irish lines by
   'Avoca Valley' (Middlebrook, p. 139).
2 Brown, Malcolm. *The Imperial War
   Museum Book of the Western Front*
   (London, 1993) p. 50.
3 Ibid., p. 55.
4 Ibid., pp. 50–1
5 Miller, Charles Cecil Imperial War
   Museum Memoir, p. 19
6 Ibid. p. 20.
7 Curtayne, Alice, *Francis Ledwidge: A
   Life of the Poet* (London, 1992) p. 177.
8 O'Sullivan, J.F.B., Imperial War
   Museum Memoir, p. 8.
9 McDonagh, Michael, *The Irish on the
   Somme* (London, 1917) p. 17.
10 Brennan, Anthony, *Imperial War
    Museum Memoir*, p. 4.
11 Cooper, Major Bryan, *The Tenth (Irish)
    Division at Gallipoli* (Dublin, 1993) p. 120.
12 Hanna, Henry, *The Pals at Suvla Bay*
    (Dublin, 1916) p. 91.
13 McBride, Peter, RTE Archive, Interview
    with Kieran Sheedy
14 King, John, RTE Archive, interview
    with Kieran Sheedy.
15 Lyon, Wallace Adelbert, Imperial War
    Museum Memoir, p. 59.
16 Gilbert, Martin, *First World War*
    (London, 1994) p. 219.
17 Hitchcock, Captain F.C., *Stand To*
    (Norwich, 1988) p. 226.
18 Hitchcock writes that one of the
    sufferers in his battalion was Lt. M.A.
    Higgins who was later killed on Vimy
    Ridge in 1917. Higgins was a brother of
    Kevin O'Higgins the Cumann na
    nGaedheal Minister who was murdered
    in Dublin in 1926.
19 Ibid., p. 202.
20 Campbell, Jack, RTE Archive, interview
    with the author.
21 Maultsaid Jim, memoir in the possession
    of the author.
22 Hitchcock, op.cit., p. 197.
23 Laird, Frank, op.cit., p. 122.

24 Killed in the assault on Guillemont.
25 O'Sullivan, JFB, Imperial War Museum memoir, p. 16.
26 Ibid.
27 Gunning, op.cit., part 2, p. 21.
28 Miller, op.cit., p. 20.
29 Campbell, Jack, RTE Archive, interview with the author.
30 Cooper, op.cit., p. 124.
31 McKernan, Michael, *Padre: Australian Chaplains in Gallipoli and France* (Sydney, 1986) p. 103.
32 Brennan, op. cit.
33 McMahon, Bill RTE Archive, interview with Kieran Sheedy
34 Brennan, op. cit.
35 Miller, op. cit.
36 Brown, op. cit., p. 51.
37 Laird, op. cit., p. 115.
38 Cooper, op. cit., p. 55.
39 O'Sullivan op. cit., p. 1.
40 Hitchcock, op. cit., p. 36.
41 De Margry, Imperial War Museum Memoir, pp. 4–6.
42 De Margry, op. cit., p. 6.
43 Gunning papers, part 2, p. 24 copy in the possession of the author.
44 Cooper, op. cit., p. 123.
45 Ibid., p. 124.
46 McBride RTE Archive
47 Starret, David Imperial War Museum Memoir, p. 71.
48 Lyon, op. cit., p. 59.
49 Lyon, op. cit, p. 60.
50 Hitchcock, op. cit., p. 196.
51 Godley, from *Letters of Lord Kilbracken and General Sir Alexander Godley* (London, no date given) p. 46.
52 Poulter, RTE Archive.
53 Hitchcock, op. cit., p. 221.
54 McDonagh, Michael, *The Irish on the Somme* (London, 1917) p. 17.
55 McElwaine Memoir, Imperial War Museum, p. 77.
56 Lyon, op. cit., p. 68.
57 Capt. E.H. de Stacpoole, 2nd Leinsters, RTE Archive.
58 Hitchcock, op. cit., p. 126.
59 Miller, op. cit., p. 29.
60 Greacen, Lavinia, *Chink: A Biography* (London, 1989) p. 41.
61 Drury Papers, vol 2, p. 49.
62 Miller, op. cit., p. 29.
63 Starret, op. cit., pp. 111–12.
64 Hitchcock, op.cit., p. 320.
65 Poulter, Terence, RTE Archive.
66 Australians referred to the killing of German prisoners as 'ratting'.
67 Graves, op. cit., p. 315.
68 This was part of a growing disillusionment with the Press which Phillip Knightley deals with in his book *The First Casualty*.
69 Hitchcock, op.cit., p. 48.
70 Gilbert, op. cit., p. 119.
71 Irvine, Tommy RTE Archive, interview with Joe Little.
72 Hitchcock, op. cit., p. 118.
73 McDonagh, *The Irish on the Somme*, op. cit., p. 17.
74 Hitchcock, op. cit., p. 119.
75 Corbally was to die of his wounds on 2 December 1916.
76 Ibid., p. 209.
77 O'Sullivan, op. cit., p. 34.
78 Wylly, Col. H.C. *Neill's Blue Caps*, vol. 3, 1914–1922 (1923) p. 91.
79 Poulter, RTE Archive.
80 Starret, op. cit., p. 112.
81 Campbell, RTE Archive.
82 McKiernan, *Padre*, op. cit., p. 103.
83 Beeston J.L. Memoir, Australian War Memorial, PR00264 p. 72.
84 Cooper, op. cit., p. 120.
85 Gilbert, op. cit., p. 222.
86 The most poignant of these must surely be the grave in a cemetry near Ypres of Pte. J. Condon of the Royal Irish Regiment who died on 24 May 1915 in a gas attack in Ypres salient. The legend on his headstone tells us that he was 14 years old.
87 Brennan, op. cit., p. 14.
88 During our interview Jack Campbell was not being entirely frank about his age. He was in fact 'only' 94. He died two years later, in Leopardstown Park Hospital, then aged 96.
89 Campbell, Jack RTE Archive.
90 Binyon, Lawrence *For the Fallen*.

Bibliography

MANUSCRIPT SOURCES

Imperial War Museum – papers of

A.R. Brennan
F. de Margry
G.W. Geddes
Sir Ivone Kirkpatrick
L.V.C. Lake

W.J. Lynas
W.A. Lyon
McElwaine
C.C. Miller

G.W. Nightingale
J.F.B. O'Sullivan
D. Starret
H.H. Stoney

National Army Museum – papers of
N.E. Drury
Desmond McWeeney

Australian War Memorial
Lt. G.G. Allardyce, letters to his father
John Joseph O'Connor, war record
Papers of Joseph Livesley Beeston
John Joseph O'Connor, war record
Statement of No. 11 Act. Flight Sgt.
James McKenzie
Red Cross Wounded and Missing Inquiry
File for David Curran, statement by
1st Air Mechanic K.L. Hudson

Somme Association – Interviews with
Jack Christie
R.T. Grange
Tommy Jordan
Letters of H. Waterman

Private Collections
Letters of Henry Gallaugher
Letters of Paddy Tobin
Diary of the Gunning brothers
Letters of William O'Reilly
Memoirs of Frank Flanagan

British Public Record Office
Letters of G.W. Nightingale PRO 30/71/3
Diaries of G.W. Nightingale PRO 30/71/3

ORAL SOURCES

Interviews with the Author
Joseph Cahill
Jack Campbell

Interviews with Richard Doherty
Harry Bennet
Thomas Gibson
R.T. Grange

Interview with Padraigh O'Raghallaigh
Emmet d'Alton

Interview with Jim Fahy
Denis Kelly

Interviews with Joe Little
Tommy Ervine
Tommy Jordan

Interviews with Kieran Sheedy

Paddy Barry	John King
John Breen	Thomas Leavy
Edward Byrne	Peter McBride
Michael Byrne	Bill McMahon
William Butler	Bill Molloy
Tommy Cusack	Jimmy O'Brien
Phillip Doyle	James Phillips
Pat Farrelly	Edgar Poulter
Michael Fitzgerald	Terence Poulter
Frank Hyland	E.H. de Stacpoole
Michael Keane	

PUBLISHED SOURCES

Barry, Tom, *Guerilla Days in Ireland* (Dublin).
Bean, C.E.W. *The Story of Anzac*, vol. 1 of the Official History of Australia in the War of 1914–1918 (Sydney, 1921).
Beckett, Ian F.W., *The Army and the Curragh Incident* (Army Records Society, London, 1986).
Bolger, Dermot, *Francis Ledwidge: Selected Poems* (Dublin, 1992).
Bredin, Brigadier A.E.C., *A History of the Irish Soldier* (Belfast, 1987).
Brown, Malcolm, *The Imperial War Museum Book of the Western Front* (London, 1993).
Connor, John, *Irish–Australian studies: Paper delivered at the Seventh Irish Australian Conference,* July, 1993.
Coogan, Tim Pat, *Michael Collins* (Dublin, 1990).
Cooper, Bryan, *The Tenth (Irish) Division in Gallipoli* (Dublin, 1993).
Crozier, Percy, *A Brass Hat in No Man's Land* (London, 1930).
—— *The Men I Killed* (London, 1937).
Cunliffe, Marcus, *The Royal Irish Fusiliers 1793–1968* (London, 1970).
Curtayne, Alice, *Francis Ledwidge. A Life of the Poet* (London, 1992).
Denman, Terence, *Ireland's Unknown Soldiers* (Dublin, 1992).
Doherty, Richard, *The Sons of Ulster* (Belfast, 1992).
Dixon, Norman, *On the Psychology of Military Incompetence* (London, 1994).
Fallon, David, *The Big Fight* (London, New York) 1918.
Falls, Cyril, *The History of the 36th Ulster Division* (London, 1922).
Feilding, Rowland, *War Letters to a Wife* (London, 1929).
Fox, Sir Frank, *The Royal Inniskillings in the World War* (London, 1928).
Fox, Sir Frank, *The Battles of the Ridges – Arras–Messines, March–June 1917* (London, 1918).
Freeman, R.R., *Hurcombe's Hungry Half Hundred: A Memorial History of the 50th Battalion AIF, 1916–1919* (Sth Australia, 1991).
Gibbon, Monk, *Inglorious Soldier* (London, 1968).
Gibbs, Phillip, *The Realities of War* (London, 1920).
Gilbert, Martin, *The First World War* (London, 1993).
Godley, Alexander and Kilbracken, Arthur, *Letters* (London, undated).
Gough, Sir Hubert, *The Fifth Army* (London, 1931).
Graves, Robert, *Goodbye to All That* (London, 1929).
Gregory, Adrian, *The Silence of Memory: Armistice Day 1919–1946* (Oxford, 1994).
Hamilton, General Sir Ian, *Gallipoli Diary* (London, 1920).
Hanna, Henry, *The Pals at Suvla Bay* (Dublin, 1916).
Hargrave, John, *The Suvla Bay Landing* (London, 1964).
Harris, Henry, *The Royal Irish Fusiliers* (London, 1972).
Brian Inglis, *Roger Casement* (London, 1973).
Jervis, Lt.-Col. H.S., *The 2nd Munsters in France* (Aldershot, 1922).
Johnstone, Thomas, *Orange Green and Khaki* (Dublin, 1992).

Kerr, J. Parnell, *What the Irish Regiments Have Done* (London, 1916).

Kettle, Thomas, *The Ways of War* (Dublin and London, 1917).

Kettle, Thomas, *Poems and Parodies* (Dublin, 1916).

Kiberd, Declan, *Inventing Ireland* (Dublin, 1996).

Kilbracken, Lord & Godley, General Sir Alexander, *Letters* (London, undated).

Kipling, Rudyard, *The Irish Guards in the Great War* (London, 1923).

Knightley, Phillip, *The First Casualty* (London, 1982).

Laird, Frank, *Personal Experiences of the Great War* (Dublin, 1925).

Leonard, Jane, *Catholic Chaplaincy*, Trinity History Workshop publication, (Dublin, 1986).

Ledwidge, Francis, *Selected Poems* (Dublin, 1992).

Lucy, John, *There's a Devil in the Drum* (London, 1938).

Lyons, J.B., *The Enigma of Tom Kettle* (Dublin, 1983.

MacGill, Patrick, *The Great Push* (London, 1916).

—— *The Red Horizon* (London, 1916).

McCance, Capt. S., *History of the Royal Munster Fusiliers*. Vol. 2: *From 1861–1922* (Aldershot, 1927).

McDonagh, Michael, *The Irish at the Front* (London, 1916).

——, *The Irish on the Somme* (London, 1917).

McKernan, Michael, *Padre: Australian Chaplains in Gallipoli and France* (Sydney, 1986).

Malthus, Cecil, *Anzac: A Retrospect* (Auckland, 1965).

Middlebrook, Martin, *The First Day on the Somme* (Glasgow, 1971).

O'Donnell, Jack, *Songs of an Anzac* (Dublin, 1918).

O'Malley, Ernie, *On Another Man's Wound* (Dublin, 1979).

O'Rahilly, Alfred, *Father William Doyle, S.J.* (London, 1932).

Orr, Phillip, *The Road to the Somme* (Belfast, 1987).

Putkowski, Julian and Sykes, Julian, *Shot at Dawn* (London, 1993).

Redmond, Major William, *Trench Pictures from France* (London, 1917).

Rickard, Mrs Victor, *The Story of the Munsters at Etreux, Festubert, Rue du Bois and Hulloch* (London, 1918).

Ryan, Mary, Browne, Sean and Gilmour, Kevin, *No Shoes in Summer* (Dublin, 1995).

Walker, G.A.C., *The Book of the 7th Service Battalion. The Royal Inniskilling Fusiliers – from Tipperary to Ypres* (Dublin, 1920).

Whitton, Lt. Col. F.E., *The Prince of Wales Leinster Regiment*, vol. 2 (undated).

Winter, Denis, *Haig's Command: A Reassessment* (London, 1991).

Winter, Jay and Baggett, Blaine, *1914–18: The Great War and the Shaping of the 20th Century* (London, 1996).

Index